B
DAVIS

Fletcher, Marvin.

America's first
Black general

$22.50

America's First Black General

America's First Black General

Benjamin O. Davis, Sr. 1880–1970

Marvin E. Fletcher

With a Foreword by
Benjamin O. Davis, Jr.

 University Press of Kansas

Published by the University Press of Kansas (Lawrence, Kansas 66045), which
was organized by the Kansas Board of Regents and is operated and funded by
Emporia State University, Fort Hays State University, Kansas State University,
Pittsburg State University, the University of Kansas, and Wichita State
University

Library of Congress Cataloging-in-Publication Data

Fletcher, Marvin.
  America's first Black general.
  Bibliography: p.
  Includes index.
  1. Davis, Benjamin O., 1880–1970. 2. Afro-American
generals—Biography. 3. United States. Army—
Biography. 4. United States. Army—Afro-American
troops. I. Title.
U53.D38F57   1989   355′.008996073   (B)   88-26122
ISBN 0-7006-0381-6 (alk. paper)

British Library Cataloguing in Publication Data is available.

Printed in the United States of America
10 9 8 7 6 5 4 3 2 1

The paper used in this publication meets the minimum requirements of the
American National Standard for Permanence of Paper for Printed Library
Materials Z39.48-1984.

For Hilary

Contents

"I did my duty. That's what I set out to do—to show that I could make my way if I knew my job."

Brigadier General Benjamin O. Davis, Sr.,
Interview, 2 June 1968

Foreword

Benjamin O. Davis, Jr.

MARVIN FLETCHER'S BOOK about my father's life covers many
details that involve me as well as my father. Even today, I can
remember as though it were yesterday, instead of more than
sixty-four years ago, the night the Ku Klux Klan paraded through
Tuskegee Institute. The purpose of its march was to state clearly
and vividly, in no uncertain terms, its opposition to the Veterans
Administration's plan to establish near Tuskegee a veterans'
hospital that would be staffed with black doctors and nurses. The
Klan felt that the jobs in the new facility should go to whites.
Our house was very close to Lincoln Gates, a hundred yards or
so from the main entrance to Tuskegee Institute's campus. The
house was on the street through which the Klan paraded; we
called it the Montgomery highway. Our house and all of the other
houses in our immediate neighborhood on our side of the highway were homes for Tuskegee Institute faculty and other employees of the institute. Across the street were business establish-
ments, a general store, a restaurant, a drugstore, and homes. On
the night of the Klan, now etched sharply in my memory, my
father and mother, my two sisters, and I sat quietly on the porch
of our house, my father resplendent in his white dress uniform
and the rest of us viewing the parade with some concern about
what was going to happen as the Klansmen marched by. The light
on our porch was an oasis in a sea of darkness, the only light
to be seen for miles around, except for the torches carried by the
Klansmen, which illuminated the masks covering their faces and
the white robes they wore. The institute's instructions had been
to avoid confrontation, but my father felt that the Davis family
should indicate what it thought about the Klan. In the end, the

Klan lost its fight, and the decision favored the black community. Today, a few miles from Tuskegee Institute, stands the Veterans Administration hospital, manned by both black and white doctors and nurses. Fletcher spends little time on this subject; he tells the story to illustrate another of the many displays of will power by my father. The whole incident impressed me. Inherent also in my father's action was his strong belief that we need never demand that people like us, but by our actions we must always demand that they respect us.

I was ten or eleven years old on the night of the Klan, and the years in Tuskegee Institute (1920–1924) were the first years I had lived with my father and my new stepmother. My earlier years had been spent with my grandmother in Washington, D.C., while my father had been stationed unaccompanied in the Philippines, my natural mother having died in 1916. My father set about training me forthwith. I recall taking music lessons on the cornet with the Institute Band. Unfortunately, my lessons were abruptly discontinued after I arrived home late for dinner one afternoon. I had stopped to play baseball after my music lesson. Thus did I learn punctuality instead of music.

I'll never forget Tuskegee Institute for many reasons, and there's one other reason related to my father that I recall. My father had returned to Tuskegee for a second tour as professor of military science and tactics during the thirties. It was 1934, and I was a second classman at West Point on furlough, visiting my parents. I had thoughtlessly walked into a white drugstore in Tuskegee town and ordered a Coca Cola. The startled white clerk served me, but this unprecedented violation of the pattern of segregation could well have resulted in an "incident" that might have damaged the fragile racial balance that existed between Tuskegee town and the institute. I went home and reported to my father, expecting a reaction of some kind, probably not good, but he simply laughed. He then told me of the incident that Fletcher relates in this book, when my father had stopped for a bite to eat at a New Mexico train station. The waiter had initially refused him service but had almost immediately profusely apologized when my father responded to him in Spanish. I had heard my father tell this story on many occasions over the years (as he frequently repeated many others of his favorite stories). The point that deeply impressed him was how deplorable it was that all foreigners, including black Africans or foreigners of *any* race, habitually enjoyed proper treatment in the United States, whereas native American blacks were routinely victims of discrimination and segregation. My father could never understand the preferred treatment of foreigners by white Americans over the unpleasant and demeaning treatment they accorded to black Americans.

I had run into similar actions by white West Point cadets in their treatment of a Filipino West Pointer, a Nicaraguan West Pointer, a Thai West Pointer, and other foreigners who were at the academy during my stay there from 1932 to 1936. These foreign cadets I have named, and others, were treated in an entirely different manner from the treatment the white cadets gave me, but I took great pride in applying my father's principle. I never demanded that they like me, but I did demand that they respect me through my actions and my reactions. My observations of this principle is in every way consistent with Fletcher's epigraph: "I did my duty."

My respect for my father had always been very great. When I was a teenager in Cleveland, I knew of no man whose achievements even approached his. My admiration for him increased in 1935, when as a second classman at West Point, I requested air corps pilot training upon my graduation the following year and had my application disapproved by the chief of the air corps on the stated basis that with no black air corps units and none planned, there was no air corps requirement for a black pilot. The fact that I was mentally and physically qualified for pilot training apparently was not relevant. It was at this point that I realized for the first time the magnitude of my father's achievement in winning a commission competitively at the turn of the century. It just wasn't possible that he could have secured the necessary recommendations that put him before the promotion board, that thoroughly examined his academic qualifications over a period of two weeks, and then miraculously forwarded the recommendation to the Washington bureaucracy that he be commissioned a

second lieutenant, U.S. Cavalry, Regular Army. And having survived the process this far, how did he manage to jump the final
hurdle? I greatly regret that I never discussed this miracle with
him. I am sure his reply to my question would have been conjecture, but it would have been interesting conjecture. I had learned
as a child all of the details of his experience, but even at this late
date, I cannot understand the War Department's action in com-
missioning my father. Perhaps I should generously conclude that
he won the commission because the people who handled his application were motivated by a spirit of fairness. Yet it was also
the people in the War Department who were determined to maintain segregation of blacks at all costs, with top priority, even at
the expense of the military effectiveness of black units.

An example of an action that the Army Air Forces could easily
have taken in 1941 was the training of all black pilots in the white-
pilot training establishment already in existence, instead of taking
the major step to build from scratch the segregated Tuskegee Army
Air Field as a training base for black pilots. Later, they made the
much-more-reasonable decision to train black navigator-bombardiers in the already-established Army Air Forces training base for
white navigator-bombardiers. Even here, they erred in putting off
this reasonable decision so long that the delay in combat readiness
of the 477th Bombardment Group (M) (Colored) was so great that
the unit's deployment to the Far East would have been several
months later than the planned deployment date. Similarly, throughout World War II the 332d Fighter Group, escorting B-17s and
B-24s from Italy to all of Europe during the last year of the war,
was always short of pilots, so short, in fact, that the Army Air
Forces found it necessary to deactivate one of the 332d's four
fighter squadrons, the 302d, in March 1945, two months before
V-E Day. This deactivation can only be described as a loss of
much-needed combat capability. In both of these cases—the 332d
and the 477th—military effectiveness was subordinated to the
desire of the Army Air Forces to maintain segregation at all costs,
even at the expense of military effectiveness.

Fletcher describes my father's struggle for a professional military assignment that would make better use of his rank, his ex-

perience, and his unquestioned expertise in cavalry tactics and operations. The insurmountable problem was that his rank, that of lieutenant colonel, would put him in regimental positions, in which he would have white officers junior in rank to him under his command. The army avoided this unacceptable situation by giving him two duty tours as professor of military science and tactics at Tuskegee Institute, Alabama. Tuskegee Institute had a Junior ROTC unit and the position of professor of military science and tactics would more properly have been occupied by a noncommissioned officer. I was much later assigned to that same position at Tuskegee Institute in 1938, putting me over the noncommissioned officer who had satisfactorily done the job alone for several years prior to my arrival. My father ultimately got two better assignments—out of the Regular Army—senior instructor of the Ohio National Guard and commander of the 369th Infantry Regiment, New York National Guard. As Fletcher describes, my father was shortly thereafter promoted to brigadier general and assigned as commander of the Fourth Cavalry Brigade at Fort Riley, Kansas. The army found itself in a box: the brigade consisted of two cavalry regiments, commanded by white colonels, whose regimental officers (other than chaplains) were all white. On 1 July 1941, after commanding the brigade for a period of several months, my father reached the statutory retirement age of sixty-four, was retired, and was recalled to active duty the next day in a more satisfactory position (from the army's point of view) as a staff officer in which he would not exercise command of white officers. His first assignment was in the Office of the Inspector General, and his mission, briefly stated, was to report upon the state of morale and discipline of army commands. Specifically, this mission was to advise the General Staff on matters "pertaining to the various colored units in the service." He visited Tuskegee Army Air Field; Camp Lee, Virginia; Fort Bragg, North Carolina; and army posts in Louisiana, Missouri, Florida, Oklahoma, Texas, and Arizona. The basic problem, as Bill Hastie, civilian aide to the secretary of war, repeatedly pointed out, was segregation, which was mandated by the War Department. Within this rigid boundary, my father could report violations of regulations, recommend the assignment of better white officers to black units, and the assignment of black officers, where possible. He could counsel white commanders on the development of better attitudes toward their black troops, on the need to provide better facilities for their troops, and the need to demonstrate a positive interest in the welfare of their men. All of this could only be an effort to moderate the effects of segregation, without really attacking the problem. My father made his visits more effective by getting information on unsatisfactory conditions—on and off bases—from Bill Hastie and his assistant, Truman Gibson. Bill Hastie, seeing no progress in getting to the heart of the problem—segregation—resigned, leaving Gibson and my father to continue a campaign to ease the effects of the policy of segregation. There is no doubt in my mind that the nature of the visits and his many recommendations, all reported by Fletcher, were of great value to the units he visited. Likewise, his advice to the General Staff on the effective handling of racial problems generated by segregation and by blacks' downright hatred of its effects was of great value to the General Staff. One of the major recommendations was that the General Staff should recognize that it had real racial problems and that all officers and enlisted people should be trained in ways to alleviate the effects of its segregation policies. Unfortunately, this extremely valuable recommendation, though later enthusiastically adopted and effectively implemented by the Air Force, was not accepted at that time. Fletcher reports on my father's membership on the Advisory Committee on Negro Troop Policies, headed by Assistant Secretary of War John McCloy. McCloy's stated position to Hastie on segregation had been that the American people's attitude toward the segregation of blacks or toward their service in mixed units was not one of the basic issues of the war. For this reason, "social issues" would not be discussed, and the emphasis of the committee would be on problems directly related to the performance of black units. Apparently, my father injected social issues that directly related to the black unit performance into committee discussions and kept them under active consideration, but the committee did not get deeply into substantive issues until much later. In the meantime, my father, at Gen. Dwight D. Eisenhower's request, departed for Europe on temporary duty.

As Fletcher strongly implies, the creation of the McCloy Committee was a War Department effort to ward off attacks by black leadership organizations on its policies of discrimination and segregation. The black Double V campaign—Victory at Home and Abroad—was popular and had captured the imagination of many blacks. Double V had been adopted and featured by the black press. Hastie had strongly opposed the building of Tuskegee Army Air Field as the sole training base for black pilots. Having lost this battle, he had fought for the desegregation of facilities on the field. The black press headlined Hastie's efforts and faithfully reported on the numerous racial problems that plagued army bases nationwide. For this reason, the War Department felt strongly that the articles appearing in the black press were inflammatory and served only to encourage black rebellion against War Department policies. The people in my units overseas in North Africa, Sicily, and Italy from 1943 to 1945 avidly read the black press, as did our relatives at home. All of us felt that the black newspapers performed their function admirably, disseminating information to us that we would not otherwise have received and pointing up to constituted authority a good many errors of its ways. The War Department might well have benefited, had it read the black press in a constructive manner and taken some of its advice. It might have learned something valuable.

Fletcher's treatment of my father's service in Europe on temporary duty is a recitation of his contributions to the European Theater. Quite properly, all of the recommendations were within Eisenhower's authority to approve or disapprove. My father did not recommend the elimination of segregation, but he did suggest many ways to deal with discrimination and segregation which, if implemented, would ease their adverse impact. Some of his very pertinent recommendations were: the establishment of a course in race relations, including black history, for all soldiers; the blanket elimination of discrimination against all people who wore the army uniform; an increase in the number of blacks being sent to Officer Candidate School; the designation of clubs by organization, not by race; and the assignment of both black and white military police in areas where black and white troops mingled. Some of these recommendations were implemented; others were disregarded.

Fletcher tells about my father's return to Washington and the continuation of his work with the inspector general and the McCloy Committee. My father made numerous inspections and investigations. He attempted to educate whites in their dealings with blacks, and blacks in their dealings with whites. He tactfully informed blacks and whites alike, when he considered their actions unmilitary. With the McCloy Committee he strongly recommended actions that were basic to improved status for blacks and improved black morale, but these were unappealing to some members of the committee. They involved ending segregation on and off base, ending the segregation of blacks' blood from whites' blood in the blood bank, and above all, fair treatment of blacks within the military. He also advocated a more active role for the committee. Evidently, McCloy still preferred that the committee restrict itself to actions directly affecting the performance of black units. As I see it, any or all of my father's recommendations, if implemented, would have measurably improved the performance of black units.

Toward the end of the book and the end of the war in Europe, Fletcher describes a major effort that my father made to reduce segregation. It grew out of the manpower shortage that existed in November 1944. In response to a request by Eisenhower for more men, the War Department sent infantrymen who had not completed training and suggested that men who were already in the theater in supply areas be used to augment the front lines. With the increased casualties from the Battle of the Bulge in December 1944, the need for replacements increased, and as a result, Eisenhower approved the integration of individual black Service of Supply volunteer soldiers into combat units. Eisenhower's chief of staff, Gen. Walter Bedell Smith, cautioned that the War Department should be informed of these plans. Instead, Eisenhower rewrote the directive, with the important change that the volunteers be formed into black platoons and that the pla-

toons, rather than the individual black soldiers, be integrated
into white companies. My father was deeply disappointed by
Eisenhower's decision; it had been his plan. He visited the black
platoons as they trained, congratulated them on their courage
and patriotism in volunteering, and explained to them just how
important it was that they make a good showing. After their
introduction into combat, he visited the army commanders to
whom these black platoons had been assigned, Gen. Omar Bradley and Gen. Courtney Hodges. After these meetings he met several small units to which black soldiers had been assigned. Black
soldiers in each case were grateful for the opportunity they had
been given to participate in battle and for the manner in which
they had been received in their companies. He also talked with
several unit officers who reported no interracial friction. In the
Seventh Army he found that Gen. George Patton had in some
cases grouped platoons to form black companies. In general,
my father was greatly pleased with even this small attempt at
integration.

Fletcher reports that my father received high marks for his
work in Europe, just as he had in the Inspector General's Office,
where Gen. Virgil I. Peterson, the inspector general, had recommended him for, and he had received, the Distinguished Service
Medal.

Marvin Fletcher has done a fine job in writing this biography
of my father. Everything about my father is here, and almost
all of it rings true to me. I can't vouch for Fletcher's analysis
of the black middle class, but I am sure that E. Franklin Frazier
knows them better than I do. I would differ slightly with Fletcher
on the reason my father entered the army. Perhaps Fletcher is
right—but I had always thought it was love for the army mys-
tique, its life, its horses, the smell of the stables, boots and
saddles, bugle calls, and martial music. But these are very minor
points. I can honestly say that Marvin Fletcher has faithfully and
truthfully presented my father, and I knew him well.

My problems in the military were not as severe as those my
father experienced. My four years at West Point were difficult,
and my two years at Fort Benning were embarrassing to me, be-

cause I was ashamed of the way the army treated my wife and me. To put it more precisely, I was ashamed that the army would treat my wife and me the way they did. I had a great deal of trouble reconciling those first six years with the "Duty, Honor, Country" I had been taught at West Point. The rest of my service, while not completely easy, was inspiring. I experienced eight years of segregation in the Army Air Forces, 1941–1949, but unlike my father, who could only peck away at the edges of segregation, I knew that outstanding performance by the black fighter units in World War II would assure us of an honorable place in the postwar Air Force. My people knew it too; they knew in the beginning that we were all fighting for the future. Fight we did, and President Harry S. Truman's executive order eliminating segregation in the armed forces came right on schedule. The Air Force was ready to integrate its black airmen throughout its structure. My base at Lockbourne, near Columbus, Ohio, was closed, and all of our officers and airmen were reassigned to the worldwide Air Force in the specialties in which they had been trained. Secretary Stuart Symington and Chief of Staff Hoyt Vandenburg imposed integration on a reluctant Air Force in June 1949. To the surprise of many, their action was an immediate success. These men had correctly determined that the Air Force would be a better military service in a better nation by the elimination of segregation. The courageous performance of black airmen in World War II helped Symington and Vandenburg immeasurably in making their decision.

Arlington, Virginia
January 1988

Acknowledgments

THIS BIOGRAPHY is an outgrowth of the dissertation that I completed at the University of Wisconsin in 1968. Given my interest in blacks in the military, I welcomed the opportunity that June to meet General Davis, about whom I had written. Several years later I began the research for this biography.

I am grateful to members of the Davis family for their cooperation and assistance. They gave me access to their father's papers and shared many of their personal recollections; however, they made no suggestions as to what I should write or how I should portray the general.

The Davis papers were supplemented with research in many collections, especially those of the National Archives in Washington, D.C., and Suitland, Maryland. Additional information was provided by a number of individuals who knew and worked for the general in his professional capacity.

I would also like to thank the Ohio University Computer Center. I used their resources in a variety of ways to produce and revise the manuscript and to index the finished product. The computer has helped immensely in this project.

Edward M. Coffman, who was my dissertation advisor and now is a good friend, constantly encouraged me to continue the project. He gave very constructive comments based on his vast knowledge of army life. In addition he helped me in my efforts to place the finished manuscript.

The greatest assistance came from my family, especially my wife, Hilary, who helped me put my thoughts into readable English. I can never thank her enough for what she has done for me.

Marvin E. Fletcher
Athens, Ohio
December 1987

Prologue: A Minority of One

HISTORICALLY, ONLY a small percentage of Americans have ever belonged to the professional military, and blacks have constituted a minute percentage of this minority. Rarer still were blacks who became officers: between 1865 and 1940 there were never more than three who were members of this select group at any one time. For thirty-nine of those years, Benjamin Oliver Davis was one of these. He entered the army as a private and became the first black to be appointed to the rank of general.

Davis was also a minority within a minority from a different perspective. Black Americans constituted a small element in the pre–World War II melting pot. Prior to 1917, most of them lived south of the Mason-Dixon line in conditions scarcely different from the slavery that they had supposedly escaped from in 1865. After 1917, although blacks began to move northward, their conditions did not significantly improve. Only a very few blacks owned their own homes, sent their children to college, or traveled abroad. Benjamin Davis belonged to this elite group.

The wealthiest blacks sought a life similar to that of the white middle class, from which they were excluded. According to E. Franklin Frazier, because there were so few economically advantaged blacks, they formed their own closely knit social group. They frequently participated in activities where wealth could be displayed, such as dances, sports, and gambling. These pursuits of the black middle class provided an escape from the realities of an America that made the color line more significant than any achievements.[1]

Frazier also asserted that members of the black middle class felt inferior to their white counterparts, and there was a fear "of competition with whites for jobs." Although they publicly demanded equality, they preferred the security of segregation.

1

"Negroes who adopt the standards of the white world create among the black bourgeoisie a feeling of insecurity and often become the object of both the envy and hatred of this class." Those blacks who succeeded in the white world may even have felt some guilt. Most blacks either could not or would not even try. Although Frazier never explicitly discussed a black professional officer in his overview of the middle class, some of what he wrote is applicable to Benjamin Davis.[2]

Benjamin Davis was an atypical member of the black middle class, because he acquired some of the trappings of the middle class without the benefit of a college education. Davis's salary allowed him to own his home, buy securities, provide his children with education, and travel. His tours of duty overseas allowed him to glimpse a life that few blacks had the opportunity to see. During the latter part of his career he was able to mingle in the black society of several major American cities; yet even then he remained somewhat isolated. He could never afford the luxury of establishing roots in a single community; he was a career officer who lived as a transient. Lastly, unlike his social peers, he worked in an institution that was thoroughly dominated by whites.

Davis was also in the minority within his professional group. According to a study by Morris Janowitz, the officer corps of the first half of this century "comprised a cross section of American society." Davis, like most of the officers, was not a first- or second-generation American, but his ancestors were not from Western Europe. His childhood was spent in an urban environment, while the typical army officer grew up in a rural or small-town setting. Few of the officers were the sons of white-collar workers. Here, again, Davis was in the minority. His education, background, and heritage set him apart from his colleagues.[3]

Davis's choice of a military career probably was influenced by his hopes for the future, whereas most officers chose the military because of family traditions and past experiences. Davis's choice of career was one of the few avenues of upward mobility. His colleagues, on the other hand, could have chosen any number of careers. While most of his fellow officers had the benefit of formal military and academic training throughout their careers, Davis did not share in this.[4]

Benjamin Oliver Davis was unique; he achieved an unprecedented success for a black man. We can use the framework provided by Janowitz and Frazier to suggest how Davis was similar to and yet different from his racial and professional peers. These authors can also provide us with some insights into Davis's reactions to different aspects of his military and civilian life. The first black general was nominally a member of both the black middle class and the professional officer corps, but because of his occupation and race, he was never fully a member of either.

1 | The Early Years: 1880–1898

ALTHOUGH ALL of Benjamin O. Davis's ancestors had been born in Virginia, only some had been slaves. The earliest person listed in the family Bible is Lucy Henry, born a free black in Virginia in January 1800. One of her daughters, also named Lucy, married Benjamin Banneker Davis, who had been born a slave in Winchester, Virginia, in May 1821, but who later purchased his freedom in order to marry her. They had nine children over the course of the next fifteen years. Their second child, Louis Patrick Henry Davis (Benjamin's father), was born in July 1844 in Winchester. Sometime between 1850 and 1854 the family moved across the Potomac River from Alexandria to Georgetown in the District of Columbia. Benjamin B. Davis got a job as a waiter, and young Louis was sent out to work as a servant.[1]

Benjamin's maternal ancestors, the Carters, had been slaves in Virginia. His great-grandmother, Judy Carter, grew up on a plantation in Northumberland County, but death and the Civil War had disrupted her life and that of her family of five. In June 1863 her three sons joined the First United States Colored Troops, an all-black regiment. The regiment fought in a number of engagements, including the famous battle of the Crater in July 1864. Hezekiah Carter later claimed that he had been wounded in the left arm by a bayonet at Fort Fisher, North Carolina. It was the only battle wound that any of the Carters apparently sustained. After the war the brothers did not return home, however; they dispersed to different parts of the country.[2]

Judy's oldest daughter, Charlotte, grew up in Heathsville, Virginia, and later became the wife of William Stewart, a farmer who was considerably older than she. Their household included three girls and a boy. The eldest daughter, Henrietta—Benjamin's mother—was born in 1855. She had a very fair complexion and

4

Caucasian features. After the Civil War the family moved to Washington, where William Stewart entered into the restaurant business. In 1868, Charlotte had a daughter, Adelaide Stewart, and later in the year, William died and Charlotte took a job first as a cook and later as a washerwoman. The Stewart children also got jobs to help support the family. Fourteen-year-old Henrietta was hired to help care for five children in the home of Albert Riddle, a Washington lawyer.[3]

Washington at this time was in the midst of a period of change and growth. In April 1862, Congress abolished slavery in the District, but as a result of the 1857 *Dred Scott* decision, none of these free blacks were citizens. In addition, freedom did nothing to satisfy the housing, health, and educational needs of the blacks. Many blacks, including the Davis and Stewart families, had come to the District with the expectation that the federal government would help them, but it did little.[4]

As the war ended, discussions of the issues of education and political rights intensified. In 1866, in a referendum, the white citizens of Washington overwhelmingly rejected the idea of sharing the franchise with blacks. The following year, ignoring this expression of the popular will, Congress granted the black males of the district the right to vote. These new voters played an important role in the District's elections over the next few years. With the municipal reforms of 1871, the form of government was changed; Congress took control, and all the residents lost the right to vote.[5]

At the same time, however, blacks did have increasing opportunities for education. In 1866, Congress authorized the use of empty army barracks for classrooms, and it designated plots of land on which schools could be built. The following year a capstone to the system, Howard University, was created. This program of education was necessary because many blacks, like Charlotte Stewart, could neither read nor write. These new schools were generally avoided by the white population, so a de facto segregated school system evolved. Some blacks attacked the dual school system as discriminatory, but other blacks supported it. As a result, segregation continued.[6]

It was in this era of both opportunity and growing discrimination that Louis Davis began his rise in society. He took a job in the household of Gen. and Mrs. John A. Logan. After service in the Civil War, General Logan went into politics and served in both the House of Representatives and the Senate. During the 1873 inauguration of Ulysses S. Grant, General Logan entrusted the care of his son, John, Jr., to Louis Davis. It was a very cold day, and President Grant spotted the young Logan as he left the ceremony at the Capitol. Grant invited John, Jr., to join him for the ride to the White House, and with the boy on Louis's knee, the two of them rode on the top of the presidential carriage all the way to the White House. The Logans appreciated Louis Davis's service, and in the late 1870s the senator used his connections in the Treasury Department to obtain a position for Davis as assistant messenger in the office of the commissioner of internal revenue, at a salary of $720 a year.[7]

Louis Davis now felt confident enough to get married and begin a family. How he met Henrietta Stewart is unclear, but they were married on 7 July 1875. For a while the Davis and Stewart families lived together in the same six-room red-brick house on Pomeroy Street near Howard University. In 1878 Benjamin and Lucy Davis moved to another home on nearby Seventh Street, but Charlotte Stewart and her youngest daughter, Adelaide, remained with Louis and Henrietta. Things began to get crowded in the Pomeroy Street house as the young Davis family grew. The Davis children were named after members of Louis's family. Louis A. Davis was born in 1876, and Mary, in 1878. The youngest child, Benjamin Oliver, was born at home on 28 May 1880; he was delivered by Amanda Eaturon, a midwife who lived at Howard University.[8]

Louis Davis began a series of moves into Washington's black-middle-class society. In the early 1880s he received a promotion to messenger in the office of the assistant attorney general, Department of the Interior, with an annual salary of $840. Henrietta also worked as a nurse, while Charlotte took care of the children. The two incomes helped the Davises to become one of the few black families in the city to own their own home. In 1893 the

Louis P. H. Davis and Henrietta Davis, parents of Benjamin O. Davis, Sr.

family moved to 1830 Eleventh Street, N.W., about six blocks from their old home, where they would live for the next forty years. Another indicator of their middle-class status was their concern for education. Both Henrietta and Louis had learned to read, and they saw to it that Adelaide and the three Davis children were sent to school.[9]

Despite the progress of the Davis family, life for the general black community between 1880 and 1900 became increasingly more difficult. Most of the gains of the Reconstruction period were lost as whites began to draw de facto racial barriers and soon followed these with legal ones: owners began to segregate areas of public accommodation, the federal government hired fewer blacks, and job opportunities were limited.[10]

Within the system of segregation, blacks demanded improved schools, and they got much of what they wanted. Lucretia Mott Elementary School, at Fourth and W streets, N.W., located near Howard University, earned quite a reputation as one of the best. In 1892 the well-equipped M Street High School was opened, but the teachers were paid less than in the white schools. Few children stayed beyond the fourth grade, and fewer still, including some girls, went on to the high school. For the middle class, most of whom were mulattoes like the Davises, career options were severely limited and becoming worse.[11]

As a young man, Benjamin Oliver was not conscious of the racial barriers that were rising around him. Pomeroy Street was still on the outskirts of the city and was not heavily settled. Both whites and blacks lived on the three-block-long street, and the children played together. Memories of these associations were mainly happy ones. Many years later he clearly remembered having gone hunting with his young friends for rabbits, squirrels, and small birds in the open spaces in the area surrounding the nearby Soldiers' Home.[12]

Life on Pomeroy Street and on Eleventh Street was not always as enjoyable for the growing boy. Benjamin's father tended to ignore the younger son, which did not bother the child because, as he noted later, "I was always uncomfortable in his presence." In the evening when Louis came home from work, the older children would climb up on his knees, but the youngest was left out. Henrietta then became the focal point of Benjamin's attentions. She was sweet and gentle and tried to make up for the lack of affection he received from his father. When punishments were meted out, Henrietta was the one to punish young Benjamin. She would merely point out that his actions made her very unhappy, which was an effective technique.[13]

As Benjamin matured, his family responsibilities increased, and he was assigned a number of small jobs. When Henrietta went shopping at the recently established O Street outdoor market, she would tell him to meet her there at a certain time. When he arrived, he was given a load of groceries to carry home. The family also owned two cows, which were pastured near the house on land between Howard University and the Freedmen's Hospital. It was Benjamin's responsibility to watch the animals.[14]

Benjamin's earliest education was at the nearby Lucretia Mott School, one of the city's few integrated schools. It was while he was a student at the Mott School that he first began to consider the possibility of a military career. Robert H. Harrison, a veteran of the Civil War and the father of one of Benjamin's classmates, organized the boys into a paramilitary group known as Harrison's Protective Zouaves. He taught them how to make wooden guns, using broom handles for barrels and boards for gun stocks. With Harrison's encouragement, the parents provided each boy with a uniform consisting of a light-green coat, red baggy pants, and a fez with a yellow tassel. He taught the boys close order drill and the manual of arms. During recess periods at school, the boys drilled and encouraged other boys to join them.[15]

After meeting some black cavalrymen, Benjamin began to think even more about a military career. A troop of the Ninth Cavalry, a black regiment, was assigned to the Washington area as a reward for their service during the Indian Wars. These honored troops were stationed at Fort Myer, Virginia, across the river from Washington. Davis took advantage of every opportunity to see the black cavalrymen, and he was especially excited when they participated in the 1893 inaugural parade of President Grover Cleveland. The mounted soldiers and the horses themselves became important to Benjamin. He read the novel *Black Beauty*, which reinforced the lure of the cavalry. As he said long afterwards, "I always longed for the day when I too would be a cavalry soldier and ride a beautiful horse."[16]

After eight years at Mott School, Benjamin graduated to the M Street High School, the city's black high school. This was his first encounter with segregation. Although his new home on Eleventh Street was close to the white Central High School, he was forced to attend the more distant black school. Education in this recently opened building was good, for twenty of the thirty regular teachers had degrees from good northern colleges and universities. This was a far-higher proportion of well-educated faculty than the white schools could claim.[17]

Upon entering M Street High School, Benjamin had to make a decision about a course of study. He had the options of taking an academic, a scientific, or a business program, but he did not even consider the last. For many students, the deciding factor was the language requirement—German or Latin. Although many students thought German was easier, Benjamin chose the challenge of Latin, because he was "more interested in trying to solve the problems considered hardest by the other boys." He also recalled, from his earlier studies of grammar, that parts of English came from Latin. As a result, he enrolled in the academic course.[18]

Not all of Benjamin's time in high school was spent with academics, for he was also a good athlete. He was a member of the baseball and football teams and in 1896 was chosen captain of the latter. In that same year, M Street High School held the Howard University team to a tie, the first time the M Street team had not lost to Howard.[19]

The thing that excited Benjamin the most during his first years in high school was the opportunity to become a cadet. "As far back as I can remember I wanted to be a soldier." He felt that being a member of the high-school Cadet Corps was the next step in that direction. An additional attraction was the fact that the cadets used weapons. Although he had fired an old Civil War musket, a breechloading shotgun, and a .22-caliber target rifle, he wanted to handle one of the new army rifles, a wish that was realized when he became a cadet. Each student was equipped with a Springfield rifle, a belt with a pouch for cartridges, and a scabbard for the bayonet. Beginning as a private during his freshman year, he gradually rose to the rank of captain of Cadet Company B.[20]

Most of the instruction in the military program dealt with learning the manual of arms and close order drill. Benjamin proved very adept at this and then at teaching others these skills. The drill instructor was Maj. Arthur Brooks, who was also the commanding officer of the First Separate Battalion, District of Columbia National Guard. Brooks was impressed with Davis's work. In April 1898 Brooks offered Davis a chance to compete for a commission in his battalion. Davis was successful and was elected a second lieutenant in Company D, commanded by Capt. John H. Campbell.[21]

As Benjamin progressed through his academic career at the high school, the family began to discuss his future prospects.

His academic course prepared him for normal school and then a teaching job in a public school. However, from the beginning, Benjamin made it clear he was not interested in teaching small children. Louis wanted his younger son to follow in his other children's footsteps and enter a career in the government. The older son was already working as a clerk in the Navy Department, and Mary was employed at the Bureau of Printing and Engraving. Benjamin's mother wanted him to enter the ministry, preferably in her own Baptist church. However, Benjamin was not interested in either of these careers; he wanted to be a soldier.[22]

During his last year at high school, Benjamin also attended Howard University as a special part-time student. He took a few courses and played football. The seventeen-year-old student met a number of other students much older than he. It was a maturing experience, and it was the only time Benjamin Davis was ever a university student.[23]

His wish to become a soldier was to be realized much sooner than he anticipated because of a conflict in Cuba. A civil war had been raging on the island since the 1870s. American interest in the war reached a fever pitch in early 1898 when the American battleship *Maine* exploded and sank in Havana harbor. In April 1898, responding to popular demands, Congress declared war on Spain. Enthusiasm for the Spanish-American War was widespread. Many blacks and whites eagerly joined volunteer military units in order to fight the Spanish and help win Cuban independence. Washington felt the war fever, as the District of Columbia National Guard increased the tempo of its drills. The black battalion began to give special attention to skirmish drills and the loading and firing of rifles. In addition they scheduled voluntary rifle practice. It was during this period of mounting tension and excitement that Company D elected Davis as their new second lieutenant. Their dreams, and those of Benjamin Davis, nearly became a reality when a notice went out mobilizing the whole District of Columbia National Guard: the troops were directed to assemble in their armories with their haversacks packed.[24]

The active military career of the District Guard was brief. On Monday, 25 April 1898, Davis joined Company D at the armory.

The battalion, along with the rest of the District Guard, marched to an open field just outside the Soldiers' Home on Brentwood Road. Expectations ran high. After arriving at the campsite, the troops were ordered to eat their lunches; but when they had finished eating, they received orders to return to the armory. What Davis called the "Campaign of Brentwood Road" was the end of most soldiers' active participation in the war. The guard had been recalled because the absence of the soldiers, many of whom were government employees, had hurt the functioning of the government itself. The recall to the armory also marked the termination of Davis's career as a member of the District of Columbia National Guard. When he could not find active duty through the guard, he sought other opportunities.[25]

2 | A Career Begins: 1898–1901

BENJAMIN DAVIS began his military career in the Spanish American War. During the next three years he served as an officer in the volunteers, an enlisted man in the regulars, and ultimately, a commissioned officer in the Regular Army.

When the Spanish-American War began, the War Department ignored the offers of the many whites and blacks who wanted to volunteer their services to the nation, but political pressure forced a change in attitude. By the end of the conflict, the War Department had accepted about two hundred thousand volunteers, including some state-organized black regiments. The percentage of black officers in these units varied from 100, in the Third North Carolina, to 0, in the Third Alabama.[1]

Congress also authorized ten federally raised regiments. In mid May 1898 the War Department began to recruit black enlisted personnel for four of the regiments (the Seventh through the Tenth United States Volunteer Infantry—USVI). The number and rank of the regiments' black officers posed a dilemma for the War Department. Although the black community wanted all of the officers to be black, the War Department was reluctant to allow any. In the end, blacks were limited to the rank of lieutenant in the line companies. Thus, power remained in the hands of the whites.[2]

The War Department's decision to create positions for black officers provided an opportunity for Davis. In June 1898, Capt. Jesse M. Lee, Ninth Infantry, invited Davis to call upon him. Lee, who had recently received a commission as colonel of the Tenth USVI, asked Davis to take a physical examination and then appear before a board of officers who would determine his fitness for appointment as a lieutenant in the Tenth. Davis gladly agreed. On 14 June 1898 he took his physical and was found fit for duty;

13

two weeks later he successfully passed his examination before the board of officers. The eighteen-year-old black man now fully expected to be offered a lieutenancy. Instead, Lee, pointing out Davis's youth, asked him to serve as the regimental sergeant major. Davis refused, because he felt that any future service in the war would be with a unit other than the Tenth USVI.[3]

Within a few days, Davis's hopes for a lieutenancy finally were fulfilled. In early July, Col. Eli Huggins sent Robertson Palmer to Washington to see if he could gather together the necessary sixty men to be mustered in as a company for the Eighth USVI. Palmer, a twenty-year-old white lawyer from Chicago, knew that if he could recruit that company, he would become its captain. Upon his arrival in Washington, he immediately approached Benjamin Davis. This was just what Davis had been waiting for. The lawyer offered the young black man the position of first lieutenant, as well as the power to name the second lieutenant, in exchange for helping him recruit the necessary manpower. Davis accepted; and they opened an office on E Street, N.W., between Ninth and Tenth Streets. Davis got a great deal of assistance from Charles E. Minkis, who had been a major in the M Street High School cadet corps. In return, Davis saw to it that Minkis became the second lieutenant in his company. On 8 July 1898 the company, now known as Company G, Eighth United States Volunteer Infantry, was mustered in, and on the twenty-first of July, Benjamin Davis accepted his commission as a first lieutenant in Company G. The official military career of this eighteen year old was about to begin.[4]

By mid August all twelve companies had assembled at Fort Thomas, Kentucky. Because most of the men and officers had little or no military background, the colonel characterized this group as a mass of "crude, undisciplined material." All of them would learn together.[5]

For Davis, as for many other volunteer officers, learning and teaching occurred simultaneously. In Company G, Captain Palmer had no military training, and Lieutenants Davis and Minkis had merely been high-school cadets. Although Davis was given the job of training the company in close order drill, he relied on the help of 1st Sgt. Calvin Tibbs, a veteran of five years in Troop L, Ninth Cavalry. Tibbs could not read and could sign for his pay only with great difficulty. For the first time, it struck Davis how significant a handicap the lack of a formal education was.[6]

Once Company G had settled into the camp routine, Lieutenant Davis had more time to meet the other officers. Young Lieutenant Minkis was replaced by a twenty-eight-year veteran of the Regular Army, Andrew J. Smith, who prior to the war had been a first sergeant, Company B, Twenty-fifth Infantry, a black regiment. Davis learned much about the customs of the service and the application of military principles from Smith.[7]

Another officer whom Davis met at Fort Thomas and who had a profound influence on his later life was John C. Proctor. Before his appointment to the Eighth Infantry, Proctor had served as a first sergeant in Troop I, Ninth Cavalry. He was a very handsome individual; he reminded Davis of some of Frederic Remington's portraits of cavalrymen. Proctor taught Davis to ride, a skill he would enjoy for many more years. They developed a close friendship which lasted long after the Eighth was disbanded.[8]

Davis also learned how to deal with a variety of new situations. On one occasion, Lieutenant Davis and two NCOs were ordered to go to the jail in nearby Cincinnati to pick up six prisoners, whom the detachment brought back and placed in the regimental guardhouse. On another trip to Cincinnati, Davis first encountered overt racial discrimination. Many of the soldiers frequently gathered at a drugstore on a corner of Fountain Square, where they would have refreshments and wait for the trolley to Fort Thomas. The presence of the soldiers became a nuisance to the proprietors, who, to Davis's surprise, announced that blacks would no longer be permitted to stop there. Discrimination also was evident at Fort Thomas, where there were three officers' messes that were divided along racial, as well as rank, lines. All of the captains and higher-ranking officers, all of whom were white, ate in one mess; the lieutenants—all blacks—ate in a second; and the field and staff officers—also all white—ate in a third. At first, Davis gave this arrangement no thought; then he noticed that two black staff officers—the chaplain, who was a captain, and an assistant surgeon—were messed with the lieutenants.[9]

In early October 1898 the regiment was ordered to Chickamauga Park, Georgia, to relieve the Sixth USVI, which was dispatched to Puerto Rico. The two-day train trip to Georgia was both exciting and discouraging to the officers and men of the Eighth. They expected that they, too, would soon be sent overseas, and this pleased them. At the same time, the regiment now had to face overt racial hostility; also, they soon learned that they were in Georgia merely to guard the supplies at Chickamauga Park. From the beginning, Colonel Huggins realized that racial prejudice would pose a "source of constant danger" to his regiment and that many southerners were "ready to distort and magnify every instance of misconduct." For Lieutenant Davis, this was the first time he had come into direct contact with widespread manifestations of Jim Crow; he found it quite distressing. He noted with annoyance the signs in the railway stations indicating "Colored—White." Unfortunately this was the first of many encounters with racial prejudice while he was in the Eighth.[10]

Many in the regiment soon became bored with cleaning the camp and guarding supplies, but Lieutenant Davis was expanding his job experiences. He was assigned a variety of new duties, indicating that his previous performance was well received. Lt. Col. Archelaus M. Hughes, who had served under the Confederate general Nathan B. Forrest in the Civil War, asked for Davis to be designated as battalion adjutant. With this position went the responsibility for all the paper work. Davis's education at the M Street High School had prepared him for this new assignment. Despite Hughes's background, the two men worked well together. A few weeks later, Davis assumed the duties of officer in charge of prisoners. There were a large number of prisoners who were serving sentences handed down during the period when Camp Chickamauga had been much larger. Some of the prisoners had received dishonorable discharges and long prison sentences; others were awaiting transfer to military prisons. Davis considered his assignment "a great responsibility," and although he found this job very unpleasant, he carried it out quite capably. As he became acquainted with the conditions of the prisoners, he began to make changes in their situation. Many of them had been kept busy moving stones from one pile to another. Davis felt that this was a waste of time, so he replaced this task with more productive ones. The men dug ditches to drain wet areas, and they constructed walks. He also tried to impress upon them the idea that they had to accept responsibility for their actions. He felt that this would help them recover their dignity. Lieutenant Davis believed it was important to treat the prisoners as human beings.[11]

Most of the duties assigned to the Eighth involved little more than waiting for orders, and leisure time grew heavy on their hands. For a while in early 1899 the regiment was under orders to go to Cuba, but these were countermanded. Camp duties continued to be dull, but leisure activities off the post became fraught with danger. White civilians in Chattanooga and other nearby towns resented the occasional visits of the soldiers and officers. The civilians harassed the military men and bombarded the War Department with requests to have the unit moved elsewhere. One day a member of the post guard discovered a flour sack that had been placed near the camp hospital. In it he found two sticks of dynamite, ready to be lit. The officers took this as a broad hint that the whites would use violence against the unit, a hostile attitude that did not go unnoticed by the regiment. Davis remarked that a visit to Chattanooga had "a most depressive effect" upon him.[12]

By February 1899 the army had decided that the regiment probably would be mustered out. A number of officers, including Gen. Nelson A. Miles, commanding general of the army, requested that the unit be kept for further service, possibly in the Philippines. All of these pleas were in vain, however; and in early March, final orders were issued to disband the regiment.[13]

Even the process of mustering the men out was not without racial problems. The discharged soldiers were involved in skirmishes in Chattanooga and Nashville. When the troop train stopped in Chattanooga, the men bought liquor and then vented their frustrations by shooting at white civilians, two of whom were wounded. Other incidents occurred later when the trains went through Nashville. The former soldiers were attacked and robbed while at the station. By the middle of March the men had dispersed, and the paper work had been filed. The Eighth United States Volunteer Infantry had ceased to exist.[14]

At this time, people began to evaluate the Eighth, especially its discipline and its black officers. The conclusions were often quite contradictory. Davis, who had learned a great deal from the experience, thought he and his men had worked well together: they had been loyal, and "they felt a great interest in my success." Colonel Huggins, who also thought Davis had performed well, suggested to Davis that he seek a commission in the Regular Army and even wrote a letter of recommendation. However, Capt. William Hughes, the mustering-out officer, had different opinions about Davis, the other black officers, and the regiment itself. Hughes felt that the black soldiers did not have the same respect for the black officers as they did for white officers, and he noted that in terms of discipline, Company G was one of the four worst companies. In his general comments on the Eighth, he suggested that it was a regiment hampered by the limited abilities of the black soldiers and the black officers.[15]

Benjamin's return to his home on Eleventh Street, N.W., brought him to another milestone. The local black newspaper reported that "Lieutenant Oliver Davis looks well since his return to the city;" however, he and his family were engaged in another discussion about his choice of career. His mother encouraged him to consider the Baptist ministry, but he had had unpleasant experiences with some of the older members of his church, and this job did not really appeal to him. Reflecting on his recently concluded tour of duty, Benjamin decided that he liked military life and that he got a great deal of satisfaction from being an officer. He wanted more. Louis Davis then tried to use his influence to obtain an appointment to West Point for his younger son. He was able to contact someone close to President William McKinley with his request, but the president's staff said that appointing a black man to the United States Military Academy was not politically feasible at that time. Despite Davis's good academic and military record, his race was a handicap. This turn of events naturally upset Benjamin.[16]

Despite this setback, he did not relinquish his dream to become an army officer. Although the route through West Point was closed, he decided to try for another volunteer commission. In 1899, Congress authorized several volunteer regiments to help occupy and pacify the newly acquired Philippine Islands. The War Department decided to fill two of the regiments with black enlisted personnel and black officers up through the rank of captain. In late March 1899, Davis applied for a commission in one of the regiments and was "strongly recommended" for the position by Colonel Huggins. Senator Shelby Cullom of Illinois and Mrs. John Logan also wrote letters of support. Mrs. Logan, a lifelong friend of the Davis family, stated that Benjamin was "of unusual intelligence and fitness" for the position he desired. Despite these efforts, he was denied a commission.[17]

Davis persevered, for there were two more paths to a commission. Because it was unlikely that he could attain the position directly from civilian life, he chose to enlist, serve two years, and then take a competitive examination for a commission. John Proctor, whom Davis saw frequently during the spring of 1899, also encouraged Davis to go with him when he reenlisted in Troop I, Ninth Cavalry. Proctor's friendship, the chance to ride horses, and the possibility of a commission convinced Davis that he should enlist; and he and Proctor did so in June 1899 at Washington Barracks.[18]

The arrival of the two men at the recruiting station in Washington coincided with the army's need for black manpower. In January 1899 the commander of the Ninth Cavalry notified the War Department that the regiment would soon have a number of vacancies, created by expiring enlistments. At the same time, Maj. Martin Hughes, Ninth Cavalry, also asked some of his old veterans, including John Proctor, to help the regiment refill the ranks. He asked them to reenlist and to find men who were capable of performing clerical duties. During his service in the

Eighth, Proctor had seen evidence of Davis's clerical abilities and thus knew that Hughes's requirement could be met. When Davis and Proctor applied for enlistment, Troop I—the latter's old troop and the one he wanted to rejoin—was already up to its authorized strength. However, Major Hughes was able to get them accepted because of their skills—one as an experienced soldier and the other as a clerk.[19]

It took the two enlisted men nearly a week to travel from Washington to Fort Duchesne, Utah, where Troop I was stationed. Their long rail journey ended at Price Station, in eastern Utah. After a brief rest, they boarded a stagecoach for the two-day, ninety-mile ride to the fort. As they neared the post, the driver awakened Davis, pointed to a green spot in the distance, and said to him, "Soldier, there's where you get off."[20]

The post and its garrison were typical of the late-nineteenth-century army. Fort Duchesne had been established in 1886 to control the Ute Indians. The central feature of the post was a parade ground. On the western edge were eight wooden houses for the officers, and barracks for six companies of troops were on two other sides. Further away were the post gardens, bakery, shops, granary, corral, and hospital. This small military world was about 170 miles from the nearest metropolis, Salt Lake City.[21]

Although the post could easily have accommodated many men, it was never very large. Usually there were one or two troops or companies, totaling no more than 150 men. During Davis's first six months at the fort, Troop I, under the command of Capt. John Guilfoyle, was the only unit present. Among the first lieutenants assigned to the troop was Charles Young, the only black officer in the army. At the time, however, Young was on detached duty at Wilberforce University. The garrison doubled in size when Troop K, Ninth Cavalry, arrived in December 1899. In July 1900, Maj. Martin Hughes arrived to take command of the post, thus boosting the number of officers present to three. The isolation of Fort Duchesne, the size of the garrison, and the few officers present were typical of the army at this time.[22]

As Davis settled into his new role as an enlisted man, he began to learn more about the army. Many of the black enlisted men had been in the service for a long time. Davis estimated that among his troop there were only five men who were serving their first term of enlistment. Troop I had the reputation of being the "Old Soldiers' Home." One such veteran was Sgt. John Johnson, also known as "Old Issue," who had already served twenty years in the Twenty-fourth Infantry and eight years in Troop K, Ninth Cavalry. Davis and Johnson spent a lot of time together, and the sergeant helped the recruit to learn the customs of the service and the history of the unit. Davis also now began to understand the role of the officer. As he later recalled it, the black soldiers regarded their troop commander as a father figure, and the commanders took their role seriously. The officers listened to the problems and sorrows of the soldiers. If they had to punish the troopers, they did so with the "usual parental attitude—This punishment hurts me worse than it does you but I must perform my duty." This familial relationship was fostered by the fact that enlisted men and officers remained together for many years. The result was a strong spirit of loyalty. These lessons had a lasting impact on the young Davis, who would recall them many years later to counter the arguments of those who claimed that blacks and whites could not get along together in the army.[23]

Many of Davis's men were illiterate, and he became fascinated by the ways they adjusted to this handicap. They learned the skills of soldiering through practice and memory. Davis recalled a first sergeant who memorized the troop's roll. When new people joined or when men reported from detached service or sick report, the sergeant would have the troop clerk enter their names and then have him repeat the roll until the sergeant had learned it. Memory also substituted for literacy at other times as well. The illiterate NCOs memorized the whole book of drill instructions, which someone read to them. Davis checked one of the NCOs by asking him the regulation governing a certain drill maneuver. The man responded with the number of the relevant paragraph and the page on which it could be found. Davis said, "I never knew him to miss."[24]

Davis had a genuine concern for his men. As troop clerk, he

soon became aware that the majority of the men could not even sign their names. Although there was a school on the post, few soldiers attended it. At the same time, many men wanted to learn how to sign the payroll properly. This became the incentive that Davis later used when he became the post's schoolteacher. Although he had no experience for this job and had avoided a career in teaching, he undertook this particular assignment with enthusiasm. He began by writing the name of each of his soldier-pupils in large letters. Each man then practiced copying the letters until he knew them all. Davis's next step was to teach them to connect the letters of their names. Once the soldiers had mastered these letters, Davis added others, and soon the students knew the whole alphabet. Eventually each soldier was able to sign the payroll. "Old Issue" was very proud of this. When asked by his comrades why he was smiling he replied: "I have done signed the payroll. That recruit has taught me to write."[25]

It was not long before Davis's efforts yielded rewards. Captain Guilfoyle had been watching Davis from the beginning. Mrs. John Logan wrote to the captain, praising Davis as an "exemplary young man." This letter prompted the captain to summon Davis, to talk to him about his education and background. Guilfoyle also noted Davis's fine work and promoted him to corporal and troop clerk. The responsibility of this job included preparing the morning report, filling out the muster rolls and payrolls, and handling the troop correspondence. Many years later, one observer recalled how Davis "could rattle a typewriter."[26]

Because Fort Duchesne was so isolated, the men had to create their own entertainment. When Charles Young rejoined the troop, he organized a brass band and several other musical ensembles. Davis was impressed by the effect that group singing had, especially while on the march. There was also a small library, located in the administration building. The collection included mainly governmental publications, and Davis spent some of his spare time there. But overall, life was uneventful at Fort Duchesne.[27]

Benjamin Davis never lost sight of his ultimate goal: an officer's commission. Mrs. Logan had written to Col. Thomas

McGregor, commander of the Ninth, that Davis was "anxious" to earn a commission by "faithful, efficient, and gallant service." The first opportunity came in August 1899, when the army began to appoint officers for the volunteer regiments that had been created to end the Philippine-American War. These were the same regiments to which Davis had applied earlier in the year. Unbeknownst to Davis, Colonel Huggins recommended him for a commission. In addition, Captain Guilfoyle asked Davis and the other black NCOs if they wanted to try for these positions. A number of soldiers, including Davis, responded affirmatively, and some of them were accepted. John Proctor was appointed a captain this time. Despite a strong letter of recommendation from Mrs. Logan, Davis's application for a commission in the volunteers was once again rejected.[28]

This setback did not deter Davis, and in the following year, when Congress authorized an expansion of the army and the officer corps, Davis got another chance. Now he had to pass a competitive examination for the Regular Army commission he sought. Charles Young gave Davis special coaching in mathematics. When the news spread around the post that Sergeant Major Davis was preparing to take a test for an officer's commission, the reactions were mixed. The old soldiers of the Ninth were surprised, and some of them told Davis that black enlisted men were not supposed to take the test. They felt that even if he could somehow pass the written exam, he would fail the physical. When Davis told these old soldiers that the regulations did not prohibit blacks from taking the test, they were partially satisfied by this response. They were more convinced, however, when Davis reported that he had gotten encouragement from Major Hughes, the post commander, and the whites in the post's Hospital Corps detachment. Despite these assurances of support, the arguments of his comrades troubled Davis.[29]

To an impartial observer, Davis's chances of overcoming all the obstacles seemed quite remote. One had only to look at the examples of those blacks who had already tried for a commission. There had been a longstanding resistance within the army to the idea of having blacks serve as officers. Although there were

more than 180,000 blacks in the Union Army during the Civil
War, there were fewer than 100 black line officers, and none of
these volunteer officers was allowed into the Regular Army after
the war. Consequently, the four new black regiments had only
white officers. During the succeeding decades, a few blacks had
been nominated to the United States Military Academy, but most
of them had not made it through the first year. It was not until
1877 that the first black graduated—Henry O. Flipper. Flipper's
military life was uneventful until 1881, when he encountered
Col. William R. Shafter, his new post commander. The officer
apparently took a dislike to Flipper and ultimately relieved him
of his duties, placed him in the guardhouse, and finally had him
court-martialed for embezzlement and conduct unbecoming an
officer. The crucial issue at the trial was the point raised by Flipper's defense counsel: "Whether it is possible for a colored man
to secure and hold a position as an officer of the army. . . ." The
fact that Flipper lost the case and was discharged from the army
would seem to indicate that it was difficult to be a black officer
in the army. Similar problems were encountered by the next grad-
uates—John Alexander, class of 1887, and Charles Young, class
of 1889. The next black to graduate from West Point was Benjamin O. Davis, Jr., in 1936. Prior to 1901 there were very few
other opportunities to earn a commission from the ranks. When
John Alexander died in 1894, Davis's own lieutenant, Charles
Young, was the only black officer in the army.[30]

Few whites encouraged blacks to apply for commissions. Most
whites believed that black enlisted men would not obey black
officers and that blacks would be out of place in the officer corps,
a world of gentlemen. There was also the fear that eventually
a black officer might be in a position to give orders to a white
officer. Both Davis and Young rejected these arguments, although
for different reasons. Charles Young felt strongly that there
should be equality between the races, and he wanted to show
whites that blacks could perform well. He believed that if Davis
could pass the tests leading to a commission, it would be another
proof of racial equality. He also looked upon Davis as a protégé
(maybe even the son he never had) and wanted him to succeed.

Davis, on the other hand, was not out to break racial barriers but, instead, to take advantage of an opportunity. He was not a militant; he was more an accommodationist, in the tradition of Booker T. Washington. Davis had seen that on his own post, blacks and whites could work together. He personally got along well with the white officers at Fort Duchesne and had also observed how well the racially mixed Hospital Corps detachment at the fort functioned. This experience further convinced him that "colored and white men can work together."[31]

In August 1900, Davis took the next step toward a commission: he submitted his application, along with strong letters of recommendation from Major Hughes and Lieutenant Young. Hughes noted that Davis had done the assigned clerical jobs with "scarcely an error or omission" and that Davis, if he received a commission, would fill the position to the satisfaction of the country. Young stated that Davis was "temperate, polite, intelligent, trustworthy, and faithful to the duties of his office." Davis also sent copies of these letters to his father in Washington and asked for his help: "Use all the pressure that you can. If I win this means a fortune for life and if I lose it will be no disgrace." The apparent mercenary nature of this letter seems out of character for Davis, but he may have felt that this argument would sway his father. Louis Davis asked people he knew to send letters of recommendation on his son's behalf.[32]

The examination for a commission was administered by a board of officers who met at Fort Leavenworth, Kansas. Davis was surprised to see Lieutenant Colonel Lee presiding. He was the same officer who, three years earlier, had tried to persuade Davis to settle for an enlisted rank rather than to try for a commission in the volunteers. Lee recognized Davis, congratulated him on his success in the army, and wished him well on the battery of tests.[33]

Over the next two weeks the prospective officers took a variety of different tests. First, a physical examination narrowed the group down to twenty-three. Next, they took a series of written tests. They knew that they had to pass every phase of the examination. The officer who coordinated the testing told them that as soon as it was apparent that a candidate could not achieve a passing grade for all the tests, he would be notified and returned to his station. Thus, no news was good news. The first series of tests were on English grammar and composition. Davis received a score of 83, one of his higher marks. Five of the twenty-three candidates quit after this round.[34]

The pressure increased: on successive days they were tested on the Constitution of the United States, international law, various forms of mathematics, geography, history, and army regulations. Davis did well in some of these and poorly on others. He received a score of 75 on the math, 73.5 on the geography, 96 on constitutional law, 92 on army regulations, but only 67 on history. The history test had included questions on relatively recent European and American events, and Davis could not answer any of the items. He knew nothing about the French Revolution or the German Empire. His complete answer to a question on the causes of the American Revolution was "English oppression and severe taxing without representation." After each examination session, Davis went to the post library and checked his answers, especially those for the history questions. This was shortly to prove to be a very helpful practice.[35]

Once the written examinations were finished, the rest of the process went quickly. The candidates had to face one hour of testing their physical skills and another hour of questioning on drill regulations and their application on the drill field. Davis got a score of 95 on this section. The board then reviewed each candidate's military record, letters of recommendation, and other supporting evidence. Davis received two scores of 100. On 12 March the board met to review all of the documents. Those candidates who had survived were ordered to appear before the board. The prospective officers waited anxiously in the anteroom. Davis, who was third on the list, was worried as he watched the first two candidates return showing no emotion on their faces. When it was Davis's turn, the board questioned him on history, the only subject that he had failed. This time he was able to give full answers to the questions. The officers were puzzled, because Davis's answers seemed to indicate that he knew information that he had not written on the examination. When the board asked him about this strange situation, Davis told them about his research procedures. He also explained that Fort Duchesne had very few books on history and none on modern (i.e., nineteenth-century) events. The board was satisfied with this response and informed Davis that he had passed. He later found out that he had earned an average score of 86 and had ranked third among the twelve men in his group who qualified for a commission. The examining board cautioned Davis not to tell those who were still waiting outside how he had done. Davis, however, left the room with a broad smile on his face.[36]

Davis's success brought a variety of reactions. The *Washington Bee* wrote that Davis "represents some of Washington's best stock." It predicted a great future for him: "His infatuation for duty, his love for obedience, will make him that brilliant military strategist of which the race is bound to be proud." They also noted that his parents were receiving congratulations from friends all over the country. However, when Louis Davis first heard the news, he did not realize it was his own son. He said his son was named Ollie, not Benjamin. It was not until Louis got home that Henrietta showed him the telegram she had received from their son. Then Louis accepted the fact that his younger son would become an army officer. Davis's close army friends were also quite happy. When he returned to Fort Duchesne, the garrison gave him a warm welcome. Those old soldiers who had tried to discourage him were most profuse in their praise.[37]

In 1901, Benjamin Davis was one of two successful black candidates for a commission; the other was John E. Green. Green had served two years in the infantry and received his commission in this branch. Davis and Green were to have their careers interrelated for the next thirty years.[38]

Although Davis passed the examination in mid March, it was several months before he received his commission. During this time his troop was ordered to the Philippines. It was part of the massive troop concentration needed to win the Philippine-American War. The Third Squadron's travel orders came through at the time Davis was finishing the testing at Fort Leavenworth.

When he returned, Major Hughes asked Davis if he wanted to stay at Fort Duchesne or go with the troop to San Francisco, the port of embarkation for the Philippines. Davis decided to go to California with the squadron. While in San Francisco, Davis saw Dr. William Purnell, a physician he had met during his service in the Eighth, who showed him the sights of the city. In the meantime, Davis anxiously awaited orders or news about his commission.[39]

Finally it was time for embarkation, and again Davis had to make a decision. He opted to remain with his regiment and travel to the Philippines. On 15 April 1901 the squadron sailed on the USS *Logan* through the Golden Gate, heading west. It was Davis's first sea voyage. Although many of the men became seasick, Davis did not, and he kept busy doing paper work for the squadron's headquarters. After eight days at sea, the vessel sailed into Pearl Harbor, Hawaii, and Davis spent three days visiting the Honolulu area. After this brief layover, the vessel departed for Manila Bay. Fifteen days later, its passengers were happy to sight land again. Davis remained with his unit, awaiting orders, and finally, four days after their arrival, he heard the long-expected news. One day he met John Guilfoyle, his old troop commander, who asked why Davis was still with the Ninth. When Davis replied that he was still an enlisted man, Guilfoyle responded with the information that Davis's commission had come through and that he was now a second lieutenant assigned to the Tenth Cavalry. Guilfoyle went back to Manila and brought out a copy of the official order. Davis was then discharged as an enlisted man and took the oath as a second lieutenant. A long-awaited epoch in his life now began.[40]

3 | Triumphs and Tragedies: 1901-1920

DURING HIS FIRST DECADES as an officer, Davis performed a variety of duties, visited two foreign countries, became a teacher, got married, and began a family. He also discovered the obstacles to advancing in his chosen profession. In the process he demonstrated some character traits that were to both help and hinder him throughout his long military career.

When he arrived in the Philippines with the Ninth Cavalry, the Philippine-American War was almost over. The Filipinos wanted their independence but were unsuccessful. The United States Army finished putting down the rebellion and then aided in the implementation of American control of local institutions. Because Lieutenant Davis had no training in either combat leadership or civil government, he had to learn on the job.

In late May 1901 the transport that was carrying Davis and Troop M, Ninth Cavalry, arrived at Calbayog, on the western coast of the island of Samar in the eastern Philippines. During the next few months, Davis led several patrols into the countryside. On the morning of 27 May 1901, he took a detachment of twenty-five enlisted men, two native guides, and four bearers on reconnaissance to Villa Real, a small town about twenty-five miles to the north of his base at Santa Rita. After marching overland for twelve miles, they found themselves at the coast. The guides claimed that they knew of no way to move ahead. Young Lieutenant Davis decided to set up camp and think about the problem. By the next morning he had devised a solution: he commandeered five boats, and with a small party, including the guides, he rowed along the coast for about one hour until they reached the village of Bongon. "At this place I found white flags of all descriptions hanging from the windows of the houses." After having acquired more guides and bearers, he began an overland push until they arrived at Villa Real that evening. Again everything was in order. When Lieutenant Davis inquired as to the whereabouts of the insurgents, he was told that none had been seen in the vicinity for over a year. The party then retraced its steps and returned to the base camp.[1]

The local diseases, on the other hand, posed a greater menace than did the insurgents. Davis was struck down with dengue fever, a tropical disease transmitted by mosquitoes, which caused him to suffer from fever and severe pain in his joints before he recovered several weeks later.[2]

In mid August 1901 the twenty-three-year-old lieutenant was assigned to Troop F, Tenth Cavalry. Later, Col. Samuel M. Whitside told Davis that the several months' delay in his assignment was normal and not because the regiment was having difficulty finding a troop commander who would accept a black officer; in fact, a number of officers had wanted him.[3]

During the next twelve months, Davis was stationed in the province of Iloilo on the island of Panay, where his duties were similar to the ones that he had performed on Samar. In September 1901 about one-half of Troop F was dispersed into small detachments. Between then and March 1902, Davis commanded a group, varying in size from twenty-five to thirty men, who garrisoned the town of Lambunao. Their major tasks were to provide a stabilizing force and to demonstrate the presence of the new United States civil government. This provided an opportunity to interact with the people, and Davis learned to speak Spanish and Visayan. The ease with which he picked up these languages demonstrated an ability that would prove beneficial throughout his military service. It was at this time that he received the first of many good efficiency reports: his commanding officer judged Davis "excellent."[4]

After nearly a year of service in the Philippines with the Tenth Cavalry, Davis and Troop F returned to the United States. He and his men joined the rest of the regiment, and they all left Manila aboard an army transport. There was a brief stopover in Nagasaki before they set sail for home. In August 1902 they arrived in San Francisco and then completed the journey to their new station at Fort Washakie, Wyoming, by train.[5]

Located on the Little Wind River, the fort was about 150 miles from Rawlins, Wyoming. The garrison included Davis, Capt. Thomas Carson, and the seventy-six enlisted men of Troop F. In December 1902, 1st Lt. Raymond S. Einslow joined the two other officers; and two years later, another troop from the Tenth and one company of the Eleventh Infantry arrived at the post. There were now seven officers, but Davis was the only black; this resulted in his complete social isolation.[6]

With so few officers present, each had to perform a variety of duties. Davis's earliest assignments were as adjutant, as head of the summary court, and as commander of the Ordnance, Signal, Engineering, and Recruiting details. When other officers arrived, he gave up some of these responsibilities, but assumed others. This variety and frequent shifting of jobs was a normal situation, given the duties that needed to be performed and the limited number of officers available to do them.[7]

One of Lieutenant Davis's major tasks was the supervision of the hunting parties. Military posts in some parts of the West, such as Fort Washakie in Wyoming, supplemented their food supplies with wild game. In October 1903, Davis and four enlisted men went on a fourteen-day trip to stalk and kill elk in the Jackson Hole area; deer were considered too small to be hunted. The hunting party covered about 275 miles on this expedition. Every enlisted man went hunting at least once a season to keep his skills sharp. When the hunters returned with the meat, it was dressed and then preserved in the post's ice house for later use.[8]

With his new career firmly established, Davis decided it was time to get married. In October 1902 he returned to Washington on a thirty-day leave, the first time he had been home since he had earned his commission. He was particularly interested in seeing Elnora Dickerson, whom he had known since he was thirteen when he had moved to his new home, one block from her house. He found her a very "pleasant person."[9]

Elnora was one of Edward and Lydia Dickerson's nine children. Both parents had been born in Virginia and had moved to the District by the end of the Civil War. Edward Dickerson had earned a living in a variety of occupations, but mainly as a porter

Elnora Dickerson Davis, the first wife of Benjamin O. Davis, Sr.

or teamster. Although he himself had no education, Edward made sure that all of his children went to school. In 1876 they purchased a house at 1711 Eleventh Street, N.W., which was valued for tax purposes at $1,800. After Edward died in 1886, the family still remained together. The educational achievements and property ownership of the Dickersons, as well as their light skin color, placed them, like the Davises, in Washington's middle-class black society. When Benjamin proposed, Elnora accepted, and they were married on 23 October 1902.[10]

Once Davis had made the decision to get married, he also began a process to accelerate his promotion. At that time, the key elements for promotion were an officer's place on the seniority list within his branch and the successful completion of a series of examinations. In August 1902, Davis asked the adjutant general whether his service as an officer in the Eighth USVI could be counted as time in rank. The army replied that inasmuch as he had entered the officer corps through an enlisted men's competitive examination, his prior service as an officer could not be considered. Three years later, however, the War Department reversed its decision and granted credit for volunteer service. As a result, Davis moved up to third on the cavalry list. This opened the way for his promotion to the rank of first lieutenant.[11]

During the intervening years, Benjamin and Elnora lived quietly in the backwater of Fort Washakie, where at different times he served as post adjutant, post quartermaster, and post commissary. He was "efficient and zealous" in the performance of these duties. In September 1903, Davis took command of a party of twenty-seven men on a two-day practice march, which went down the Little Wind River from the post and then returned. For three months in 1904 he was the instructor at the post school for enlisted men. On several different occasions he was placed in charge of the post exchange. His efficiency reports during this period indicate that he was doing well as a company officer. One officer commented that Davis was "as competent to command as any Second Lieutenant I have ever met."[12]

The early part of Davis's career as an officer coincided with an increased emphasis on officer education. Efforts of such leaders as Secretary of War Elihu Root resulted in educational programs for enlisted men and officers. The school at Fort Washakie was expanded to serve more students for a longer term, as new programs for officers were required at each post, and service schools grew. Lieutenant Davis eagerly participated in the officers's school, where each officer lectured the others on a particular topic. In the 1902-1903 term, Davis studied Cavalry Drill Regulations, Small Arms Firing Regulations, and Administration. At the end of the course he was examined by a board of officers and was declared proficient. The following year his daily recitations were good enough to exempt him from the term's final examination. For this course he wrote an essay on "The Training of the Troopers for Duty with a Small Cavalry Patrol." Captain Carson showed his pleasure with Davis's work by nominating him in May 1903 for the course at the General Service and Staff College at Fort Leavenworth, Kansas. Although Davis was not accepted, his nomination was indicative of his high level of performance.[13]

Second Lieutenant Davis also participated in several competitive athletic events, though without much success. Many of the black troops enjoyed baseball and played it well, and at isolated posts, officers also took part in the games. Davis, who had athletic abilities, played in some of the games. In June 1904 he injured his knee playing baseball; this caused him to hobble for two weeks. The previous year he had been one of four cavalry officers to participate in the Tri-Department Competition in Pistols, which was held at Whipple Barracks, Arizona. He represented the Tenth Cavalry against competitors from the Departments of California, Columbia, and Colorado. On the way to the match he experienced another incident of prejudice when he stopped at the train station in Las Vegas, New Mexico, for a bite to eat. A waiter told him that they did not serve blacks, but when Davis responded in Spanish, the man apologized profusely. It annoyed Davis that the waiter accorded a foreign black the respect that he denied to a native black. This unpleasant reminder of the prejudice that a black man faced in America may have had an impact on Davis's performance in the pistol competition, for he failed to place among the top twelve finishers.[14]

Davis's performance as an officer and his movement up the seniority list soon made him eligible for promotion. In May 1904 he traveled to the regimental headquarters at Fort Robinson, Nebraska, to appear before a promotion board, whose members quizzed him on a variety of topics covered in the post officer's school the previous two years. He earned a passing score in every area, but this performance was not good enough, given his position on the promotion list at the time. Davis tried again the next year, after his time as a volunteer officer was taken into account. He was given another series of examinations, and this time he earned an average of 84.72. The board recommended him for promotion, and the army approved. After four years as a second lieutenant, the twenty-seven-year-old Benjamin Davis became a first lieutenant.[15]

The army had a difficult time assigning the newly promoted black officer, because it was the policy to limit the assignment of black officers to the black regiments. Davis requested that he be reassigned to the Tenth; he also suggested that if no immediate vacancy were forthcoming, he could be switched with 1st Lt. John Wagner of the Tenth, who wanted to transfer. This was the solution. The available opening was in the Third Cavalry, but the army did not want to assign Davis to this white unit. The War Department, disregarding the request of the regimental commander, ordered Davis back to the Tenth. On 21 April 1905 he reported for duty with Troop M at Fort Robinson, where he remained for four months before being ordered for duty as professor of military science and tactics (PMS&T) at Wilberforce University. This was to be the first of many tours of detached service.[16]

Wilberforce, in central Ohio, had been established in 1856 by the Methodist Episcopal Church, North. By the late nineteenth century the African Methodist Episcopal (A.M.E.) Church, a black denomination, had begun to support Wilberforce, which had evolved from a preparatory school into a small university. During the early 1890s it established a military program, so its need for black officers as instructors provided a solution to the army's problem of assigning them to a white line regiment. Both Charles Young and John Alexander served tours of duty as teachers at the school. When Young returned to the Ninth Cavalry in 1899, the school's military program was without a teacher, so over the next few years the school's administration sought to have Davis assigned to them. Although the War Department offered to send some retired white officers, the school indicated that it wanted a man "of our own race variety." In 1905, Horace Talbert, secretary of the school, visited Secretary of War William Howard Taft to present his request to Taft personally. This time Taft told Talbert that Davis would be assigned in time for the beginning of the fall term.[17]

Davis was not very happy about this new assignment, because Wilberforce was a church-dominated school, and Davis felt he would be out of place there, especially after having lived and worked with soldiers for so long. In many ways he was correct: it took him a while to adjust to this new environment, and in some ways he never did. The school officials professed to be shocked by his barracks language. On his first Sunday at Wilberforce, Davis did not go to church. President Joshua Jones asked Davis why he hadn't attended, and Davis responded that he did not want to go and if Jones did not like this, then he could ask Washington to relieve Davis. Jones backed down. A similar conflict occurred when Davis had some liquor delivered to his house, in violation of a school rule that prohibited alcoholic beverages on the campus. Davis hoped that the delivery would go undetected, but a bottle fell out of the packing case and broke on the ground. The school officials were horrified and publicly protested, but the young officer ignored them. Conditions at the school did not really develop to his liking, but he decided to finish his tour of service. Charles Young had encouraged Davis in this goal and had challenged him to teach the young students some discipline. Davis believed that continuing at his post would set an example of this quality for the students.[18]

Young also helped the new instructor by renting Davis a furnished house. The rent of $24 a month just equaled the army's allowance for housing. It was a comfortable house, with an attached stable. Davis bought a horse to use in his teaching and "to keep myself in the proper physical condition." After several years of living in Young's house, the Davis family decided to buy their own home. They also bought a piano, rugs, pictures, and two beds (one large, one small). The latter was for Olive Elnora Davis, their first child, who was born in April 1905.[19]

Teaching military subjects at Wilberforce was difficult since only three hours per week were allocated for military instruction. In an effort to instill discipline, the students were required to wear their uniforms to morning chapel and to classes. They were to be punished for infractions of these rules. Davis addressed the students at the beginning of each academic year and tried to make them aware of the necessity for self-discipline. Despite these efforts, he felt he was being sabotaged by the lack of support he received from the school's president.[20]

The disagreements between Davis and Wilberforce's President Jones soon involved the War Department. Davis reported a number of incidents in which his attempts to discipline students had been nullified by President Jones. "Under the present conditions the military professor deems it impossible to properly perform his duty." The army's response was to ask Davis to prepare a full report about conditions at Wilberforce.[21]

Charges and countercharges flew between Davis and President Jones. In his report, Davis gave a number of examples of the school's unwillingness to accept his conception of discipline. The General Staff analyzed the report and concluded that while Davis had some legitimate complaints, many of the problems had stemmed from his "excessive demands." Jones responded to the two reports with an attack on Davis: he called Davis "somewhat unreasonable, very much inclined to find fault and to complain about little things that cannot be prevented." This exchange of letters brought the controversy to a temporary halt, Davis continued as military instructor, and conditions at the university did improve, though the basic problem remained unsolved. The controversy demonstrated a lack of flexibility in Davis's relations with the school administrators that was to recur.[22]

Despite the problems at the school, Benjamin and Elnora did enjoy the company of the faculty and of black people who lived at Wilberforce and nearby Xenia. These social opportunities were a change from their more solitary life in Wyoming. In June 1906 many famous people, including Booker T. Washington, attended the golden jubilee of the university. Davis, however, was more interested in talking with William T. Anderson and George W. Prioleau, black chaplains in the cavalry regiments.[23]

Teaching at Wilberforce was not limited to the classroom. In January 1907, Davis gave a paper to the Sodalian Literary Society, a campus group, on "Military Training in Civil Schools." The speech reflected the ideas then current in the military—that training must go on in peacetime so that the country would be prepared for wartime emergencies. According to Davis, rifle training should be emphasized, shooting galleries ought to be constructed, and money should be allocated for weapons and ammunition. He also argued for a system of national military training to create a true reserve force. With these ideas as a framework, one can see why Davis was so insistent upon improving the quality of the program at Wilberforce and why he kept trying to get President Jones to support his ideas on discipline.[24]

Davis's views on discipline were further put to the test by the furor that erupted over the Brownsville incident of 1906. In December of that year, President Theodore Roosevelt discharged without honor three companies of the Twenty-fifth Infantry because the men had refused to confess that they had shot up the town of Brownsville, Texas. The black community was outraged at Roosevelt's order and demanded that he rescind it, which the president refused to do. Privately, Davis felt that the decision had been made and that it should be obeyed. Over the next few months a series of speakers at Wilberforce attacked Roosevelt and supported Senator Joseph B. Foraker, who defended the black soldiers. At the 1907 commencement, Foraker spoke on the theme "Stand up for Your Rights and Make Everybody Else Stand up for Them"—an idea that Davis, too, believed and practiced, although he could not support the senator on this particular issue. Eventually a few of the men were allowed back into the army. It was an injustice that disturbed blacks for many years.[25]

During the summers of 1906, 1907, and 1909, Davis was an instructor for the District of Columbia's First Separate Battalion. Each year, Davis inspected the unit, supervised its drills, and watched its field exercises. The three maneuver camps gave Davis a rare opportunity to serve with troops and to experience some pseudo-combat situations. "Many things which I have studied in the Garrison Schools I have seen actually executed in the field and I now have a conception of these things that I could not have obtained in any other way." The D.C. militia leaders found his work "very satisfactory" and frequently requested his help, and the War Department was most willing to cooperate. During the 1909 maneuvers in Massachusetts, Davis was asked to organize a bicycle corps, whose members were given special instruction in reconnaissance, reporting, and carrying of messages. However, it soon became clear that the bicycle squad was road bound. This experience convinced Davis that bicycles would not replace horses in any war situation. When the exercises ended, he was commended by Brig. Gen. Ernest Harris, commander of the District's National Guard.[26]

Army regulations supposedly limited detached duty to three years, so Davis anticipated his departure from Wilberforce. After the annual inspection in the spring of 1908, however, President Jones wrote the War Department that the military program "has grown in value, favor and interest with students and faculty." Jones believed not only that Davis had become "a real necessity" to the university, but also that the idea of another tour of duty would be acceptable to the lieutenant. Without consulting Davis, the War Department agreed to this request and assigned him for another year.[27]

The 1908-1909 school year was not to be a happy one, as Davis clashed with the new president, William Scarborough, over an old issue—discipline. Although it appeared to Davis that Scarborough was not supporting him, Scarborough nevertheless asked the War Department to retain Davis for another term. The War Department ignored the request, however, and assigned another black officer, Lt. John E. Green.[28]

After the 1909 National Guard summer camp, Davis was reassigned to his old regiment, the Ninth Cavalry. He arrived at the regimental headquarters, Fort Ethan Allen, Vermont, in late November, but one week later he received the news that he was being reassigned to the American Legation in Monrovia, the capital of Liberia.[29]

The United States had very few military attachés at the time, and most of them were usually assigned to the American embassies in countries that were major military powers. The exceptions involved the black officers (Young, Green, and Davis), who in the years before World War I were detailed to the predominately black countries of Haiti and Liberia.

The independence of Liberia was threatened by its British and French neighbors, and in 1908 the United States government dispatched a commission to investigate the situation. The commission recommended that the United States government back a private loan to Liberia to help refinance its debt. The commission also proposed that a few United States officers be lent to Liberia to help train its frontier police. These ideas were incorporated into the loan agreement that was concluded in the following year. In line with the agreement, Ernest Lyon, the United States minister, requested that Davis be assigned as military attaché. He regarded Davis as a "bright young lieutenant. . . . He would not only be of great assistance to me but would also be a good agent for the government to have in that Republic." Lyon also wrote to Davis, who was then on leave in Washington, to inform him of this proposal and to ask him to consider taking the position. The minister said that Davis's presence in Liberia would serve as an "inspiration" to the people.[30]

The proposal placed Davis in a quandary. He had just finished a four-year tour of detached duty, and he wanted to return to his regiment. Realizing that he could, however, "be of service to the United States in this capacity," Davis accepted. He believed that as an attaché, he would be closely involved with training Liberian troops.[31]

Over the next few months he prepared for his overseas tour of duty. He first made arrangements to take his wife, Elnora, and five-year-old daughter, Olive, with him to Africa. Then he reported to the War Department, where Matthew Hanna and Henry D. Todd, Jr., members of the General Staff, gave him a series of background briefings. Most of the discussions centered on the

Captain Davis in his office as military attaché in Liberia, 1911

duties of a military attaché. As they outlined Davis's major task, it was to send home reports on the military forces of Liberia, including their organization, strength, staff, training, morale, and mobilization system. In addition he was told to keep the United States informed about important military events. The overall purpose of these efforts was to help the War Department prepare monographs on the country. While Davis was authorized to visit different parts of Liberia in order to perform these duties, Hanna told him that he must keep "a strict regard for economy." The new attaché completed his orientation in early January 1910, but he and his family did not sail from New York until 2 April. After a three-day stay in Liverpool, England, they departed for Africa on the *Landanna* and arrived in Monrovia a week later.[32]

Although Davis thought he was well prepared, Liberia proved to be more primitive than he had imagined. This became clear on his first day in the country. There was no breakwater at the port, so the *Landanna* had to anchor some distance out in the harbor, and the Davis family was rowed ashore in a small boat.

During the next weeks, Davis set up his working space in the legation. He installed a large desk, typewriter, and other office furniture; and on the walls of his new office he placed a map of West Africa and a timetable of the local steamship line. His request for an interpreter was approved, but other requests, such as for a telephone, were denied on financial grounds.[33]

Living conditions in Liberia presented a problem. For a while the Davises enjoyed their new environment. Young Olive learned some of the native dances, and among her playmates was Gabriel Dennis, who many years later was to become Liberia's secretary of state. At the same time there were problems. The Davises found little native food that they could eat, so they had to import canned goods from the United States and Europe. This was quite a drain on an already limited budget. Another cost was the expected participation in the various diplomatic functions. All three Davises found the tropical climate difficult, and almost always one of the three was ill. Benjamin himself had frequent attacks of blackwater fever, which caused him to lose more than twenty-five pounds during his first months in Liberia.[34]

Davis's observation of the Liberian Army and militia proved to him that they were inept. This view and his proposed solutions were included in the reports that he sent to both the United States and the Liberian governments. As Davis became better acquainted with the condition of the Liberian forces, he concluded that the government could not really control them. In April 1911 he saw a mob of about 120 soldiers mutiny and threaten the secretary of war with violence unless they were paid. This group finally dispersed when its members became convinced that no money was available. The event made a vivid impression upon Davis: it strengthened his belief that the army and the militia were "worthless and should be reorganized." This impression was confirmed on his trips to other parts of the country. In mid 1910 there was an uprising of some tribesmen who lived near Cape Palmas, about two hundred miles south of the capital. Upon investigation, Davis found the Liberian Army trying to starve the natives into submission. He returned to Monrovia and reported the situation to Minister Lyon. This report on the fighting at

Cape Palmas and the other descriptions of the condition of the Liberian military establishment were part of the traditional functions of a military attaché, but they did not satisfy Davis's desire to improve the Liberian Army.[35]

Once Davis had familiarized himself with the military problems, he tried to promote the necessary reforms. In February 1911 he discussed these issues with Liberia's secretary of state. Encouraged by his reception, Davis later sent the secretary a memo detailing Davis's plan for the reorganization of the military. His proposal was designed to encourage efficiency; it began with a recommendation that the office of secretary of war be abolished. Davis went on to suggest that the army should be run by five Americans, including three NCOs and two officers (John E. Green as the quartermaster and Davis as lieutenant colonel and chief of staff). While the plan was not adopted, the Liberian government took note of Davis's willingness to serve. Several months later they asked him if he would accept an appointment in the Liberian Army, but he was afraid that accepting the position would jeopardize his hard-earned status in the United States Army. Apparently he had not completely dismissed the offer, however, because he asked the War Department if the United States government would still be interested in having him work closely with the Liberian Army. There was no immediate response, because this query raised a constitutional issue. After considering the matter, Chief of Staff Leonard Wood informed the secretary of war that as an American officer, Davis could not become part of the Liberian Army without violating the United States Constitution. On the other hand, Davis could act as an advisor, said Wood, provided Davis did not accept any compensation for his work. By the time the United States government reached this decision, Davis was no longer in Liberia.[36]

While the United States government was deliberating, Davis became even more frustrated. The Liberians had not accepted his ideas, and his own government did not seem to care. Finally, in July 1911, he wrote to the War Department, requesting an end to his assignment. In this note, Davis pointed out that he had been absent from a troop command for six years and that the tropical fevers were ruining his health. Despite the constant use of medication, he found it difficult to work. His poor health convinced the War Department that he should be relieved from his post in Monrovia. In late October the three Davises left on the *Cedric*, a British steamer. They stopped in the Canary Islands and London en route home and were back in the United States by November 1911.[37]

During the next month, as Davis and his family acclimated themselves to the cooler climate of Washington, he gave some thought to his experiences and their meaning. His first task was to brief his old friend and successor, Charles Young, on the conditions that Young would find when he arrived in Monrovia. Then Davis turned over his files, records, codes, and field-safe combination. Finally he related his experiences and recommendations for the Liberian Army to some staff officers. He made clear to them his frustration at being unable to really tackle the problem of army reorganization. Davis pointed out that sending an officer to Liberia merely to give advice was "a waste of time and energy." Young apparently learned from his predecessor's experiences and frustrations, because during his four-year tour of duty he was able to carry out many of the reforms that Davis had suggested.[38]

When Lieutenant Davis returned to Washington, he found that he had been reassigned to the Ninth Cavalry, which was now stationed at Fort D. A. Russell, Wyoming. When he arrived there in January 1912, he was assigned to Troop I, then under the command of Capt. Kenzie Walker, an officer whom Davis had first met during his days as an enlisted man at Fort Duchesne. Shortly thereafter, Davis was given the command of the regimental Machine Gun Platoon, a position he would hold during most of this tour with the regiment.[39]

Davis's family life returned to a more normal existence, although this took some doing. In February and March 1912 he was sick in his quarters with tropical fevers, and he had to take a daily dose of five grains of quinine for a number of months. However, he soon regained his health and strength. At the same time his family had grown from three to four. On 18 December 1912, Elnora gave birth to a son, Benjamin O. Davis, Jr., who brought joy to their small household. On the other hand, their social life was greatly restricted. Other officers and their families generally ignored the Davises, and there were few black civilians in nearby Cheyenne with whom they could socialize.[40]

In 1913 the Ninth Cavalry was transferred to the Mexican border, because there had been an attempted revolution in Mexico in 1912, and at times the fighting spread across the border. Several groups of rebels strayed across the boundary or purchased arms and tried to smuggle them back into Mexico. The United States government assigned the troops to patrol the border, preserve American neutrality, and calm the residents of the area. Most of this duty involved long rides through arid, treeless terrain. While there was little fighting in the region, the men on the patrols never knew when something might happen. Davis felt it best that his wife and children return to Washington, where they remained as long as the situation was unstable. When things calmed down, they were able to visit him.[41]

During his three years on the border, he served first with Troop B and then with Troop K. For some periods he commanded the troop, while for others he was second in command. Generally his unit patrolled the part of the border between Hachita, New Mexico, and a point midway between Naco and Nogales, Arizona. Individual troops were assigned to a certain section of the boundary for a period of about three months and then made a number of day and night marches from their stations. After a while they would be rotated back to the regimental headquarters in Douglas, the midpoint, and another group would be sent out as replacements.[42]

Davis was aware of the racial problems that his cavalrymen might encounter, so he tried to defuse them. In Cheyenne the troops had grown accustomed to a lack of segregation in the places they frequented. The attitude along the border was somewhat different, as Davis had already discovered in 1903. His fear was reinforced by a rumor that circulated shortly after the regiment arrived in Douglas. There were reports of trouble between the Ninth and the local citizens, although the sheriff told the War Department that there was no truth to the rumors. Racial conflict was always possible with the black units, however, and the regimental officers were aware of this. Davis tried to avoid any hostility by acknowledging racial separation and the power of the local law-enforcement officers. When his troop was assigned to an area, he would make it a point to ride ahead to the town and contact the sheriff and mayor. He would explain the mission of the troops and ask if he could detail an NCO and several privates to help keep the peace when the soldiers were off duty. In every case the local authorities thought this was an excellent idea and allowed him to control his own men. At the same time, Davis tried to impress upon his men the danger of trying to break racial barriers. He explained "that we could do a better job if we had the cooperation of the citizens among whom we were placed." This acceptance of the local customs worked, and though he disliked the situation, he believed that he could not change it by himself. It was typical of his approach to race relations: try to avoid conflict whenever possible and work quietly to encourage change.[43]

In April 1913, Davis and his troop saw some real action when forces under the command of Gen. Alvaro Obregon attacked Naco, in Sonora Province. Troop B, which Davis then commanded, and Troop C were camped across the border at Naco, Arizona. Early one morning, Davis was awakened by the sound of heavy firing, and while he was hurriedly dressing, two bullets passed through his tent. The units mounted up, galloped across an open space under fire, and dismounted behind some barricades. Although several of Davis's men were wounded by the Mexican bullets, he and his men kept their composure and did not fire back. After a while the shooting ceased, but several days later the unit came under fire again when a group of Yaqui Indians tried to cross the border. Fortunately there were no casualties. The skirmish at Naco was the only combat that Davis was to experience during his three years on the border.[44]

At this time, Davis received low ratings on his efficiency reports. One officer noted that Davis was "a good officer in that he is attentive to duty, thorough, and careful." Another officer felt Davis was "ordinary" and "too fat" for cavalry duty. The predominantly negative comments were summed up by the statement that Davis "lacks initiative and enthusiasm." Despite the criticism, by early 1915, Davis had become eligible for promotion to the rank of captain. In February of that year he reported to an officer examination board, where he underwent a thorough physical examination. During the course of the next two weeks he was subjected to a series of oral and written questions on topics relating to his skills as an army officer. After reviewing test results and in spite of the lackluster efficiency reports, the board recommended that he be promoted. In December 1915, at the age of thirty-seven, he became a captain. The news reached him in Ohio, where he was readjusting to life at Wilberforce.[45]

After the departure of Lieutenant Green in 1913, Wilberforce University was without a professor of military science and tactics (PMS&T) for several years, and it was making a strenuous effort to try to fill the position, which the army ignored. The officials at Wilberforce persevered and used their political connections, this time with success. In mid 1914 the General Staff studied the situation and decided that Davis could be made available by the end of the year. Despite the earlier problems with Davis, Scarborough expressed pleasure at his impending return; he thought Davis was "every inch a man and a gentleman such as our boys ought to have as a model."[46]

The next two years were professionally easy and uneventful. Davis's personal situation was quite different. He left Douglas, Arizona, on 19 February 1915 and reported to President Scarborough at Wilberforce three days later. Soon the rest of Davis's family joined him. At first the school authorities were pleased with his performance, and in his 1916 efficiency report they noted that he was doing "creditable work" in the military program.[47]

Life at Wilberforce was more pleasant than it had been at the military bases. Riding had always been a favorite form of recreation for Benjamin, and he didn't stop after he left his cavalry unit. During this tour he kept two horses, Billie and Price, for his private use at the school, and he rode frequently. But in the midst of this happiness, tragedy struck. In February 1916 the family grew again with the birth of Elnora Dickerson Davis. Since the previous two deliveries had been easy, his wife chose to remain in Wilberforce. Mary Dickerson, her sister, came from Washington to be with Mrs. Davis during the delivery, which was uneventful. However, several days later Mrs. Davis developed an embolism and died. This tragedy left Benjamin with three young children: Olive, age eleven; Benjamin, Jr., three; and the infant Elnora.[48]

During this family crisis, Sadie Overton, a teacher at the school, proved to be of great help in taking care of the young family. She, too, was a member of the small black middle class. Her father, Lawrence Overton, had been a member of the Mississippi lower house in 1876-1877, at the end of Reconstruction; and later he had become a teacher. His wife Izella, who was in her early twenties when they were married, had been born in Arkansas in 1855. Sadie, their third child, was born in Macon, Mississippi, in April 1880. Learning was important to Lawrence, and all three of his children received college educations. Before coming to Wilberforce in 1914, Sadie had taught at Clark University in Atlanta and at Lincoln High School in Kansas City. In 1915 she was made director of secondary practice at Wilberforce, and the following year she received a bachelor's degree from the University of Chicago. She continued to take summer courses and in 1919 received a Master's degree from Ohio State University. The Davis children took a liking to Sadie, and young Benjamin told his father that he should marry her. It was a suggestion that Davis would soon consider, but a dispute with Wilberforce intervened.[49]

Elnora's death had created significant problems for Benjamin, and his official duties had suffered. Problems with student discipline became worse, and finally, in early 1917, he asked to be relieved of duty at the school and to be returned to active service. The conditions at the school, Davis thought, created a situation in which he was "unable to render service commensurate with my rank, pay, and allowances." The army investigated the complaints and found that there was merit to them. The inspecting officer reported that Wilberforce wanted Davis "simply for the advertising . . . it gives them."[50]

The reaction of President Scarborough to Davis's memo was

to counterattack. In Scarborough's view, Davis merely wanted to leave so that he could look after his children. The complaints, wrote Scarborough, were justifications for this requested move. The president felt that another problem was Davis's inability to function within the institution's structure. The War Department, after studying these comments, decided that Davis should be relieved of duty at Wilberforce and that no officer would be detailed to take his place.[51]

Davis spent the period of World War I in the Philippines while his children remained in Washington with his parents. Captain Davis returned to the Ninth, which was then stationed at Camp Stotsenburg, Luzon. When he arrived in July 1917, the garrison consisted of the entire Ninth Cavalry, a battery of field artillery, and a battalion of Philippine Scouts.

In the following month an incident occurred in Houston, Texas, which was to have an impact throughout Davis's career. A battalion of the Twenty-fourth Infantry that had been stationed in Houston, Texas, encountered the typical southern hostility. When several soldiers were beaten by a white policeman, a mob of armed soldiers rampaged through town, killing sixteen whites and Hispanics and wounding others. A court-martial ordered thirteen of the soldiers to be hung for their crimes, and the sentences were carried out before the government had announced the action. Later trials resulted in more hangings, although President Woodrow Wilson did commute other death sentences. Blacks were outraged by the whole affair, which smacked of the injustice of Brownsville. This reaction reinforced the War Department's reluctance to use blacks in combat or to have large concentrations of black troops in the South. These ideas influenced not only the policies of World War I but the next conflict as well, and they were to affect Davis's career in many ways.[52]

As the war in Europe progressed, many Regular Army officers, including Davis, were rapidly promoted. Davis's rise disturbed the regimental commander, who feared that the black officer would soon become a squadron commander. Therefore, the commander recommended that Davis be returned to the United States, possibly to command one of the Negro units that were

The Davis children—Olive, Elnora, and Benjamin, Jr.—about 1917

being raised to fight in France. "I do not think it advisable that he be continued for duty in a command as mixed as that now at Camp Stotsenburg." The adjutant general denied the request, with the note that there was no place for Davis in the Europe-bound army. This reaction was consistent with the army's policy of preventing blacks from assuming positions of authority in the black regiments, mainly labor units, that were being sent to France. This goal was more important to the authorities at the time than were the more local problems that would be caused if Davis assumed the position of squadron commander. Other officers, for different reasons, also tried to get Davis transferred from the Ninth. The only response from the War Department was to suggest that Davis might be given a command with the Philippine Scouts, but this idea was rejected by his regimental and department commanders. As a result, Davis spent the war years far away from the fighting in Europe.[53]

Davis performed several different roles, the first of which was to command the supply troop. Then he was made the post quartermaster. When he received a promotion to major, he became commander of the Third Squadron of the Ninth, a position that he held until the middle of 1918. In June, Davis received a promotion to the temporary rank of lieutenant colonel in the National Army and was then given command of the First Squadron. He also served as provost marshall and, in the process, improved his command of Spanish. All of this work was performed quite capably. Col. Thomas Dugan, in his 1917 efficiency report on Davis, noted that Davis was doing a good job. Dugan thought that Davis was an officer who was "much interested in his profession."[54]

Although Camp Stotsenburg was far from the European battlefields, the war was not ignored by the Ninth Cavalry. In August 1918, Davis delivered a lecture to the post officers' school on "Cavalry in the Present War." His sources were the books and journals available at the post. The lecture began with a discussion of the German, British, and French cavalries and their roles in the war. He stated that, in his opinion, the absence of German cavalry early in the war had led to the Germans' defeat at the battle of the Marne. Davis concluded his lecture with a discussion of the future role of the cavalry, which he believed would be a key offensive weapon. Reflecting on his research, he decided to suggest a reorganization of the standard cavalry regiment. Among his recommendations was a proposal for the arming of the troopers with bayonets and hand grenades. These ideas were typical of many attempts by cavalry officers to adapt their arm of the service to changing conditions. All such suggestions were ignored.[55]

Not all of his time was taken up with training, for he found occasions to travel and increase his knowledge of Spanish. In October and November 1918, Davis spent forty days on a tour of China and Japan, including several days in Yokohama. He retained pleasant memories of his experiences in Japan. "I found them a very delightful people." Later he obtained a two-volume Spanish encyclopedia, which he read in his spare time. Soon he was able to read and translate without the aid of a dictionary. He hoped that this newly improved skill might prove beneficial later on.[56]

Travel and study, however, did not relieve his loneliness. When he left the United States in mid 1917, he had assumed that his assignment in the Philippines would be for two years, so he had made arrangements with his parents to care for his children. By 1919 he learned that overseas duty during the war period had been extended to three years. The army denied his request to return briefly to the United States to make other arrangements for his children. Sometime after he had left the United States, he had decided to marry Sadie Overton, and he longed to see her again. His financial situation necessitated that he postpone this event until his planned return to the United States in 1919. This plan was frustrated by the army's change in troop-rotation policies. His loneliness increased, and during this time, Sadie and Benjamin wrote many letters to each other which substituted, to some extent, for the other's presence. After one cross-country ride with some cavalry recruits, Benjamin wrote: "I am sure I imbibed some of their youth. Now if I could just top the whole day off with you. Wouldn't that be great." Finally, Benjamin decided not to wait any longer. He made arrangements for Sadie

Sadie Overton Davis, the second wife of Benjamin O. Davis, Sr.,
about 1940

to come to the Philippines, and they were married in Manila in
December 1919.[57]

A great deal of racial strife existed in the United States in 1919,
and it even touched Davis in the Philippines. He had thought
that he had developed good relations with the officers at Camp
Stotsenburg, including his new commander, Col. John W. Heard,

a Mississippian. Colonel Heard, however, had a different opinion. In his 1920 efficiency report on Davis, Heard asked to have the black officer removed because the colonel preferred white officers and did not like mixing races within the officer corps. Davis also began to feel that others in the United States did not think so well of him. When he did not receive orders returning him home, he began to suspect that prejudice was involved: "I am getting to the point where I am beginning to believe that I've been kept as far in the background as possible." Shortly afterwards an article in the *Army and Navy Journal* triggered a violent response from Davis. A black officer was denied a chance for a promotion examination because blacks were "deficient in moral fiber, rendering them unfit as officers and leaders of men." In a letter to Sadie Overton, written in July 1919, Davis described the discrimination that blacks had faced in the recently concluded war, especially in their efforts to become officers and to have their successes recognized. Davis felt that the United States was a great country, "but unfortunately it possesses many little folks" who were promoted only because they were white. On the other hand, blacks were not advanced because of their race. "Every day we have seen evidences of discrimination. That is why I am here today." The discrimination hurt him deeply, but he stayed in the army, he wrote, because of his poverty. However, all of these experiences had convinced him that someday he should try to find a place "where I can be without contact with" whites. His feelings of loneliness, separation, and lack of advancement had brought out a side of his personality that rarely showed.[58]

In the months after his marriage, however, conditions seemed to improve. The army authorized travel around the islands, so that the officers could improve their knowledge of the area. Benjamin and Sadie made a trip to the resort area of Lake Lanao. In March 1920, they returned to the States, where he was reunited with his young family and Sadie began her role as mother to his children.[59]

The three children had lived with their grandparents Louis and Henrietta Davis while their father had been overseas. The period was not a happy one. The youngsters were separated from their father, their mother had died, and they felt that Louis Davis was not very friendly. However, the other set of grandparents, the Dickersons, provided the love and affection that seemed to be lacking at the Davises' home. The children frequently visited down the block. Ernest Dickerson bought young Benjamin a wagon and helped him to get a paper route. On a number of occasions the boy would stay overnight with his aunts and uncles, and in the morning, his Uncle Ernest would leave a quarter on the window ledge for Benjamin to find. The three children were happy to see their father and new mother, and they looked forward to being all together at his new station, Tuskegee, Alabama.[60]

The reunion of the Davis family brought Captain Davis to the end of another phase of his career. During the preceding decades he had experienced some personal and career highs and lows. He had been frustrated by his inability to convince the Liberian government to make the changes that he felt were necessary and to get the authorities at Wilberforce to enforce what he saw as the proper level of discipline. As his career advanced, he had been allowed to spend ever-shorter periods of time on troop assignments. He spent World War I far away from combat and the professional rewards that it might have brought. He suffered the death of his wife and endured being separated from his children for three years. Yet there were some positive accomplishments during this period also. Davis had risen from a second lieutenant to the permanent rank of captain and had been a lieutenant colonel during much of the war. Despite the army's dislike of the situation, he had commanded the white officers in his squadron and had generally received good efficiency reports. He had resolved his personal problems with his marriage to Sadie, a good person with whom he could share the rest of his life.

Davis's personality began to be clear as he matured. Generally he would accept the insults of segregation but would try to work behind the scenes to ameliorate them. On the other hand, he was not very tolerant of blacks who he felt did not appreciate his talents. As he began the 1920s, his future appeared to be looking up, but he was to find the next decades equally as trying as the last. His rise in the army and up the economic ladder was to continue.

4 | A Holding Pattern: 1920–1940

DURING THE 1920s and 1930s, Benjamin Davis slowly advanced in rank, but his assignments were far from the centers of army life. Finally, in 1940, he reached a new pinnacle for black officers—the rank of brigadier general.

Davis's first assignment after his return from the Philippines was as professor of military science and tactics (PMS&T) at Tuskegee Institute, Alabama. He found the position different from his previous teaching assignment at Wilberforce because of changes in the laws governing such programs. The courses of instructions had been regularized, and student quotas had been established to maintain the programs. The PMS&T was to regard himself, in terms of administration, as if he were commanding a unit in the Regular Army. Junior-level programs, such as Davis's at Tuskegee, were to be "practical with a few lectures and demonstrations." The goals were to provide instruction in basic infantry subjects, to develop discipline, and to increase public awareness of the program.[1]

When Davis arrived in Alabama, he found the school officials very cooperative. Initially Tuskegee provided him with a small house, but the following year they began construction on a larger one. At his suggestion they built a two-story eight-room cottage. In addition to a bedroom for each of the three children, there was a living room and a dining room. This was to be the family home for the next three years.[2]

Davis had been assigned to Tuskegee while he was still a captain, but by the time he arrived, he had been promoted, as had John E. Green, to the rank of lieutenant colonel. With Green at Wilberforce, both of the black officers in the army were now on college duty. Davis knew that military studies played a minor role in Tuskegee's academic programs, so he tried to design a course "with the least practicable interference" with their other classes. Instruction was scheduled before the start of classes at 9 A.M. The cadets were organized into a provisional regiment of infantry, with a headquarters company and two battalions of four companies each. This structure, which was typical of a Reserve Officers' Training Corps (ROTC) program, allowed many practical lessons to be taught through the "application method." The cadets were required to wear their uniforms and polished shoes on school days and to conduct themselves with dignity and not "at any time lean against trees, posts, buildings." All cadets were required to make up their beds and to sweep and dust their sections of the dormitories. Davis usually inspected the student dormitories at 7:30 A.M. and reported any student who might still be in bed during inspection. He made sure that students who violated the rules were disciplined, and the school officials supported him in this.[3]

In 1923 the program was inspected by Gen. David Shanks, commander of the Fourth Corps. During the two-hour visit, Shanks inspected the unit and addressed the students on the concept of training civilian soldiers through the ROTC. General Shanks was quite impressed both with what he saw and with Davis's contribution.[4]

While Davis found success in many of his ROTC duties, there were also some problems. The army prescribed gallery rifle training as part of the program. Shortly after he arrived, Davis submitted a requisition for 48,000 rounds of ammunition and for iron gallery targets. The response of Tuskegee's president, Robert R. Moton, was a low-key rejection; while he would not stop the requisition from going forward, he would not endorse it. "In view of our local situation, outside of the institution, I doubt very seriously whether it would be the best thing for us to bring in such an amount of ammunition." Moton suggested that Davis bring the issue to corps headquarters; then, perhaps the army would excuse the cadets from target practice, "because of this local situation, which, to say the least is delicate." Five days later, Moton came up with a proposed solution: Davis and his men could go directly to Atlanta to pick up small portions of the ammunition. The army fully supported Moton, and the corps commander told Davis that he would not approve anything that a college's president would not agree to. Davis was so upset that he considered leaving. The army blamed the crisis on the fact that Davis was a "little overconscientious in the performance of his duties." By the end of the 1921 school year the army believed that Davis understood the situation and recommended that the issue be considered closed. Davis reluctantly accepted the army's position. Although Moton was quite graceful in his refusal, unlike the manner in which Jones and Scarborough had previously handled similar situations, it still rankled Davis. This was one of the disadvantages of teaching ROTC in a black school in the South.[5]

Other of Davis's activities were only tangentially related to his duties as PMS&T. In November 1920 the school observed the second anniversary of Armistice Day. Davis was master of ceremonies for the program which was held in the college chapel. A number of veterans gave short talks, followed by music from the Tuskegee band, songs by the old soldiers, and a speech by Tuskegee's vice-president, Warren Logan. The following month, Davis addressed the local chapter of the Young Men's Christian Association on the issue of profanity. This marked the beginning of a two-week campaign to abolish profanity from the college campus.[6]

Davis's college duties were not very onerous, so he was able to spend a lot of time with his children, whose ages were fifteen, eight, and four. For the first time, Sadie had a direct hand in their lives. She wanted to ensure that they got a good education. Sadie taught Elnora how to read even before she was due to begin the first grade; as a result, Elnora started her formal education in the second grade. Sadie told the children that they must spend some time every night reading a book, and the parents installed a special reading light near each child's bed. Sadie also encouraged them to play music, and the two younger children began piano lessons. Benjamin, Jr., and Elnora attended a small school at Tuskegee Institute. Because the school was very poorly equipped, Sadie and Benjamin decided to send Olive to Atlanta University

High School. The Davises realized that while some things might be denied them or taken away because they were black, learning, once acquired, was something that they would always have.[7]

Discipline, the same approach that Davis used with his ROTC students, was an important element in the lives of his family. He organized their lives into a daily schedule, with a set time for getting up, practicing their music, and eating. He wanted his children to serve as models for the cadets, and he told them so. Each of them was responsible for some chores, such as washing and drying the dishes. They would take turns in the jobs, and Olive would assist whenever she was at home.[8]

Usually, things ran smoothly; but sometimes, as is normal with growing children, there were problems. The approaches that Sadie and Benjamin took to resolving the issues reflected their different backgrounds. If something distressed Sadie, she would wait until things calmed down, and then let them know about it. On the other hand, Benjamin adopted a variety of different techniques to enforce the rules. At times he would use his parade-ground voice to make his feelings known. On other occasions, he would spank the children. Once Elnora cut her own hair. When Benjamin found the hair and the scissors, he questioned her. Feeling threatened by his tone of voice, she denied having done it. Then he spanked her and made it very clear that she was being punished for lying, not for cutting her hair. Benjamin, Jr., once was spanked when he came home late from play and missed dinner, thereby violating the schedule. In general, life was a contest of wills between the two males.[9]

Living at Tuskegee was like being on a little island, with the black community isolated from the white world around it. When the first movie theater was built in Tuskegee, no blacks were permitted to enter. The owners then built another one for blacks only, in an attempt to get more patronage, but this did not work. The Davises saw their first movies on the Tuskegee campus. Playing cards was another form of amusement for the whole family. The children began with such games as old maid and fish and then graduated to adult games. Bridge became a popular form of entertainment, which the four Davises played frequently. In addition the adults joined several bridge clubs. Other leisure activities were quite varied but always within their small segregated world. In December 1921, Davis and seven other members of the faculty and administration spent a week fishing at Coden-on-the-Bay, near Mobile. On Charles Young's birthday, Davis gave a talk about him to the local chapter of the fraternity Omega Psi Phi. According to one witness, it was an "intimate and illuminating" presentation. Certainly, Benjamin was one of the few people who could have done this.[10]

While Davis's family life and social life were improving, relations with the army were not always on such an even keel. During the early 1920s the army, under budgetary pressure from Congress, began to discuss possible cuts in enlisted and officer numbers. Like many officers, Davis believed that enough had already been done and that the army was already below the size necessary for "domestic security." Despite a variety of similar pleas, the army went ahead with plans for the cuts. The first step was to establish officer-elimination boards. On 30 June 1922 there were 10,972 officers, which the army hoped to reduce by about 1,500 by the end of the year. Of the 667 lieutenant colonels, including Davis, they planned to eliminate 90. Davis managed to survive this reduction, but he constantly had the feeling that the army was still looking for a chance to retire him. At the time of his 1920 physical he weighed 190 pounds, the level at which he had been after his recovery from the tropical fevers of Liberia. By the time of his next physical in May 1923, Davis, who was five feet nine inches tall, had gained 11 pounds. The examining physician noted that he was "inclined to be stout" and needed to lose 35 pounds. Davis felt that this warning meant that if he did not lose the weight, he would be retired. He began to exercise more, and he went on a strict diet. He and Sadie worked together to devise a food plan that eliminated all fatty foods and limited others. As a result, Davis lost 50 pounds, but the next physical examination revealed traces of albumen, a protein, in his blood. The doctors congratulated Davis on his weight loss but recommended a diet that excluded red meat and salt. After a later medical exam at Maxwell Field, he was found to be free of all physical ailments. Davis was very proud of his weight loss, and he maintained his slimmer figure. He used the episode as a lesson for his children: if he could discipline himself to do this thing he wanted, so could they.[11]

In that same year he used a similar display of will power to deal with the Ku Klux Klan. The problem arose when the Veterans Administration decided to establish a hospital at Tuskegee and to staff it with local black civilian doctors and nurses. Feeling that these jobs should have gone to area whites, many of the citizens objected, despite the fact that the patients would all be black. While discussions continued in Washington, the Klan moved to take matters into its own hands. When it became known that the Klan would parade through the campus area, Moton told the staff, including Davis, to stay indoors and avoid any confrontation, but Davis ignored the warnings. During the parade, all members of the Davis family sat on their front porch, with the light on, watching the white-robed marchers. Davis, to emphasize his stand, wore his dress white uniform. By this gesture he showed the southern whites what he thought of their attitudes. In the end, the black community won its struggle, and the hospital was staffed solely by blacks.[12]

Because most of the officers assigned to junior ROTC programs held the rank of captain, or lower, Davis felt that his assignment was somewhat demeaning for him as a lieutenant colonel. In February 1922, Davis, in a letter to the adjutant general, complained that he was unable to give the proper course of instruction to the cadets, especially in small-arms target practice. In addition, Davis noted that conditions in the South did "not permit my family to enjoy the advantages and comforts permitted in other sections of the country." He requested a transfer to any other part of the country or to any foreign-service duty, with the exception of Liberia. Moton, believing that he had to protect the program at Tuskegee, told the army that he could not agree to this request, but he phrased his refusal in a very sympathetic manner.[13]

Moton wanted Davis to remain as PMS&T, but other people were interested in seeing Davis leave, even though this raised

Lt. Col. Benjamin O. Davis, Sr., in 1923

the issue of who should replace him. Garnet Wilkinson, who was assistant superintendent of schools in the District of Columbia, tried to have Davis moved to Washington. Wilkinson's first step was to speak to the adjutant general, who, Wilkinson understood, agreed that, if Davis would apply, he would receive a transfer to the District of Columbia. Wilkinson shared this information with Davis and suggested that Davis offer, as a basis for the move, the "health of your wife or your self, or desire to enter a wider sphere of influence, or for other reasons that may appeal to military men." Davis wrote the suggested letter, but he couched it in different terms from those outlined by Wilkinson. In addition to the reasons already stated in the February 1922 letter (program omissions, segregation), Davis pointed out that service in the black high schools of the District and at Howard University would be of more use to the country than the work he was performing at Tuskegee. The army took the request under advisement and queried Moton regarding his choice of a possible replacement. The Tuskegee leader asked for Lieutenant Colonel Green or, if this was not possible, the retention of Davis. After considering the matter for several months, the army finally rejected the idea. The army thought that this transfer would create more problems than it would solve; therefore, Davis remained in Alabama.[14]

Wilkinson, who was not discouraged by this turn of events, tried a new approach that involved other black leaders. The first indication of this new tactic was when Davis received a letter from Emmett Scott, treasurer of Howard University, in which Scott wrote: "It has always seemed fitting to us that you should have this berth." Shortly thereafter, Wilkinson again discussed the issue with the War Department. The army raised the point that a shift of Davis to Howard would harm either Tuskegee or Wilberforce. Because both schools wanted a black officer and because there were only two in the army at the time, the removal of Davis from Tuskegee to Howard would have meant that one of those other schools would be without a black officer to head its ROTC program. While Wilberforce had a senior program and therefore needed a Regular Army officer, Tuskegee did not. On the other hand, Tuskegee had a great deal of political clout. Once again the army decided to leave Davis where he was. Wilkinson was determined to wait, but Davis tried to force the matter.[15]

Davis used the occasion of the 1923 Tuskegee ROTC inspection to recommend that his program be eliminated and consequently that he be transferred. In his mind the issue of the canceled target-practice program was enough to demonstrate that he could not really carry out the necessary level of instruction to meet the army's requirements. Not surprisingly, Moton objected to the proposal to eliminate the program but not to the idea of transferring Davis. The president continued to insist that it would be unwise to have a program of target practice, for it "might contain a hostile suggestion." General Shanks concurred with Moton's view of the matter: transfer Davis, but retain the program. Shanks said, "I do not feel that he is fitted for the important position which he holds." The chief of cavalry and the chief of infantry concurred with these recommendations; however, the Fifth Corps's commander, who was the supervisor of the Wilberforce ROTC unit, objected. He pointed out that if Green were transferred, the War Department would only be shifting the problem to the Fifth Corps. At that point the army again decided to do nothing, although it knew that the issue could not be postponed indefinitely. In the following year, both Davis and Green would have to be relieved because their tours of college duty would expire.[16]

During the remainder of 1923 and part of 1924, Moton, the War Department, various area commanders, and some politicians wrestled with the problem of the new assignments for Davis and Green. The possible solutions were limited by the army's continued adherence to the principle of not assigning black officers to troop commands. To help his own cause, Davis wrote a note to Maj. Edward Burr, in the office of the chief of cavalry. Davis appealed to Burr for a change in his duty assignment. Davis brought up the problems that he and his family were facing in the South. As a solution, Davis listed five possible assignments that he would be willing to accept. His first choice was the Eighth Regiment, Illinois National Guard, a black unit. Second was an assignment to the Fifteenth New York, a black National Guard regiment that had not yet received federal recognition. The last three suggestions included service with the First Separate Battalion, District of Columbia National Guard; duty with troops in the Philippines; or assignment to the Tenth Cavalry. Commenting on this request, the chief of cavalry recommended that Davis receive another assignment but that "he *not* be assigned to regular troops." The General Staff now also discussed the issue of relieving Davis. Col. William R. Smedberg, Jr., of the General Staff noted that "it is considered highly undesirable that these officers [Davis and Green] be assigned to units of the Regular Army." The only available alternatives were the black National Guard infantry units. However, the decision was again deferred.[17]

As the end of Davis's tour of duty approached, the issue of his next assignment had to be faced. Disregarding set policy, the Militia Bureau decided that Davis, a cavalry officer, could serve with an infantry National Guard unit. The next step was to find out which area commander would be willing to have Davis in a National Guard unit under his general command. The Sixth Corps commander responded very briefly: "Not desired this Corps area." Other commanders gave the same response. One staff officer noted, after studying these negative responses, "No one seems to want him."[18]

During this impasse, Superintendent Wilkinson and President Moton made moves to have Davis receive a good assignment. They appealed to black politicians and to President Calvin Coolidge, but in vain. Secretary of War John W. Weeks dismissed these arguments. According to Weeks, the army was trying to find an assignment for Davis in which "he will be of most value to the country and where he will have a standing commensurate with his rank." Finally, in July 1924, the different branches and bureaus agreed to assign Davis as instructor to the Second Battalion, 372d Regiment, Ohio National Guard. Although Davis did not end up in Washington, as he had desired, he was able to move out of the South, so this was a partial answer to his many requests.[19]

The issue of a federally recognized black National Guard unit for the state of Ohio had been unresolved for a number of years. The solution to this problem coincided nicely with the War Department's need to find a spot for Davis. A small black unit from Ohio had served in World War I, but it took four years of lobbying by the National Association for the Advancement of Colored People (NAACP) and other groups to convince the army to convert this unit to a National Guard one. In 1924 the four Ohio companies became the Second Battalion of the 372d Infantry. Other battalions of the regiment were assigned to Massachusetts and the District of Columbia. The battalion's four companies were located in Cleveland, Columbus, Cincinnati, and Toledo. Altogether the unit contained about fifteen officers and three hundred enlisted men.[20]

As instructor, Davis was responsible to both the federal government and the state of Ohio. According to army regulations, an officer in his position was under the orders of the corps commander but was on loan to the state. Davis submitted reports on his work to the Militia Bureau and his corps commander but not to the state of Ohio. While actual teaching was to be done by personnel of the Ohio National Guard, the instructor was to attend all drills at his own station. In cases in which the assigned unit was divided among several cities, the instructor was to visit the other locations as often as possible. Before Davis began his assignment, he received a ten-day course at corps headquarters. He was oriented on what was expected of him, the pertinent national laws, local conditions in Ohio, methods of training, and how to conduct himself in his role. For the next five years, however, Davis was mainly on his own.[21]

The family members settled in Cleveland and began to develop new friendships. Shortly after they arrived, they purchased a home. The children continued their education, but now in the public schools of Cleveland, which were de facto segregated by demographics and by the actions of the Board of Education. Up to this point, Elnora had attended schools with only black children and had found it hard to understand what Benjamin, Jr., was talking about when he related a story about his experiences in school with white children. The parents explained briefly about racial differences but did not dwell on the issue. Benjamin, Jr., did very well at Cleveland's Central High School, which housed about 60 percent of black students in senior high school. In 1928 when he was a senior, Benjamin, Jr., was elected president of the class and head of the student council; he also won a number of awards. The next fall he entered Western Reserve University. Two years earlier, Olive Davis had completed her work for an undergraduate degree from Western Reserve University. Before she began graduate study, Olive and her parents took a tour of Europe. Benjamin, Jr., and Elnora spent the summer in Washington with the senior Davises. In the fall, Olive resumed her education at Western Reserve. After she had graduated with a Master's degree in Social Service Education, she began to teach at Bluefield State Teacher's College in West Virginia.[22]

The family's new social circle involved other members of Cleveland's black middle class. Sadie found a friend she had known during her childhood in Mississippi. Another close acquaintance was Jane Hunter of the Young Women's Christian Association (YWCA), who was instrumental in the founding of the Phillis Wheatley Association, an all-black component of the YWCA. Sadie also formed the Cleveland chapter of Delta Sigma Theta, the sorority that she had become an honorary member of at Wilberforce. Both Benjamin and Sadie were also involved with several bridge clubs.[23]

Benjamin's professional activities and the widely dispersed companies of the Second Battalion followed a routine. He journeyed by car to each of the different companies. Another feature of Davis's yearly routine were the semiannual battalion inspections conducted by Regular Army officers. During the summer the unit spent two weeks at Camp Perry, on the shores of Lake Erie. This was the the only real period of training for the regiment, and Davis worked hard to take advantage of it. During one weekend at the camp, the battalion held a special review and invited the soldiers' families and friends, as well as political leaders, to view it. In 1925 the parade was reviewed by Governor A. Victor Donahey and Adj. Gen. Frank Henderson, who were very pleased at the splendid showing of the companies. There was much more to summer camp than parades however; field exercises, drill, and rifle instruction were also emphasized. The weeks at Camp Perry were the closest that Lieutenant Colonel Davis was to come to a semblance of actual field service until the late 1930s.[24]

In general, National Guard duties and the biweekly drill sessions took up little of Davis's time. He was receptive to suggestions for other assignments or more work. He kept in touch with Garnet Wilkinson in Washington and worked with him on a number of occasions. In 1925, Wilkinson requested, again, that Davis be assigned to ROTC duty in the District of Columbia, but the War Department turned him down. On a number of occasions, however, the army was willing to allow Davis to attend the annual review of cadets from the Washington high schools.[25]

In 1928, Davis's four-year assignment with the National Guard was due to end, and the customary discussion of his reassignment began again. In June of that year, Maj. Howard Gilbert asked Ohio's adjutant general, Frank Henderson, if Davis could be continued with the battalion. According to Gilbert, Davis "has been of inestimable value to this organization and to be deprived of his services at this time would work a severe hardship on all concerned." Davis did not agree, for while he appreciated Gilbert's kind thoughts, he wanted to be assigned back to the cavalry "or given an assignment more commensurate with my rank and length of service." General Henderson could not honor Davis's request, because he had already written to the army that he concurred with Gilbert's suggestion. The army replied that Davis was going to remain with the battalion at least until the end of the 1929 training period. The fact that John Green still had another year to serve as PMS&T at Wilberforce University complicated matters.[26]

In early 1929, Davis saw another opportunity for a good assignment, because the army had requested volunteers for foreign service. Davis tendered his services, but he was turned down. Instead he continued to serve the battalion, with time off for his usual duties with the competitive drill in the District of Columbia and for service as instructor at a ROTC camp at Tuskegee Institute. Moton again requested that the status of his school's program be reinstated to a junior level and that Davis be returned as PMS&T. Although Moton was refused by the War Department, he appealed to President Herbert Hoover directly. Again his request was denied. Moton shared all of this with Davis and concluded, "Tuskegee needs you very much." The army disregarded Moton's pleas and resolved the issue by reassigning Davis to Wilberforce University. Providentially, Green's term had ended, and the army was able to save travel funds by assigning Davis within Ohio.[27]

By this time in his career, Benjamin was earning the highest possible annual salary for his rank, about $5,700. This figure alone placed him in the top 6 percent of all income earners in America. Before they returned to Wilberforce, some members of the family vacationed in Europe. Benjamin, Sadie, and Olive sailed from Montreal in early July 1929. They spent much of their time in Paris, which allowed Benjamin to brush up on his French. These family summer trips to Europe were made possible by their hard work and frugality. Sadie made the children's clothes and often bought things on sale. The parents wanted their children to have what others in their social circle had but not to be ostentatious in their display of it. Although they could have afforded household help while in Cleveland, as they had had student help at Tuskegee, Sadie reserved this only for special occasions. Some of the money they saved went toward the purchase of stocks and bonds. These investments did well during the 1920s, and as the decade drew to a close, their material possessions included their own home and a car, as well as stocks and bonds. This represented quite a change from Davis's early days in Utah and Wyoming.[28]

Sadie and Benjamin's return to Wilberforce in September 1929 was a homecoming for them, but it was a new experience for Elnora, the only child who accompanied them. Olive and Benjamin, Jr., remained in Cleveland. Earlier in the year, Olive had married George Streator, a Memphis-born black whom she had met while she was teaching. Benjamin, Jr., lived with them during his first year at Western Reserve University. Benjamin and

Sadie enjoyed life in Xenia, and they purchased a house about three miles from the campus. Many of their old friends still lived there, and they were able to establish a social life rather quickly. It was partial compensation for the type of assignment the army had given Benjamin.[29]

Davis had succeeded Lt. Col. John Green as PMS&T at Wilberforce. Although the students had predicted that Davis would keep the unit "in the top shape that he is bound to find it," the army had other opinions about the condition of the program. In 1929, Wilberforce was the only senior ROTC unit in the country that was rated "unsatisfactory." Davis worked hard to improve the conditions, which were made difficult by a number of academic, financial, and demographic circumstances. Several students had to be dropped because they had not taken some required courses, such as plane trigonometry and logarithms. Although the school expressed interest in the military department, it had a hard time providing the necessary supplies and uniforms. In addition, there were only a small number of eligible male students. Despite the handicaps, the army found great improvement when the program was inspected at the end of the 1929-1930 academic year. The problems that Green had had with the organization probably reflected his frustration with the army and its assignment procedures. As a result he had decided that he would retire when he had finished thirty years' service, and he did so in November 1929. This left the fifty-two-year-old Davis as the only black officer in the army. The following March, Davis was promoted to the rank of colonel, "on the basis of seniority." He thus became the highest-ranking black officer in American history to that point. The *Chicago Defender* noted that this was "a much deserved honor."[30]

One of Davis's first assignments as a colonel was as an escort to black Gold Star Mothers. Many American mothers and widows were unable to visit their relatives' grave sites in Europe, and some well-meaning individuals thought that this was a problem that the government should resolve. Responding to this desire, in 1929, Congress authorized pilgrimages to the European cemeteries by the mothers or widows of people who had died during World War I. The army was placed in charge of this operation.[31]

The black community protested the army's decision that the program would be segregated. Many of the black newspapers and the NAACP attacked the administration on this issue. They urged black women to stay away from the whole proceedings. "Far from making the world safe for democracy, the late war has not made the world safe for anything." In a rebuttal memo for use by the president, the War Department claimed that the decision was the result of "careful consideration of the interests" of the people involved.[32]

With the War Department's decision to conduct a series of segregated tours, a possible position for a black officer was created, and Davis lobbied for it. The army felt that the officers involved in the program should "possess a high degree of tact, be sober and dependable in habits, and be qualified in all respects to conduct parties of mothers and widows." The chief of cavalry submitted the names of nine officers, but Davis's was not included. Realizing that the army would not nominate him to such a posh position, Davis described the situation to President Moton in hopes that he would put Davis's name forward. While Davis condemned the Jim Crow policy that the army was in the process of applying, he felt it offered him an opportunity. "Let a colored officer . . . look after the colored Gold Star Mothers." He then listed his qualifications: "As you know I have travelled over the battlefields. I have a speaking knowledge of French." Moton took the hint; several days later he wrote to Secretary of War Patrick Jay Hurley about Davis's merits, including his knowledge of the country and the language. The army accepted the suggestion, and in mid April they added Davis to the list of officers assigned to the pilgrimage. Davis thanked Moton: "I cannot adequately express to you in words my appreciation for this action of yours."[33]

Once Davis had received the news of his inclusion, he began to make plans. In May 1930 he asked the army if he could take his wife, daughter, and a friend or two with him to France. His plan was to take everyone on the first trip in July and then for the rest of them to return with him to the United States with the second group in early September. The army approved this request. Elnora was left in Washington with her grandmother.

While the army paid his fare, Benjamin paid the fares for the rest of his family.[34]

When the first group of black pilgrims arrived in New York in early July 1930, they met Davis, who was to be their shipboard guide, as well as the five nurses who were to accompany them throughout the sea voyages and the tour around France. They began with a ceremony at City Hall to honor the black pilgrims, which was similar to the ones the white widows received that year. The next day there was a brief ceremony at the dock, at which time Colonel Davis said a few words. The group then departed on the *American Merchant* for France.[35]

The journey to France and the ensuing tour were uneventful. There was little to do during the voyage, but Davis made sure that everyone was well cared for, and he saw to it that they had a variety of activities. Once they landed at Cherbourg, a European-based group of army officers took over the direction of the tour. After a day of sightseeing, the group gathered at the Arc de Triomphe for a wreath-laying ceremony at the tomb of France's unknown soldier. During the next two weeks the women had a brief tour of France, which included a visit to the grave sites of their sons or husbands. Each woman was given a floral wreath to place on the grave, and later they were presented with three copies of the photographs taken of this ceremony. While the women were touring, so were Davis and his family. After traveling around France, the women all returned to Paris and then took the boat train to Cherbourg, where Davis met them. The return voyage was uneventful, and after a brief visit to Coney Island, the first party dispersed. Three days later the second group of black pilgrims arrived in New York City, and Davis was back at work.[36]

The experiences of the second group of black pilgrims were not really different from those of the first, but the newspapers paid less attention to it. Davis again made a little speech prior to the departure for their thirteen-day trip to France. On 7 September 1930, the second group of black pilgrims and Davis and his family returned to the United States. After this summer adventure in Europe, Davis did not go back to Wilberforce; instead, he reported to Washington to prepare for his next assignment, which he expected to be another trip to Liberia.[37]

Several times during the late 1920s the Liberians had requested Davis as military attaché, but the army was reluctant to send him. The situation changed in early 1930 as chaos reigned in Liberia and the government had to resign because of a report that condemned their participation in the practice of slavery. The State Department decided that the United States needed to prop up the regime and that military assistance was to be part of this aid. The army was reluctant to send anyone to Liberia because it felt that little of military value would come out of the assignment. If the State Department were interested, said the army, then it would have to support the position itself, for the attaché in this case would be working more for the State Department than for the army.[38]

The State Department now realized that if it wanted Davis as an attaché, it would need to convince the army with more than words. Secretary of State Henry L. Stimson stated that Davis's presence in Monrovia would be of great help, "both because of his previous experience there and because of his abilities and personality." Stimson also indicated to Hurley that if the army did not have the funds for a Liberian attaché, the State Department would be willing to pay for travel, entertainment, and a post allowance of $1,500. This monetary inducement was enough for the army, which offered the position to Davis.[39]

In early June 1930, before his first visit to France with the Gold Star Mothers, Davis went to the State Department to discuss the assignment with the people who were directly interested in the matter. After considering the opportunity and discussing it with his family, he decided to go to Africa, but then he had second thoughts. "Liberia is not a very inviting place for one who has been there." In the end, he wrote to the State Department that he would go if there was a real need, but he would not go "as an ornament." Coincidentally, President Moton chimed in with another request for Davis's service as head of the ROTC program at Tuskegee. Moton noted that Davis had already been in Liberia and had then been quite sick. "I realize the embarrassment to which the War Department may be put in making an adequate assignment to Colonel Davis; but it should not be necessary to kill him in order to escape such embarrassment." The War Department, under this pressure, said that Davis could be relieved from the attaché's position but that it was up to the State Department to make the move. The State Department agreed, and Davis was reassigned to Tuskegee.[40]

While Colonel Davis was making arrangements for a new assignment, Benjamin, Jr., was applying for admission to the United States Military Academy. After one year at Western Reserve, in 1930 he had transferred to the University of Chicago for continued study. Oscar DePriest, a black Republican congressman from Chicago, asked Colonel Davis whether he thought his son would be interested in an appointment to West Point. In the winter of 1931, Davis came to Chicago and the two Benjamins visited Congressman DePriest. Benjamin, Jr., agreed to take the entrance examination. It was not a sudden decision on his part; it was something he had been thinking about for several years. One of the factors that influenced the decision was his desire to fly, which was abetted by Charles A. Lindbergh's trans-Atlantic flight in 1927. In addition, Benjamin, Jr., did not want to try any of the other careers that the black middle class had traditionally chosen, such as education or dentistry. Finally the failure of Alonzo Parham, a black cadet who flunked mathematics and had to leave the academy in 1930, presented young Davis with a challenge. Colonel Davis had never really channeled his son's thinking but had led by example. Although Benjamin, Jr., failed on his first effort at the entrance examination, he passed it the following year. In the fall of 1932 he entered West Point. It would prove to be a difficult four years for him, facing the silent treatment from the cadet corps, but he had his father's example to guide him in dealing with adversity.[41]

While his son was adjusting to Chicago and then West Point, Benjamin and Sadie were readapting to Alabama. In December 1930 he returned to Xenia to pack his belongings. Because his assignment had not been definite, Sadie and Elnora had remained in Xenia after the return from France in September. The new assignment in Alabama meant that the family was able to stay together and that Henrietta Davis could come down from Washington to visit them. Benjamin was happy that he had avoided a long separation from his family, for this meant "much to all of us at our time of life." They sold the house in Xenia and moved to Alabama in early 1931.[42]

Davis's services were still in demand throughout the country. In early 1931 the Eighth Regiment, Illinois National Guard, was about to lose the officer assigned to it. Oscar DePriest and the regiment's commander, Col. Spencer Dickerson, wrote to the War Department and asked for Davis's services. DePriest thought Davis would do an excellent job and get a good response from the men because he was black. The War Department denied the request on the grounds that Davis had been at Tuskegee for less than a year. On the other hand, Davis was assigned to the 1931 Gold Star Mothers' Pilgrimage. Davis again made arrangements for his family to accompany him. This time he decided to take his mother, his wife, and his youngest daughter with him on the first trip, and they would all return on the last trip several months later. "Mrs. Davis and I know Paris very well and have no trouble taking care of ourselves after our arrival there," he said. After the end of the term at Tuskegee in May, the Davis family left for New York to begin another summer abroad.[43]

Davis conducted three parties to France during the summer of 1931. One of the passengers felt that Davis was a "lovely host" to the pilgrims. "He really was a real big brother to them and went out of his way to make them very happy indeed."[44]

Benjamin was in Paris only periodically during the summer, but the rest of his family stayed there the whole time. All of them had a variety of interesting experiences. One evening they went to see Josephine Baker, but because she performed in a state of undress, the family was worried about whether Henrietta would like the show. She assured them that she would. In fact, wrote Benjamin, "My mother is having the time of her life." Members of the Davis family spent most of the summer in Paris and used the time to improve their knowledge of French. They stayed at a hotel where no English was spoken, and they hired a tutor for

Elnora. Benjamin sometimes sat in on the lessons. They also accompanied one of the pilgrim parties in its sightseeing tours of Belgium, Holland, and England.[45]

The pilgrimages continued for two more summers, with Davis making the trip with the black pilgrims. "I welcome the opportunity of getting north of the 'Mason and Dixon's Line' if only for a few months." When he was not on trips to Europe, Davis would return to his work at Tuskegee, where things continued much as before.[46]

Davis was a well-known figure on the Tuskegee campus, and the students came to accept his military ways. On one evening a week the students would march to chapel. Davis would be there, arriving five minutes before the 7 P.M. service. The PMS&T would sit by himself, except when the principal attended and joined Davis. The whole campus knew Davis for his military bearing and his punctuality. It was accepted that if one made an appointment with Davis, one had better be on time. Davis would arrive a few minutes before the scheduled meeting, wait until the appointed time, and then leave. In general, Colonel Davis had a reputation for being a stern man, but he was well liked by students and faculty. His emphasis on discipline was a target for satire in a 1935 student publication. "He made himself stand at attention all day because one night he failed to salute when he thought of a superior officer in the United States Army." However, this same publication concluded its remarks about Davis with the note: "You won't find a better friend on the grounds."[47]

Davis's performance as PMS&T was well received by the army inspectors. The usual rating given to the detachment in the yearly inspections was "satisfactory." In 1933 there were nine units similar to Tuskegee in the Fifth Corps area. Tuskegee had the second-largest enrollment (634) of these schools, but it was one of only three that were rated as satisfactory; the other six were rated excellent. During the years that Davis was PMS&T at Tuskegee, only once, in 1936, did the unit receive a rating of excellent. Whether this was an indication of Davis's ability, his dissatisfaction with the job, or the prejudice of the inspector is difficult to determine.[48]

While Davis was stationed at Tuskegee, a number of people, including himself, sought his reassignment to another post. In mid 1933, shortly after his return from Paris, Davis visited the chief of cavalry, Gen. Guy V. Henry, to ask for a better assignment. Henry, after discussing the matter with the adjutant general, reported to Davis that he would have to remain in Alabama. In a memo written several months later, Davis reiterated his frequently expressed belief that as a black man in Alabama, he was subjected to racial disturbances and insults "hurled at him by any white hoodlum." He noted that while the army did not seem to want to assign him to a position where he could command whites, there were some alternatives, which included two black National Guard regiments, one of which was the 369th of New York. He also noted that he was the only officer on the active list who was assigned to full-time duty with a 55c ROTC unit. The army's internal response to this request was "Take no action."[49]

Davis did not give up his efforts. First he asked President Moton to use his influence to help obtain a position for Davis as PMS&T at Howard University. In addition to the reasons Davis had mentioned to the army, he told Moton that his mother was ill and he wanted to be near her. Moton wrote to the president of Howard University for his assistance. Nevertheless, the army still rejected this idea. Not deterred, Davis next visited the State Department to see if it had a position he could fill. He told staff members there about his continued interest in Liberia and its problems, but nothing came of this hint. Three years later, in 1937, he wrote a note to Lester Walton, the United States minister in Liberia, "I am wondering if Liberia could use me in connection with any military program to meet any probable contingency that may arise in connection with its exploitation by any foreign power." Walton referred this note back to the State Department. The minister interpreted this note as a request by Davis for a Liberian assignment, and this time the State Department raised the issue with the War Department. The army informed the diplomats that the slots for military attachés were already filled and that they could not possibly detail Davis.[50]

While Davis was trying to find a new assignment, some army officers were considering whether he should be retired. The chief of cavalry studied Davis's efficiency reports for the previous twenty years and divided them into favorable and unfavorable comments; the latter outnumbered the former. Most of the favorable reports were from the period after Davis began his service with the Ohio National Guard. For example, in 1928, Col. Edgar A. Fry wrote that Davis was "a loyal officer who makes every effort to carry out instructions of the service with success." Also included were the favorable comments that Davis earned as a result of the Gold Star Mothers' Pilgrimage. Most of the unfavorable comments came from the years when Davis had served as a troop commander; his white superiors did not like him very much. Another source of derogatory comments stemmed from his dispute with Moton over rifle practice and ammunition at Tuskegee. Summarizing all of this, Col. Llewellyn Oliver of the staff noted that Davis's age and rank, his generally "satisfactory" ratings, and the difficulty of finding him suitable assignments that were commensurate with his rank—all suggested that he probably should be retired; but once again the army decided to do nothing. Given this attitude toward him, Davis's chances for promotion were remote.[51]

Despite this, some blacks, who were not fully aware of the army's feelings, began to put pressure on the military for a promotion or an assignment to match Davis's rank and service. In 1934, Charles E. Houston, of the NAACP's legal staff, raised this point, among others, in a letter to Chief of Staff Gen. Douglas MacArthur; but the general did not reply to Houston. Moton decided to assist Davis, who had told Moton that he wanted to remain in the service until at least 1936, when Benjamin, Jr., was due to graduate from West Point. Moton urged Davis to stay on as long as possible so that he could be promoted to the rank of brigadier general. In June 1936, Moton wrote to President Roosevelt to urge him to promote Davis: "I feel it will make the Negroes generally very happy." Because of the election and the importance of the black voters, it was a year before Moton received a response, which was negative. The army claimed that because the sixty-year-old Davis was within four years of retirement, he could not be included on the promotion list. If the administration and the army felt that this rejection would end the agitation, they were to be disappointed.[52]

While Davis's career seemed to be at a standstill, the rest of his family was making great strides. When Benjamin, Jr., graduated from West Point in 1936, it was an important occasion for the whole family. He had become the first black to graduate since Charles Young had done so in 1889, and Benjamin, Sr., was very proud of his son's achievement. Within a few days of graduation, Benjamin and Agatha Scott were married. Elnora received a bachelor's degree from NYU in 1936 and a master's degree from Columbia the following year. After graduation, she accepted a position as a teacher at Wilberforce University High School.[53]

While Sadie and Benjamin spent most of each year in segregated Alabama, their life was enlivened by a number of visitors. During the summers, Benjamin, Jr., and later Agatha and Benjamin, would visit them. The two men spent part of their time riding and another part playing cards. In general, relations among the four of them were quite good. Benjamin and Sadie never interfered with the lives of their children, and they all visited back and forth. Another frequent guest in Alabama was Henrietta, who had chosen to give up living by herself and so spent varying amounts of time with her children.[54]

For years the army had resisted efforts to move Davis from Alabama, but a vacancy at Wilberforce forced their hand. In 1936 and early 1937 the chief of cavalry noted on Davis's record: "No assignment available. Cannot be moved." But shortly after the second rejection, the situation changed. Wilberforce's PMS&T, Lt. Col. Frederic W. Whitney, a white man, ended his term of service. Originally the army had planned to replace him with another white officer, but Wilberforce's President Ormonde Walker requested Davis. The army was now able to satisfy Walker and grant Davis's longstanding desire to leave the South.[55]

Colonel Davis's fourth assignment to Wilberforce University was brief and much more pleasant than his earlier ones, but it was still disquieting to him. The school had made the first two years of ROTC compulsory for all male students. Before Davis's arrival, few students had seen ROTC as a very exciting career choice, and it had little prestige on campus; but Davis changed all that. The presence of a black officer, his immaculate uniform, and his military bearing all gave ROTC a positive image. Davis had that command bearing that impressed people. As head of the program, Davis had a relatively easy schedule. He taught a few sections for the seniors, and he supervised the rest of the program. Although the work load was not very demanding, Davis applied his usual energy. He learned the names of all four hundred cadets, many of whom he still remembered when he met them in the course of his duties in World War II.[56]

Elnora, Sadie, and Benjamin lived in Xenia while Benjamin was stationed at Wilberforce University. Because of Benjamin's relatively brief work day and his short distance from campus, he had a considerable amount of free time. Some of this was spent riding, as he had done during his previous tour there and while at Tuskegee. Generally the Davises stayed away from campus-centered activities. They continued to associate with their friends and to play cards for amusement. One campus event that they did attend was the annual military ball, which was held in the gymnasium and was a great social occasion for the students. While being a PMS&T was not very taxing, the assignment itself was very frustrating for Benjamin. He was a senior colonel with more than thirty-five years of service, but he was relegated to the backwaters. The chances for promotion still did not look very bright, and he continued to consider retirement. Then, in mid 1938, things began to change.[57]

In 1938, Davis became the instructor and then the commander of the 369th New York National Guard, headquartered in New York City. The army first detailed him as the unit's instructor, but New York's governor quickly moved to make him the regimental commander as well. New York's black community had for many years expressed its desire to have all the officers' positions in the regiment filled by blacks. Appointing Davis helped both New York's Governor Herbert H. Lehman and the army. Lehman was able to designate as commander a highly qualified black officer who had no political ties to the state, while at the same time the assignment allowed the War Department to send Davis to a position that suited his rank and length of service. Lehman announced Davis's appointment with the comment "I believe that the state of New York and the 369th Regiment are indeed fortunate to obtain the services of such a well qualified commander." In general the black press was equally enthusiastic about the appointment, although it was worried about the issue of segregation in the army and about the discrimination that Davis had previously faced.[58]

As commander and instructor of the 369th New York, Davis was in a different position than he had been as an instructor with the 372d Ohio a decade earlier. According to army regulations, Davis could accept a commission in the National Guard, with the permission of the president, but only for a four-year term. Because Davis was scheduled to retire in 1941, the length of term of the appointment did not pose a problem.[59]

The transfer of authority occurred during the summer and early fall of 1938. In June, Benjamin, Sadie, Benjamin, Jr., and Agatha went to New York to attend a regimental dinner and review. The elegant banquet was followed by a concert by the regimental band, and then the two male Davises went to the armory for the review. There was a large crowd on hand for the event, and Colonel Davis was cheered as he was escorted across the floor. He made a few brief remarks: "It is a great pleasure for me to be here with you this evening with such a regiment. I feel that we will be competent and capable to fulfill all the duties which our commander-in-chief may assign us." The next step in the transfer of authority occurred several months later at the summer encampment. Governor Lehman was present, along with Albert Einstein and twenty-five thousand other spectators, to witness the ceremony at which Davis officially took command of the regiment. Governor Lehman made a five-minute speech, but Davis merely bowed and saluted. He was now commander of the 369th.[60]

The ceremony also marked the beginning of a whole new life for Sadie and Benjamin. Initially they lived in the WPA-built

Dunbar Apartments on Seventh Avenue. Several years later they moved to a larger place on 162d Street. Benjamin had room for his piano, and he began to take lessons to improve his technique. Sadie and Benjamin also had the opportunity to see many movies, a pastime they both enjoyed. Benjamin was able to integrate his leisure activities into his duties. For example, on 9 July 1940, they went downtown to see "All This and Heaven Too" in the morning, and then the colonel went to the armory to work in the afternoon and evening.[61]

In addition to a variety of personal activities, the New York assignment also meant an increase in official social functions. In August 1939, Davis made a brief welcoming speech to Mayor Fiorello LaGuardia when the mayor attended a meeting of the Medical and Dental Associations at the Abyssinian Baptist Church in Harlem. Many of the military reviews of the 369th also became social events; these usually involved dinner dances preceding the troop exercises. During the summers, Benjamin, Jr., and Agatha would join Sadie and Benjamin for these events. On other occasions, Olive and George Streator would accompany Sadie and Benjamin.[62]

Every day, Davis spent some time at the armory, and he returned in the evenings for meetings and the weekly drills. His apparent goal was to re-create the Regular Army in his regiment. In a speech to the officers in September 1940, he pointed out some of the lapses from his model. He pointed out that they often failed to use military language while issuing commands or filing reports. His key point, however, was the role of military customs: "In the military service rank is everything. The basis of discipline is respect for superiors. Military discipline requires only that relationship which a gentleman demands *by his conduct* from others who are gentlemen." This was certainly the philosophy by which he himself had lived for many years, and he encouraged his regiment to emulate him.[63]

In 1939, Governor Lehman had asked the federal government whether he could convert some of the state regiments, including the 369th, to antiaircraft units, but the army had turned him down. The army firmly believed that the 369th was not "suitable" for conversion to this task. By the middle of 1940 the army was beginning to change its attitude. In early April 1940, Colonel Davis went to Washington to discuss the issue with Chief of Staff Gen. George C. Marshall. Davis told Marshall that in his opinion, more than one New York regiment should be converted. Only in this way, said Davis, would it prevent the black community from feeling that they were being shunted aside. Marshall came out of the meeting with the feeling that Davis could manage the conversion, and Marshall notified the New York National Guard and the chief of the Coast Artillery of his conclusions. As a result, in mid 1940 the change was announced and was well received by the black community and by the press, who saw the conversion of the 369th to an antiaircraft regiment as a way of demonstrating that blacks could serve in all branches of the military service. The conversion process was successful, and Davis's role in it left General Marshall with a favorable impression.[64]

During 1940, Davis's approaching retirement became the subject of public discussion. The *Pittsburgh Courier*, as part of its campaign for black equality, continually requested the army to make a commitment for a black division, "and when it is won and the division is formed, Colonel Davis will command it." Others hoped that Roosevelt would realize the political capital that could be made from such an appointment. If Davis harbored any hopes about a promotion, especially after all the talk, they were probably dashed when the promotion list was announced in late September 1940. Although the president appointed eighty-four new generals as part of the army expansion, Davis was not one of them. As the *New York Age* headlined: "Pres. Appoints 84 Generals, Ignores Col. Davis."[65]

As the election campaign continued, rumors about additional appointments began to circulate. Some black newspapers reported that Davis was upset by his failure to be promoted and was planning to retire, but Davis denied this. The reports, however, spurred people to write letters of protest. One old soldier compared Davis's position to that of Charles Young in 1917. Young, on the eve of the war, was denied promotion to the rank of colonel and then was retired by the army. "If America fails the Negro, why should the Negro not fail America?" When people wrote directly to the War Department with complaints, they were informed that Davis was too old to be promoted. "Only in exceptional cases were colonels nominated who were above the age of fifty-eight. Colonel Davis is now over sixty-three years of age." The army argued that Davis's age would have prevented his serving for more than a short period of time. However, on 26 October 1940, only a few days before the 1940 election, the government announced another list of promotions to the rank of general, and the name of Benjamin O. Davis was included.[66]

The determining factors were not recorded, but there certainly were political considerations involved. At that point in the presidential campaign, FDR's try for a third term was encountering difficulties. The black community, which had given Roosevelt many votes in 1936, was upset by governmental policies. This anger had been expressed to Roosevelt in a meeting involving Walter F. White, A. Philip Randolph, and T. Arnold Hill. Although they complained about discrimination in the armed forces and the defense industries, the resulting press release seemed to indicate that the black leaders supported the government's policies. The black press seized upon this, and eventually the White House issued a clarification; but the damage had been done. The anger at discrimination in the defense build-up was also expressed in other comments in the black press. For example, Roy Wilkins, in his syndicated column, said that normally little pressure could be applied, "but this is election time and Mr. Roosevelt is asking for votes." The Republicans saw an opportunity. In a series of advertisements in black newspapers, they pointed out what the Roosevelt administration had not done for blacks, including the omission of Davis from the last promotion list. Walter White, for one, advised the Democrats that "the only way the damage could be repaired would be to take steps immediately to end discrimination in the armed services and industry." The same kind of advice was given to the White House by Will Alexander, an advisor to the Roosevelt administration on racial matters. By mid October these events and others had helped to convince some that Wendell L. Willkie, FDR's opponent, had a chance to win. Then came Davis's appointment. The timing strongly suggested that political considerations were at work.[67]

Secretary of War Henry Stimson also perceived that Davis's appointment was motivated by politics. On 22 October 1940, Undersecretary of War Robert P. Patterson discussed with Stimson the possibility of appointing a black man to be civilian aide to the secretary. In this discussion, the first on this issue, there was no mention of new appointments to the rank of general; they attributed the possible appointment of a black civilian aide to Roosevelt's electoral problems. On the following day, Stimson and Patterson, joined this time by General Marshall, again discussed the issue of the civilian aide but made no mention of a new general. Two days later, things had changed. Stimson noted in his diary: "As soon as I reached the office this morning General Marshall was ready for me with a list of new proposed General Officers, including the colored Brigadier General whose proposed appointment by the President gave the occasion for the appointment of others whose appointments from the standpoint of national defense were rather more important." After discussing Davis's appointment with Marshall, along with a number of other officers that were to be promoted, Stimson and Marshall went to the White House and received FDR's approval for the entire list. Later that day, Stimson, when discussing the issue with Secretary of the Navy Frank Knox at a cabinet meeting, indicated his displeasure with the appointment of Davis. From this evidence it is clear that the appointment originated from the White House and that, like the appointment of William Hastie as civilian aide to the secretary of war, it was a "symbolic statement" with political motives.[68]

While the appointment was a surprise to Davis, it was well received by him and others. Davis's diary notation for the day is very matter-of-fact: "Associated Press called about noon notifying me of my promotion." The news was followed by many congratulatory calls and telegrams. Most of the black press was ecstatic. The *Amsterdam News* used one-and-one-half-inch headlines to say, "Col. Davis Promoted." In its stories, the press paid tribute to Roosevelt's "courage" in making the appointment. On the other hand, the *New York Age*, a pro-Willkie paper, said that the appointment was "an empty honor." In addition to Davis's having been passed over several times, it felt that Davis could provide little "useful service in his new capacity." Certainly the timing and coverage could not but help FDR on election day. This was the tenor of much of the mail that Roosevelt received. There was very little negative feedback, either in the mail or in the white press's coverage.[69]

Despite the promotion, Davis's career was progressing more slowly than those of his contemporary white officers. During the 1920s, Davis had been a little younger than the average lieutenant colonel. In 1925, Davis was forty-eight according to the army's records. The average lieutenant colonel in that year was almost fifty years old. However, during the 1920s the typical officer spent a little more than four years in that rank, while Davis spent ten. Davis also spent more time as a colonel than the average—ten years, as compared to seven. He continued to be among that small group of officers who had not attended a professional school. In 1940 only 22 percent of the generals had no higher education, but Davis was one of that group. The average age of the other generals in that year was fifty-nine, which meant that Davis was older than his peers. The additional years that he spent at the various ranks did benefit him. By the end of the decade he was receiving the maximum salary for his rank, $7,200 per year. This placed his income in the top 5 percent of family incomes for that period.[70]

With the appointment, Davis's tenure as commander of the 369th drew to a close, and he received a new assignment. During his last few weeks as commander of the regiment, a number of parties and events were staged in his honor. Davis was touched by them. At the same time, other honors were bestowed upon him. Omega Psi Phi, a black fraternity, selected him to receive its second annual achievement award for outstanding service. In early January 1941, Benjamin and Sadie left New York and drove slowly westward to Fort Riley, Kansas. The new assignment that Brigadier General Davis had been given was as commander of the Fourth Brigade, Second Cavalry Division. For the last few months of his planned army career, he could look forward to service with his beloved horse soldiers.[71]

The promotion to brigadier general brought to a happy end two decades of being out of the military mainstream for Benjamin Davis. Again it had been a period of personal and professional highs and lows. All of his family had enjoyed his tour of service with the Gold Star Mothers' Pilgrimage. His three years with the New York National Guard had given him the satisfaction of troop command and the personal pleasure of living in an urban area. He also took pride in the success of his children. Especially significant was his son's graduation from West Point, following in the footsteps of Charles Young. On the other hand, there were a number of disappointments. The years at Tuskegee, the Ohio National Guard, and Wilberforce had done nothing to advance his career. The whole fiasco of his assignment to Liberia was disconcerting. During the period he received no professional education, and much of the time he lived in rural areas with small black communities. However, all of the disappointments took on a new gloss with his promotion in 1940. Whether it was politically motivated or not, the sixty-three-year-old Benjamin Davis was now a brigadier general. Although he was due to retire in mid 1941, many surprises were still in store for him, including eight very productive years of active duty.

5 | World War II— Inspector General: 1941–1942

ALTHOUGH GENERAL DAVIS began 1941 in Kansas, he soon found himself in Washington. The beginning of World War II marked the start of the most rewarding period in Davis's long life of public service. In early 1941, Davis began his assignment as commander of the Fourth Cavalry Brigade. It was a new organization, made up of units, including the Ninth and Tenth Cavalry, that were not in a state of combat readiness. During the 1930s the Ninth had been stationed at Fort Riley, but the Tenth had been broken up into small detachments at Forts Leavenworth and Myer and at West Point. Much of their duty had been to act as servants and horse groomers.[1]

Once Davis had assumed command, he began the process of bringing the brigade to active-duty status. By May, Gen. Terry Allen, commander of the Second Cavalry Division, of which the brigade was a part, reported to Washington that the Fourth Brigade was making good progress and "should finish fast in spite of a slow start." He felt that even though one half of his division was white and the other black, this unique organization could be made to work.[2]

One problem that complicated the training was the fact that the recreational facilities were segregated. Davis objected when the United Service Organizations (USO) in nearby Junction City took steps to see that their facilities were kept separated. He did not understand why segregation needed to be brought into an area where it did not already exist, but he won only a temporary victory in this particular effort to prevent this.[3]

While his official life was busy, Benjamin's social life was quite restricted. He and Sadie lived on the post, at 5 Barry Street, near General Allen. The brigade officers were quite proper in their social relations with the Davises, but no more than that. When the Davises first arrived at the post, the officers came to call, as was required by army etiquette, but there was no further interaction. Social activities were limited by segregation outside the post and by military custom within it. The Davises could not go to the segregated movie theater or to the officers' club. As a result, their social contacts were limited to Benjamin, Jr., whom the army had assigned to be his father's aide, and Agatha, Benjamin, Jr.'s wife. On many evenings the four would gather to play bridge, which was quite competitive, with the men playing against the women. Riding was another form of recreation for Benjamin, who tried to ride daily, sometimes with unsettling results. On one occasion in early April, his horse, Big Parade, "refused a jump but I didn't. The ground was soft and I wasn't hurt."[4]

Retirement was an ever-present issue as Davis's sixty-fourth birthday drew nearer. When he first arrived at the post, he was questioned by reporters on the issue of his retirement. He replied: "I think I have done my share but if the War Department desires me to continue to serve in the national emergency, I will have an open mind." As the date approached, he asked the army to appoint a replacement to command the brigade; however, he did say that he was still available for further duty "should the Department feel the need of my services."[5]

Simultaneously, some civilians were trying to exert pressure on the War Department to retain Davis on active duty. Louis Lautier, a reporter and secretary of the Committee on Participation of the Negro in National Defense, started such a campaign. He wrote notes to key congressmen, asking them to introduce bills to retain Davis. Lautier thought that this action would boost the morale of the black troops and thus would aid the army. Lautier also sought and was granted the help of Emmett Scott, a respected educator. Scott wrote to several influential legislators that retiring Davis would serve to confirm the theory that Davis's initial appointment to the rank of general had been purely political. Scott was not very optimistic that these arguments would have any impact; however, Congressman Ulysses G. Guyer of Kansas and Senator Harry S. Truman of Missouri did introduce bills into Congress that sought to retain Davis on active duty with combat troops.[6]

The army opposed these proposals and consulted with Harold Smith, director of the Bureau of the Budget, to see if a negative response would be acceptable to the administration. When the army received assurances that it would be, Secretary Stimson followed through. On 25 July 1941 he informed Congressman Andrew J. May, chairman of the House Committee on Military Affairs, that the War Department was opposed to Guyer's bill on the grounds that no special legislation should be passed to aid individual officers. As a result of this recommendation, the bills never came up for discussion.[7]

While Congress was considering these proposals, the War Department had already begun planning to use Davis's services after his mandatory retirement. In early June, General Marshall queried Davis about working in the office of the inspector general (IG), "as inspector and advisor in connection with matters pertaining to the various colored units now in service." Although there were some problems as to what his rank and pay might be, Davis immediately accepted the position. On 28 June, orders were issued for Davis's retirement and his immediate return to active duty. This pleased many blacks. Even the New York Age, which had questioned the motives behind the initial appointment, felt that Davis's retention was "reassuring news."[8]

One can only hypothesize why the army decided to retain Davis on active duty but away from the command of combat troops. It is likely that General Marshall realized that the continued expansion of the army would result in more racial friction. Davis appeared to be a moderate on the race issue who they knew would not seriously challenge the army's basic policy on segregation. Furthermore, they probably hoped that this appointment might placate the black community.

During the following weeks, Davis concluded his assignment with the Fourth Cavalry Brigade and moved to Washington. Because he had not lived there after he had joined the army in 1899, he had to buy a home. A three-story brick house at 1721 S Street,

N.W., was purchased for $12,000. It would be his family's home for more than twenty years.[9]

After a ten-day leave to set up his new residence, General Davis reported to the IG for his new assignment. He was placed in charge of what was referred to as a "Special Section," within the office of the IG. The current inspector general, Maj. Gen. Virgil I. Peterson, had two assistants, Brig. Gen. Howard McC. Snyder and Davis. The mission of the IG was to inquire into and report on the operations of the army. These inspections, Davis noted several months later, were for the purpose of "promoting efficiency and economy, to observe and report upon the state of morale and discipline, condition and unpreparedness of commands, and other activities to fulfill their respective missions, to determine whether or not law and regulations are being complied with, and to report upon the general, economic and administrative efficiency of Army activities." Specifically, Davis was assigned the mission of advising the General Staff on matters "pertaining to the various colored units in the service."[10]

Davis soon found himself involved in such an issue when two colonels were asked to move in order to set up an office for him. When they objected, Davis and his clerk were moved to two rooms separated from the other IG offices. This separation also affected other aspects of Davis's work. There were no real dining facilities for blacks in the War Department; so rather than eat in a segregated lunch room elsewhere, Davis skipped lunch.[11]

The problems that occupied Davis remained constant throughout the war, although their severity increased as the war progressed. There was discontent among the black population because of the military's policy of segregation. This applied to interracial contact both on and off a base. As the army grew in size during the 1941 mobilization, this problem escalated. New training facilities had to be established, and segregation was introduced into all of them, in the South and also in the North, where it had not existed before. The soldiers also felt that they received discriminatory treatment by the military police, most of whom were white. Still more problems arose when the soldiers left the base and came into conflict with civilian police officers.

In order to avoid these problems, the men were often confined to the bases, which had limited and always segregated recreational facilities. All of these factors created racial tensions which the white officers of the blacks units were unable to handle. Most white officers did not relish this assignment, and few of them understood the concerns of their troops. As a result, morale was poor, and friction between the races increased.[12]

Davis's initial assignments set the pattern for much of his work during the first two years of the war: he conducted inspections of black units, and he investigated racial incidents that had already occurred. For example, in late July and early August 1941, Davis traveled back to Tuskegee, Alabama, to inspect the new flying facilities that were being developed there. He viewed the facilities that were being constructed for the student fliers, talked to many of the pilots, including his son, and observed the training procedures. After meeting with Capt. Noel Parish, the officer in charge, Davis filed a report on the situation and made suggestions on how to deal with the racial problems; but he did not criticize the segregated unit or the separate facilities.[13]

Several months later, on a similar mission, Davis traveled to Camp Lee, Virginia, to view the quartermaster training facilities. William Hastie had already sent over a series of complaints about conditions there which he had received via the NAACP. Davis met with the enlisted men and officers, including the Eighth Medical Battalion; viewed the training and recreational facilities; and watched the men in action. In a talk with the post's officers, he reminded them that they needed to forget any preconceived ideas about race and that everyone had to work to achieve victory. This talk and the visit itself helped to alleviate some of the problems. Davis himself was pleased with the morale of the soldiers and the condition of the facilities. He was later quoted in the black press as being enthusiastic "about the new Jim Crow service club and the recreation program provided." This and other inspections served a variety of functions. The inspector's visit gave the black soldiers a chance to voice their complaints to the high-ranking black officer, and his report apprised the IG of conditions that black soldiers were facing. Furthermore, the whole process gave the War Department an opportunity to get favorable coverage in the black press.[14]

Davis also dealt with incidents of violence in which he sought to discover the cause of the problem and make recommendations to prevent its recurrence. Fayetteville, North Carolina, was the scene of several racial disturbances in early August 1941. Groups of black soldiers from nearby Fort Bragg got into a number of fights with the MPs, in which one MP died and three others were wounded. One black soldier was also killed, and three were wounded. From 12 August to 11 September, Davis headed a board of three officers who went to the area to conduct a thorough investigation. The board obtained sworn testimony from ninety-one witnesses, studied affidavits submitted by other investigating officers, visited the scenes of the incidents, and got the assistance of the FBI for laboratory tests on weapons and bullets; but despite all that work, the board was not able to determine who had killed the soldiers. Davis was also anxious to expose the cause of the problems. He felt that much of the trouble was related to the poor leadership of some unit commanders. However, since many of the problems stemmed as much from basic army policies as from individual officers' deficiencies, there was really little hope for solutions.[15]

Davis also made his views on the race issue known in the discussions within the War Department. As he noted in his diary, color "is indeed a great problem for the white man. A little color affects him greatly." He talked with General Peterson and wrote reports to the staff on his impressions of the condition of black troops. In a detailed report issued in late November 1941, Davis noted that the first black soldiers entering the army during the 1940/1941 expansion had been subjected to "radical propaganda designed to make them dissatisfied under any conditions." The situation was made worse, wrote Davis, by the poor quality of the officers who had initially been assigned to the black units. By late 1941, Davis thought conditions had improved: there were better living quarters, and the unit officers had made some efforts to help the troops deal with nearby communities. "The men are finding out for themselves that the propaganda spread before them prior to induction is not true, and much of this unrest and dissatisfaction seems to have disappeared." Davis also pointed out that morale was quite high when black officers were assigned to the black units. He believed that the end result was "an improved feeling on the part of the colored population toward the national defense effort."[16]

Davis's optimistic reports were unlike those simultaneously being submitted by William Hastie, which reiterated the problems and also criticized the clashes with southern whites and the limited possibilities for the promotion of black officers. Hastie's solution was to bring an end to segregation and the barriers to black advancement. This emphasis on problems, rather than progress, was obviously not what the leadership wanted to hear, and Davis's words were much more acceptable. The army's reaction to Hastie's proposals—namely, total rejection—reinforced Davis's belief in the "quiet approach."[17]

While the army tried to ignore Hastie, the black press continued the pressure. The army made plans for a conference involving a number of leading editors from the black community and key military personnel in order to provide the black press with information about the ways in which the War Department functioned and "to endeavor to create better relations between the army and the Negro public." The Office of Public Information asked a number of departments, including the IG, to detail a spokesman, so General Peterson sent Davis. The conference was originally scheduled for 3 December but was then postponed to 8 December.[18]

Although the War Department was in great confusion on that day, because of the Japanese attack on Pearl Harbor on the preceding day, the conference was still held. Hastie made some introductory remarks, and General Marshall then briefly welcomed the editors. The next group of speakers represented those army agencies whose policies and decisions affected the lives of the black servicemen. Davis described in general terms his activities at the IG. "No complaint has been too small to receive attention, and I have listened to them all." He reiterated the points made earlier in his report to the General Staff—namely, that the soldiers had been stirred up by special interest propaganda and that some of the unit officers did not understand the problems of the black soldiers. In a remark clearly directed at the press, Davis noted that wherever "the army is allowed to work out the situation in its own way," morale was good and constantly improving. In addition, Davis talked about the investigations he had conducted. He thought that these inquiries had been effective. Davis concluded his talk with this statement: "We are alert and on our toes, and it is 'Full Speed Ahead.' " There were no questions following his presentation.[19]

Davis also participated in a variety of other public-relations events. In early November 1941 he went to Chicago to take part in two public ceremonies. First he placed a wreath on the monument to the members of the Eighth Illinois who had died in World War I. After this he was escorted to a black Service Men's Club by bands from the two local black high schools and some military units. Chicago's Mayor Edward Kelly was the chief speaker, but Davis also made a brief speech, after which there was a reception for him at the club. At Christmastime, Davis made a radio broadcast directed primarily to the black troops, the program and spirit of which were well received by the War Department.[20]

As American participation in the war began, Davis's level of activity increased. As the number of drafted black troops grew, all problems that had existed prior to 7 December 1941 got larger and more menacing. These included the attitudes of commanding officers, the hostility of southerners, the inadequacy of facilities, the segregation within the army, and the opposition from the black press and the black soldiers to conditions. Davis was among the vanguard who tried to moderate the policy of segregation, as during the first eight months of 1942 he continued the activities he had begun in 1941.

During the first weeks of 1942, Davis went on a three-week survey trip which covered posts in Louisiana, Missouri, Oklahoma, and Texas. At Camp Livingston, Louisiana, he tried to defuse a potentially dangerous situation. The reputation that Davis had gained from his investigation at Fort Bragg gave him prestige with the enlisted men and officers. He spoke very plainly to the latter and emphasized that though they were in the South, the black soldiers should be treated as men, according to regulations. In addition he stressed the idea that their conduct was helping to shape the future and that they should return the men to civilian life "with a good taste in their mouths." In his report to the IG on the situation at Camp Livingston, he noted that the soldiers "seemed to be bewildered." They believed that they had tried both to keep out of trouble and to follow local racial customs, yet problems still persisted. The soldiers thought that the black MPs were being discriminated against in terms of equipment and assignments, which in turn, according to Davis, lowered the morale of the troops. His recommendations included a request that black MPs and white MPs be treated alike and that the regulations concerning equality of duties be adhered to.[21]

Davis's reviews continued during the next few months as he listened to and dealt with the complaints of individual soldiers and officers. While this was a traditional role for an inspecting officer, it was particularly important in this situation. At times, Hastie or Gibson would provide Davis with background information or relay complaints that they themselves had received. While at a post, Davis became familiar with a variety of problems: soldiers told him about concerns for their dependants, problems with company officers, or uncertainty about future assignments. Davis wrote down each soldier's name, rank, company, and complaint; then he noted how they were to be handled. On occasion, time did not permit him to meet with everyone who wanted to see him. When he visited MacDill Field in Tampa, Florida, in March 1942, about one-third of the eighteen hundred black enlisted personnel lined up to talk to him. Because he could not meet with all of them, he enlisted the aid of the chaplain and the NCOs to group the men with similar complaints and then to select representatives to speak for each particular problem. Then Davis spoke to the first sergeants of each of the units to get another viewpoint on the situation. He came to a variety of conclusions, including his often-stated view that much of the trouble arose from the officers' failure to win the confidence of their men.[22]

On a number of these 1942 inspections, Davis met with local black civilian officials. In April he addressed the Fifth All-Southern Negro Youth Conference at Tuskegee Institute, Alabama. Speaking about black contributions to previous American wars, he pointed out that blacks had participated from the colonial period onward: "From Boston Commons to the battlefields of Europe, Negroes have distinguished themselves by gallantry far beyond the call of duty." Davis also mentioned to his listeners a major theme of his work in the war: "What we do desire is equal opportunity to share in the obligations of citizenship and in the hardships of preparation for combat on the same basis as other people." Usually combined with inspections of local facilities, these visits were featured by the black press and helped to build up morale as well as the army's view of Davis's usefulness.[23]

During the first half of 1942, Davis also had to deal with investigations of racial disturbances, a process that he found quite trying. One of the most difficult of these situations began at Fort Dix, New Jersey, in April 1942, where the soldiers became very upset about segregation on and off the post and a riot ensued. When the investigating officers, including Davis, arrived, the soldiers gave them little cooperation. It seemed to be a silent revolt. Although the inspectors were able to report on the causes of the riot, nothing was done to deal with its basic causes.[24]

This constant activity began to wear Davis down. In 1941 he took only about twenty days of leave of absence, scattered throughout the year, and in 1942 he only had seven vacation days. The constant round of inspections and investigations, public appearances, and travel began to affect him. In mid May 1942 he became ill and had to report to Walter Reed Hospital for several days. After a rest and a checkup, he was released, although he spent the remainder of the month in the Washington area. Even then he was busy with activities in the War Department and with official functions. The rest and the slower pace were healing, and by the beginning of June, Davis was his old self again and ready to resume his active schedule.[25]

Davis was soon confronted with one of his most difficult challenges. The racial situation that he encountered at Fort Huachuca, Arizona, was similar to that on other posts, except that it was magnified by the larger number of black troops present. It was there that the army assembled, at one time or another, the two black combat divisions. The isolated location of the post, the mostly white officer corps, the segregation of facilities, and the paucity of recreational activities all contributed to the problems, which included low morale and a high rate of venereal disease. Before one of Davis's trips to the post, he noted in his diary, "I do not look forward with pleasure to this trip."[26]

In late July 1942, Davis left Washington for his first visit to Fort Huachuca. He was quite busy as he toured the post, talked with officers and men, and watched the soldiers train. One of his first activities was to meet post commander Col. Edwin N. Hardy. The officers and the men were informed that if they wanted to talk to the general, they would have to submit their names, and each person would then be assigned a time. Officers were the first to talk to Davis, and they complained about the overcrowded quarters, the shortage of proper supplies, the segregated officers' club, and the refusal of the officers' barber shop to serve blacks. Davis pointed out that it was War Department policy to provide separate but equal facilities for black units. On the next day, Davis talked to a number of enlisted men. His general attitude was sympathetic, but he understood the difference between discrimination and discontent based on the hardships of army life. Before Davis returned to Washington, Colonel Hardy sent Davis a memo detailing his personal observations about the post. While Hardy thought morale was all right, he believed that the black press was too prone to criticism and that this was leading the soldiers to believe that they were being treated unfairly. After collecting this information, Davis returned to Washington and reported to General Peterson, who in turn conveyed his findings to the General Staff. Davis thought that in general operations at Fort Huachuca were going smoothly. The worst problem concerned the officers' clubs. He felt that on a post that had a preponderance of black personnel, the clubs should not be labeled for a particular race. General Peterson agreed with Davis's recommendation that this practice be changed.[27]

Although Davis's life was strenuous and kept him away from home for long periods of the time, his family ties remained strong. He wrote to his wife at least every other day. His love for Sadie and his home life shone through many of his letters: "I hope all has gone well with you. I have had a long day but I have thought of you." Benjamin and Sadie kept in touch with the progress of their family, even though the visits with Olive and Benjamin, Jr., were less frequent because of wartime conditions. Elnora spent this period teaching at Maryland State College in Bowie. Because it was close to Washington, she would visit her parents frequently, at times taking the train in for dinner or coming in for weekend visits. Davis was able to see his son during his inspections at Tuskegee, but he learned the news of his son's promotion to lieutenant colonel from a wire, to which the parents responded with a congratulatory telegram. Although Davis's trips away from home were demanding, tiring, and lonely, he felt that the work was rewarding because he was making a contribution to the war effort.[28]

Another aspect of General Davis's work, which also continued from the prewar period, was having to advise the War Department on how to handle the racial problems generated by its segregation policies. The issue of race relations was again the subject of a report that Davis and Peterson prepared for the General Staff. In his draft report, Davis proposed that racial problems should be recognized and that all soldiers and officers should be trained in ways to avoid difficulties. He also noted that blacks "deeply resent[ed]" the War Department's policy of segregated facilities, including its introduction into areas where it had not existed before. He made it very clear that while blacks supported "the cause of Democracy," they did not accept the way in which the government was organizing its manpower resources to win the war. Davis also thought that the army, "the best agency for bringing about the necessitated change in attitude," should impress upon whites the need for better race relations. He believed that this could not occur as long as the military prohibited most inter-racial meetings through its policy of segregation. Unfortunately, many of these ideas were omitted from the final memorandum, although Peterson did include Davis's suggestions for training to deal with racial problems and the idea that blacks should not be sent to areas in which racial mores were different from those they were used to (i.e., do not send black troops from the North to train in the South). Peterson did include a note that Davis was opposed to limiting the role of blacks to only certain aspects of the war effort. The idea that good leadership was needed for the black units was well received by the General Staff, which passed this on to its subordinates.[29]

Although Peterson did not include the meat of Davis's suggestions on the racial issue, he did think highly of Davis's work and recommended Davis for a Legion of Merit. In his statement, Peterson noted that Davis had worked for many years in the army but that in the recent past, his contributions had been very great. The recommendation was not accepted because the staff thought Davis's work in these areas was not yet finished.[30]

Another aspect of Davis's role in the War Department in 1942 was his appointment to the Advisory Committee on Negro Troop Policies, which was a response to the increasing pressure on the War Department to do something to put an end to discrimination and to implement integration. In some ways the committee was an attempt to defuse the attacks from the black community, for there had been no real change in the fundamental idea that the war should not be used to bring about social change. As Assistant Secretary of War John McCloy, the head of this new committee, told Hastie: "I do not think that the basic issues of this war are involved in the question of whether Colored troops serve in segregated units or in mixed units and I doubt whether you can convince the people of the United States that the basic issues of freedom are involved in such a question." When Undersecretary Patterson created the committee in late August 1942, William Hastie was not appointed to it, nor was he even notified about it until a month after it had been established. Appointees to the committee included Davis and officers from other parts of the army whose actions affected the black troops. As far as McCloy was concerned, social issues were to be ignored; only those problems directly related to the performance of blacks would be discussed. Although this was the committee's aim, the basic problems could not be ignored, and Davis kept them before the committee.[31]

At one of the first meetings of the committee, Davis brought up a small matter, but one that he believed was important for the morale of the black soldiers. He was continually bothered by the way in which individual commanders used the word *Negro*. He thought that some people pronounced it like *Nigra*, a word that particularly upset many blacks. As a result he suggested that the committee recommend the use of the word *colored*, a term that Davis himself used in his correspondence and reports. The suggestion was not adopted. At this point in the committee's existence, nomenclature was the kind of issue that it was discussing, as the group sought to define its role. It would not be until the end of 1943, partially at the prompting of Davis, that more substantive issues would be addressed.[32]

Before Davis could get too involved in committee work, he received a new assignment—special duty in England. The United States' racial problems spread overseas when the first black service units arrived in England in early 1942, and reports about this situation began to drift back to the United States. When Cyrus L. Sulzberger of the *New York Times* visited the United Kingdom in mid 1942, he wrote a memo to Service of Supply (SOS) with his findings. He believed quite strongly that no more black troops should be sent to the United Kingdom and that the ones who were there should be concentrated in the port cities, instead of being scattered around the country. Nothing was done to follow up on these ideas, and the racial problems continued to grow in intensity. Dwight D. Eisenhower, the American commander in the European Theater of Operations (ETO), decided to seek help. In early August 1942 he asked Washington to detail Davis as advisor to the commanding general of SOS. General Peterson was not very enthusiastic about letting Davis go, because Peterson thought that Davis was contributing a great deal by his IG work. After several weeks of discussion, Davis was finally ordered to Europe on one-month temporary duty, with a departure date of 19 September 1942.[33]

Davis's first wartime tour of duty in Europe began with a circuitous flight from New York to England via Canada. During a layover, Colonel Abbott, an officer in G-1 (Personnel), told Davis that Eisenhower had been trying to get Davis assigned for more than two months but that Peterson had tried to prevent it. According to Abbott, Eisenhower prevailed because he argued that he needed Davis very badly. After five days of traveling, Davis arrived in London.[34]

Davis began his visit to Britain by meeting the senior United States commanders. Davis and Eisenhower talked about what Eisenhower expected Davis to do: namely, investigate the racial situation and make recommendations. Then Davis was introduced to Lt. Gen. John C. H. Lee, the head of SOS in the ETO. The two, along with Lee's aide, then took the train to Cheltenham, General Lee's headquarters. From the beginning, Davis thought that Lee was sympathetic to the plight of the blacks and that he looked favorably on Davis's efforts. After spending the night in Cheltenham, Davis began inspection trips to the bases where black and white soldiers were stationed, usually returning to Cheltenham or London in the evening. He expressed the belief that his trips were giving him "much valuable experience."[35]

On a visit to Northern Ireland, Davis also conducted an inquiry into a racial incident. He talked with American soldiers and policemen and Irish civilians. The news of Davis's work quickly reached the American black press, whose members were able to reassure their readers that Davis was on the scene, investigating problems. After finishing his work, he left for England on the evening of 8 October. As he approached the car ferry, he met Lt. Farrell D. Lowe, the officer escort at the boat. Lieutenant Lowe helped Davis's driver find the correct stop on the ship and then escorted General Davis to his cabin. Lowe asked Davis if everything was satisfactory; then he saluted and left. Altogether, Lowe had met Davis for about five minutes. Two years later, when Davis was next in Europe, he encountered Lowe again, recalled him by name, and congratulated him on his promotion to the rank of captain. It was typical of Davis's phenomenal memory for names and faces. A day after his return to England, he sub-

Brig. Gen. Benjamin O. Davis, Sr., and Maj. Gen. John C. H. Lee "somewhere in England" during World War II

mitted a report to General Lee on the murder of the black soldier. The SOS commander was impressed with the work and asked Davis to accompany him on another inspection tour. This pleased Davis, who thought that Lee was an officer who understood what he, Davis, could contribute.[36]

Davis became somewhat of a celebrity in Britain, where he met many famous people. One day, while walking in London with Adm. Harold R. Stark, U.S. Navy, Lady Astor hailed Davis from her car. She stopped, got out, and Stark introduced Davis to her. She invited Davis to lunch to meet Lord Astor. He accepted, and two weeks later he visited Cliveden as their guest. He found Lady Astor "charming." He was also interviewed by the *Times*. He told the reporter that some American whites resented the way in which the British had treated the American blacks, but blacks were "profuse in their praise" of British conduct. Later during a November trip to Bristol, he met Eleanor Roosevelt, who was in the area visiting a variety of installations including Red Cross clubs. She encountered Davis at the club set aside for blacks, the first such institution in Britain. She was quite impressed with him and his work, as she told Walter White the next month at a conference at the White House. In addition to meeting celebrities, Davis was also asked by the American Embassy to make a speech over the British Broadcasting Corporation.[37]

One of the major successes of Davis's time in England was an increase in the number of blacks admitted to Officer Candidate School (OCS). Blacks believed that they were not being allowed into the programs because of their race. Davis discussed the issue with General Lee, who agreed to create a board of officers, with Davis as its head, and authorized it to admit ten black candidates to the program. Later, Lee increased this number to fifteen. The board sent in its list of nominees in late October, and General Lee approved all of them. This was a great accomplishment, Davis thought, and "well worth my trip."[38]

Despite the accomplishments and the encounters with important people, as the month of his original assignment came to an end, Davis began to wish that he could go home. In some ways he enjoyed being a celebrity, but he missed his wife, and the English weather was hard on him. He found the houses cold and the coin-operated electric heaters not very effective. He began to be frustrated. For example, on one of his visits he saw a group of Canadian soldiers, some black, some white, in the same unit in which there was no color prejudice: "A border line makes so much difference." He thought that he could convey this idea of racial harmony to the United States leaders, but he found that most of them did not want to see it. Eisenhower, however, wanted Davis to stay, and after some negotiations with the War Department, Davis was ordered to remain for two additional weeks.[39]

Before Davis departed, he submitted his final report on the racial situation to General Eisenhower. According to Davis, one source of the racial friction that had occurred had been caused mainly by certain whites who resented having blacks associate with British women and objected to the absence of Jim Crow in Britain. Blacks, on the other hand, liked the treatment they received from the British. One black soldier asked, "Who are we over here to fight, the Germans or our own white soldiers?" Another source of trouble, according to Davis, was the inability of some unit commanders to control their men. He believed it was necessary to get experienced and able officers to command black troops, and he noted that General Lee was working to correct this aspect of the situation. The report concluded with a series of recommendations for Eisenhower. One proposal involved a course in race relations, including black history, for all soldiers. He recommended that Americans who entered Britain be inculcated with the idea of team work and cooperation. Davis suggested that all soldiers should be informed that "it is desired that there be no discrimination against any persons wearing the uniform of our Army." Another recommendation concerned the military police. He thought that they should be closely supervised and that where black and white troops mingled together, there should be both black MPs and white MPs. In the area of entertainment, Davis proposed that freedom of association be allowed and that clubs be designated by organizations, not by race. On the other hand, blacks should be instructed that while the British were sympathetic to them, they did not really understand Jim Crow. General Davis proposed that the black soldiers be told: "Your relatives and friends back home are depending upon you to show our allies and comrades that you can perform this duty with dignity and honor becoming American citizens." General Lee passed on the report to Eisenhower with his approval of the proposals. A number of these suggestions had already been acted upon; some were put into practice after Davis left; and some were ignored. Davis's report did not overlook the existence of discrimination, but he tried to suggest ways to deal with it.[40]

The army released parts of this report to the press, emphasizing that Davis had thought that racial problems were not serious in Britain. The reactions to this were varied. The *Afro-American* commented that Davis had played down the issue of racism, and it blamed Eisenhower for his failure to discipline the white troops. On the other hand, Joseph Julian, writing in the *Nation*, implied that Davis's study of racial conditions was cursory and that he had missed much of the discrimination going on through-out England. Julian's suggestion on how to deal with this problem, however, was right in line with Davis's: education of the troops. The impression that came across in some of the press was that Davis was ignoring the racism and that he was suggesting that there was too much emphasis on color and the race issue. For some of the militants, this was too much; it indicated to them that Davis had given in to the establishment. If Davis's full report had been issued, however, it would have shown that he was not oblivious to the situation but had put a positive emphasis on correcting the problems. Davis was part of the establishment, yet he was not willing to go outside of it to try to make changes. As he wrote on a number of occasions, he thought that he was making progress and that he had found a sympathetic ally in General Lee. Alleviation of the racial problems could only come from higher in the chain of command, but, wrote Davis, "I think it is a case of 'they just won't see it.' "[41]

Many people were pleased with Davis's work in England and told him so. Shortly before Davis departed for the United States, General Lee wrote him several nice notes. The SOS commander said that for him, it had been a "distinct pleasure" to work with Davis. He was happy that the two "seem to view all these matters with practically a single eye." Several days later, Davis responded with a note, in which he informed Lee that he hoped a way could be found so that he could continue to work for him. "I would be pleased to command a Base Section made up of colored troops, or to render any service you desire." Lee was unable to make this arrangement, but he kept a fond memory of Davis. A year later he wrote to Davis, congratulating the latter on his son's fine performance in the air war over Italy. Lee reiterated his hope that Davis would be able to return again, a hope that was fulfilled in 1944. Other officers on Eisenhower's staff also thought highly of Davis's work and believed that he contributed much.[42]

Davis returned to Washington on 15 November 1942, about two months after he had left. After a brief leave of six days, he then went back to work. One of his first tasks was to report to General Peterson on his activities in Europe. Davis sent Peterson a copy of the memorandum he had written for Eisenhower. Several days later, Davis was back in the field on a special investigation in Phoenix, Arizona. It was a difficult one, involving two groups of black soldiers who were fighting each other. "This is the toughest proposition I have had yet," he wrote; conditions had not changed.[43]

With Benjamin Davis's return to the IG, the first phase of his activities in World War II came to an end. During the previous two years he had gone from commanding a cavalry brigade to becoming a key cog in the IG office. After his brief retirement, he began the really significant phase of his military career. His work with race relations took on increased importance after the entry of the United States into World War II. There were only three blacks who were high enough in the War Department to have any influence. Because of their approaches, Hastie and Gibson seemed to have little clout; but Davis had some impact on the implementation of policy, for he generally followed the established rules. Although he was not a flaming militant on the race issue, at least publicly, he did not accept racial discrimination and segregation, and he made that clear in many of his reports to his superiors in the War Department. He did not ask for special treatment, but he did ask for fairness and equality. When this chance was not offered—as was usually the case—he tried to deal with the problems that arose. His skills in this area made him valuable to the War Department, both internally and in its relations with the black community, especially the press. This also made Davis attractive to General Eisenhower, when the latter began to have racial problems among the troops in Great Britain. As a result, Davis took his techniques and ideas to that country for a two-month period in late 1942. Some of his ideas were adopted, especially by General Lee, with whom Davis developed a good working relationship. When Davis returned to the United States in late 1942, the racial situation remained a persistent irritant both to blacks and to whites. During the next two years, however, several things were to change as the War Department began gradually to modify its racial policies; and Davis was to play a role in this process.

6 | World War II— New Directions: 1943-1944

THE RACIAL TENSION in the army intensified in 1943, and there were racial disturbances in black units in the United States and overseas. The causes were obvious, but the army resisted doing anything drastic. Early in the year, William Hastie resigned his position in a dispute over segregation; but General Davis remained in the forefront of the army's small-scale effort to ameliorate the situation.[1]

Throughout 1943, Davis continued to function within the inspector general's office in the same manner as he had during the previous year. He conducted a comparable number of inspections and investigations, and he continued to visit posts where there were complaints by soldiers or officers. He went to Fort Clark, Texas, because a white officer, during an inspection of a barracks, had found a black newspaper and made derogatory comments about the black women pictured in the paper. As Davis noted, these comments "were offensive, unbecoming, and caused a great deal of resentment on the part of the enlisted men." Davis also pointed out that segregation, as it existed on the post, also disturbed blacks. In the post theater, black officers had to sit with the black enlisted men, but white officers were allowed to sit in a special section. The officers found this situation "very humiliating and distasteful." After his visit, Davis recommended that there be an investigation into the fitness of the officer who made derogatory comments about blacks and that segregation on the post be discontinued; he also suggested that soldiers be denied permission to leave the post unless they understood the local racial mores and were willing to accept them. Davis wanted the army to enforce its regulations concerning equality of facilities, but he also realized that he could not do anything about segregation in civilian society.[2]

Davis tried to help officers who were not used to dealing with black troops. He advised one second lieutenant that calling the soldiers "niggers" was wrong and suggested that the young man consult with some of the older officers. "In the Regular Army the use of any references whatsoever to race by officers on duty with colored troops was 'taboo.' " On the whole he seemed to feel that where the officers were sensitive to the racial issues, morale was good.[3]

Davis also tried to deal with some of the special concerns of the younger black officers. In August 1943, during a visit to Fort Devens, Massachusetts, several officers complained about slow promotions. He agreed but said there was little he could do about it. On another occasion, a black officer asked Davis's advice on how to handle a situation in which a black officer was superior in rank to the whites around him. While the black was worried about possible problems, Davis recommended that the officer not be concerned about this. As he commented to Sadie, "the colored folks thought more about it than the white folks."[4]

One black officer, who observed Davis dealing with these problems, thought that Davis was "all soldier." He was ramrod straight in his posture, and he spoke decisively. He gave the feeling that he knew what was expected of officers and soldiers. His manner was positive, and he listened carefully when the soldiers came to him with their complaints. Although he did not seem to respond directly to their individual problems, he made careful notes and tried to deal with their legitimate concerns. On the other hand, as an old army man, he had little patience with those who did not follow regulations or who wanted to make the army like civilian society.[5]

In July 1943, Davis and Gibson returned to Fort Huachuca to investigate problems in the Ninety-second Division, the second black combat division to be activated. They found that the situation had become "nasty" and quickly learned just how deeply rooted the problems were. On 18 July, Davis participated in the dedication ceremonies of the Andrew Foster Memorial Baseball Field. When Gen. Edward M. Almond, division commander, arrived, he was greeted by boos and noise, which Davis thought showed "unusual disrespect" for Almond. At other times, white officers had been pelted with rocks while driving in nearby towns, and one white officer had been attacked while sleeping in his tent. The discontent began to surface as Davis and Gibson talked to the officers and men, whose chief complaints were the promotion policy, segregation of the officers' mess, the lack of contact between black officers and white officers, and the poor quality of officer education.[6]

Upon returning to Washington, Davis and Gibson reported their findings and tried to suggest solutions. They believed that General Almond was so concerned about the carrying out of military duties that he "overlooked the human element" in training. Davis pointed out that the absence of a reaction from the black soldiers was misinterpreted by Almond. Davis believed that over the years, blacks, in response to oppression, had developed, "as a defense mechanism, the ability to present a calm outward appearance." However, a little incident might trigger a big reaction. It was his contention that the incident at the dedication of the athletic field was such an event. According to Davis, this had shocked Almond and had made him more aware that something was wrong. Davis's report recommended a change in the promotion policy and an end to segregation of the facilities that were available to the officers.[7]

The black press did not take such a sanguine view of conditions at the post. In September 1943 the *New York Amsterdam News* published an article describing Fort Huachuca as "Hell on Earth." It incorrectly stated that Davis and Gibson had found conditions at the post to be excellent. Gibson protested to the paper, and Davis defended himself to John McCloy. Davis wrote the chairman of the Negro Troop Committee that most of the complaints were the result of individual problems, not acts of discrimination by the army. This response, while correct, skirted the issues of segregation and discrimination.[8]

William Hastie's resignation led to a more responsive army leadership on the issues of race relations. In early 1943 he learned that the Army Air Forces were going to establish a segregated Negro Officer Candidate School. This had been one of the few

A publicity picture of General Davis during World War II

areas of integration, and Hastie saw this new school as a regres-
sion in policy. He was also upset that he had not been notified
of the proposal; therefore he resigned. Davis, in a personal note,
expressed sorrow that Hastie was leaving the War Department.
"I know that you have been unable to accomplish many things
that you desired. . . . I hope that you will not separate yourself
from the interest of the colored soldier." In response, Hastie sent

Davis a copy of his letter of resignation, in which Hastie pointed out the problem areas: segregation, lack of combat for blacks, and the possibility of segregation in officer training. At the same time, John McCloy sent Davis a copy of the letter and suggested that it might be a topic for future discussion of the committee.[9]

The next few months witnessed some changes. Truman Gibson, Hastie's assistant and replacement, began the process when he asked McCloy to provide him with information on the relationship of the civilian aide's office to the Advisory Committee. At the same time, Davis was trying to get the committee to address the more significant issues. He argued that the existing situation only helped the enemy. Davis urged the committee to step in and call upon the army to indicate, by 15 March, the steps it was taking toward this end. The proposal came up for discussion at the 22 February 1943 meeting, but it was tabled because of the "improving situation." Because Davis was not present at the meeting, he could not argue his case. It is certain that he would not have agreed that things were improving.[10]

Instead of trying to address the problem of racial friction, the Advisory Committee took up the problem of how to best utilize Army General Classification Test (AGCT) class-5 blacks. Black units had a higher proportion of soldiers in this bottom category than comparable white units had. As a result, many organizations included men who were not able to handle the assigned tasks. In late 1942 and early 1943 the army began to discuss possible plans for screening out 90 percent of the class-5 men in combat units, sending many of the excess to service troops, and discharging the rest. The McCloy Committee began to consider this issue in February 1943. Gen. Idwal Edwards, assistant chief of staff for personnel and training, sent a memo to the committee members, in which he stated his belief that black class-5 men who were currently in combat units would be better off in service units. Davis thought that this proposal was "a step in the wrong direction;" he argued that the loss in morale and the criticism from the black press would offset whatever efficiency could be gained. Despite his misgivings, however, Davis reluctantly agreed to support the proposal. When the plan was implemented in mid

1943, the army tried to screen the class-5 men during their induction period. As Davis suspected, objections were raised, and racial bias in the placement test was suggested. Again Davis was unable to convince the committee to recognize the inherent racism in their policy decisions.[11]

At the next meeting of the Advisory Committee, Davis brought up another grievance with blacks—the failure to transfer black combat units overseas. He noted that three black infantry regiments and two black artillery battalions had been in training for a very long time and that they were getting restive. In addition, the delay in assignment was convincing the black population that there was no intention to use blacks in combat. Davis stressed that for morale purposes, if for no other reason, it was important to send some black troops to combat zones as soon as possible. McCloy asked the black officer to prepare a definite recommendation for the next meeting of the committee, as well as a report on the status of the Ninety-third Division, the one that had been activated first. Within a week, Davis responded. He argued that if a suitable division could not be found, then one regiment could be sent. In an effort not to antagonize the committee and thereby jeopardize a favorable response, Davis did delete one sentence from an early draft of his memo: "Colored combat troops and the colored population are becoming quite restless."[12]

The issue of overseas deployment did come up on 2 April 1943 at the next committee meeting. Davis restated his plea for the use of black combat troops without delay. The discussion that followed did not really address the points that Davis had made. In the end, the committee agreed to ask the secretary of war to discuss the use of black combat troops at his next press conference. This disappointed both Davis and the black community.[13]

As racial incidents began to increase in frequency and severity, Col. Joseph Leonard, secretary of the committee, issued a memo to its members, in which he suggested that the causes of the unrest were discrimination in transportation, harsh treatment by civilian police, limited recreational facilities, segregation by race on the bases, the slow promotion of black officers, and the use of epithets such as "nigger." He called for actions to remedy these complaints "as far as possible." Obviously, Davis had failed to convince Leonard that the real causes were segregation and the quota system.[14]

Leonard's memo became the central focus of the 28 June 1943 meeting of the Advisory Committee. McCloy proposed that a subcommittee be formed to draft a letter on the subject for the chief of staff. Truman Gibson pointed out that the problems more often existed in the individual commands, especially those that had a large number of southern officers. The civilian aide also indicated that most officers' messes were segregated and that the War Department's policy against segregation on post PXs and movie theaters was not clear. General Davis added: "In the early 1900s soldiers mixed and there was no race problem." Only since 1918 had the War Department policy been "everything equal but separate." The committee decided to place Davis as head of a subcommittee that also included Brig. Gen. Miller G. White, Personnel; and Lt. Col. Willard Renshaw, Army Ground Forces. They were instructed to draft a letter for the chief of staff and to report back to the Advisory Committee within the week.[15]

Both Truman Gibson and Colonel Leonard responded quickly by providing Davis and the others with their observations. Gibson noted that the black soldiers had become dissatisfied because they thought their efforts were futile; he also suggested that tensions could be minimized if men were treated equally and if they were protected while in uniform. Furthermore he noted that officers who did not want to serve with black troops should be transferred. Colonel Leonard took a somewhat different approach. It was his belief that while there were problems, there should be "no discrimination in favor of negro troops in the way of compromising disciplinary standards." He also noted that while blacks were "of lower average intelligence" than whites, they could make good soldiers. He suggested that black units should be organized with white officers but that blacks should be introduced as second lieutenants and then gradually replace the white officers. This analysis of the problems proceeded from the general view that racial conditions were actually better than the public realized and that only a few small changes needed to be made.[16]

The Davis subcommittee put forward most of Leonard's ideas, which the Advisory Committee, in turn, generally accepted when it next convened, on 2 July 1943. In the letter that the McCloy Committee prepared for the chief of staff, it noted that dissatisfaction was widespread and was a serious problem. The contributing cause was "real or fancied" incidents of discrimination or segregation. Conflicts had arisen because of "the failure on the part of commanders in some echelons to appreciate the seriousness of the problems and their inherent responsibilities." While there should be no discrimination against blacks, declared the committee, there should be none in their favor. Discipline must be maintained. To this end, the committee thought the chief of staff should bring the seriousness of the situation to the attention of key officers, who must in turn communicate to their subordinates that they should treat people equally, provide equal facilities, and try to remove the causes of friction with civilians. General Marshall accepted these suggestions and, on 14 July 1943, issued them to the heads of Army Air Forces, Army Ground Forces, and Army Service Forces. However, Marshall ignored the committee's suggestions for specific responses to racial problems. The Advisory Committee had tried to grapple with the manifestations of discrimination and racial turmoil, but because the basic problems were not addressed by the committee and because even its mild recommendations for oversight were ignored by Marshall, not much progress could be expected.[17]

For the remainder of 1943 the McCloy Committee dealt with some of the less pressing aspects of the race issue. It drafted legislation to make it a federal crime to attack a soldier who was engaged in the performance of duty. After discussions within the War Department, this draft legislation was presented to Congress, which referred it to the Judiciary Committees. The committees tabled it, and despite lobbying by the Advisory Committee, the legislation progressed no further. Another topic that the committee tackled concerned the attitudes of the black troops. A number of studies had been done by Special Services of these views, and

Davis suggested that these findings be publicized more widely. The result was the pamphlet "Command of Negro Troops."[18]

Later in 1943 the Advisory Committee considered a report that evaluated the combat efficiency of the Ninety-ninth Fighter Squadron. This segregated organization was created in 1940 only after a long struggle to overcome the resistance to the idea of black pilots, who were trained at a segregated facility at Tuskegee Field, Alabama, where they faced a maze of obstacles created by the Army Air Forces in their effort to maintain the walls of separation between the races. Finally, in 1943, this first group of black flyers was transferred to the Mediterranean Theater, where it flew missions in North Africa, Sicily, and Italy. During the committee's discussion of the report, Davis stated that "the War Department goes on the theory that colored fliers are inferior." He pointed out that the unit did not consist of a select group of top-quality personnel; rather, they were novices who did not have the benefit of numerous seasoned leaders and the experience of veteran flyers. He argued that the War Department should not scrap the whole air program over the results mentioned in one report. In the end, the committee decided to ask Col. Benjamin O. Davis, Jr., who was then in the United States in order to assume a new command, to appear before them to discuss the issue. Without reviewing the matter with his father before the meeting, Colonel Davis assured the committee that while there had been problems in the beginning, the Ninety-ninth was improving and would soon reach a high standard.[19]

The committee's failure to make a decisive response on the issue of the Ninety-ninth bothered General Davis, who tried to get its members to realize the implications of a continuation of the status quo. In a long memo to John McCloy, Davis outlined his feelings: "The colored officers and soldiers feel that they are denied the protection and rewards that ordinarily result from good behavior and proper performance of duty." Davis then proceeded to list a number of specific complaints: the lack of combat service, the hostility of southern civilians, the War Department's failure to protect the black soldiers' rights, and the introduction of Jim Crow on military bases. Finally, Davis raised the issue of the Advisory Committee's effectiveness. He noted that the officers on the committee had other responsibilities that consumed large amounts of their time. "I believe the problem is large enough and serious enough to warrant the establishment of a bureau with General Staff representation to devote full time to the study of the conditions surrounding the colored soldier." Basically, Davis believed that it was "utterly impossible for any white man to appreciate what the colored officers and soldiers experience in trying to develop a high morale under present conditions." This indictment of army policy and the McCloy Committee was quite severe but was certainly valid. That Davis was willing to be so open in his feelings indicates his high level of frustration. McCloy responded by asking Colonel Leonard to study the points raised by Davis and possibly to draw up proposals for consideration at the next meeting of the committee, which was scheduled for early 1944.[20]

Davis's responsibilities were not limited to committee discussions and inspections, for in mid 1943 he was assigned as military aide to President Edwin Barclay of Liberia when he visited the United States. Accompanying Barclay was President-elect William V. S. Tubman, a military aide, and a personal attendant. Because Barclay was a guest of the United States, Secretary of State Cordell Hull asked the War Department to assign a brigadier general to act as military aide. Stimson designated Davis, with the concurrence of the State Department and Colonel Leonard. Davis traveled with the Barclay party to a variety of functions, including several state dinners at which Davis was able to mingle with high governmental officials, including President Roosevelt. The Liberians and Davis also visited a number of tourist sites in the area, such as Arlington National Cemetery, after which they left for a three-week tour of the eastern United States.[21]

The first days of the tour were like a homecoming for Davis. After a brief visit to Akron, Ohio, the group went to Xenia. "I saw many folks I knew. I received as much attention as the President." They were given a tour of Wilberforce, and Davis noted that the area had grown considerably. Later that day they drove

on to Columbus, where they were met by the mayor and a welcoming committee that included both blacks and whites. They
then proceeded to the state capitol, where they were met by Governor John W. Bricker. During the next days they visited Buffalo
and then Philadelphia, where they toured the Sun Shipyards and
Barclay addressed nearly three thousand black shipworkers. The
last stop was New York, where the Liberians stayed for about
two weeks. Barclay was pleased with Davis's work and, in the
following year, conferred upon him the degree of Commander
of the Order of the Star of Africa.[22]

Davis also served the War Department when it attempted to
improve its relations with the black press. Many officers believed
that the black press's coverage of the army was one of the causes
of the racial disturbances. As part of the Advisory Committee's
study of these issues, it recommended that countermeasures be
taken to respond to "inflammatory gossip, rumors, or propaganda." The Bureau of Public Relations made an earnest effort
to improve its relations with the media and the black community. Early in the year the bureau put together a radio program
about black soldiers, which was entitled "Fighting Man." In the
initial script there was to have been a two-minute interview with
Davis, but this was deleted because he could not be in Washington at the time of the broadcast. When the press published reports concerning discrimination in Europe, Davis was consulted
about a rebuttal. However, the major role that Davis played in
this area in 1943 involved escorting a group of black reporters
to Louisiana to view some maneuvers that involved black troops.
Davis, who spent May fourth through tenth with the press in
Louisiana, was prominently featured in the resulting stories,
which also had good things to say about the maneuvers and the
general state of morale in the units involved, including the
Ninety-third Division. After the end of the maneuvers, Gibson
reported to McCloy: "General Davis was unusually helpful in
the many informal discussions conducted during the trip." While
overall relations with the black press improved, Davis was not
immune from attack. At one point he was accused of having
urged that the Red Cross segregate blood, one of the facets of

Brig. Gen. Benjamin O. Davis, Sr., and Col. Benjamin O. Davis, Jr.,
holding a press conference in 1944

segregation that really disturbed black Americans. Following
standard procedure, Davis did not respond publicly to this charge,
which he knew was false.[23]

Although Davis was busy with official duties, he still found
time to keep track of his children. He saw Olive and Benjamin,

Jr., infrequently, since their jobs kept them away from Washington. However, Benjamin, Jr., did return during the year to report on the progress of his flying unit, and father and son were reunited. The general was present during his son's press conference, and a number of pictures were taken of them together. Benjamin and Sadie frequently saw Agatha and Elnora, who were both working in the Washington area. At Christmastime, Elnora married a young lawyer from Chicago, James McLendon. Benjamin and Sadie also had some time for activities together. In October they went to a concert by Duke Ellington and Lena Horne, but Benjamin did not enjoy the music, saying, "I guess I'm not modern." Later that day, Olive joined them for a visit to the ballet, which he really liked: "It was beautiful." On other occasions, Benjamin had a chance for pleasure reading, among which during 1943 was Douglas Southall Freeman's *Lee's Lieutenants.* Another favorite activity was sitting on the front porch of their house. These activities normally had to be sandwiched in around his official functions and trips.[24]

As the year progressed, General Davis was given a number of honors in recognition of his achievements. In August, Colonel Hardy, commander of Fort Huachuca, asked the army's permission to name a football stadium at the post after Davis. Hardy noted that the staff at the post tried to name public facilities at the fort "for distinguished Negroes." The inspector general turned down the suggestion because he believed that the "duties required of General Davis" would not make this a wise choice. Another possibility, this one brought up by the black press, was that Davis be named commander of the Ninety-second Division; but it, too, was rejected, this time because of Davis's age. However, General Peterson did not think Davis was too old for his IG duties. "His dignified and courteous manner and the esteem in which he, as the senior negro officer in the Army, is held by members of his race, together with his understanding of their problems, have rendered his services to this Department, and to the army at large, of great value in assisting in the solution of matters involving negro troops." Other honors came from outside the army. Atlanta University awarded an honorary degree of Doctor of Laws to Davis "in recognition of the value of his services."[25]

During 1943 the focus of Davis's activities began to shift. While he continued his inspections and investigations, he became more involved in prodding policy makers, through the Advisory Committee, and in public-relations activities. At the end of the year, his suggestions for a revitalization of the Advisory Committee were being considered by Colonel Leonard. These would form the focus of some of Davis's activities in 1944.

Davis continued to try to encourage the Advisory Committee to confront the causes of racial unrest. At the 4 January 1944 meeting, Davis stated: "The War Department has to take decided action. The colored people are fighting segregation. The Army is the best agency to solve the problem." The immediate reaction of the committee was to postpone consideration of Davis's idea, in favor of taking up McCloy's proposal for a manual on how to command Negro troops. McCloy then appointed a subcommittee, including Davis, to study the issue and make recommendations for the whole committee.[26]

While the committee ignored Davis's broad call for action, it did react to his indictment of the group itself. In a postmeeting memo, Leonard argued that the committee had only been created to act in an advisory capacity on policies in regard to Negro troops. He believed it had accomplished something toward that goal in the areas of personnel problems and the training and utilization of Negro troops. Other members who commented on Davis's proposal echoed Leonard.[27]

A major topic of discussion at the next meeting was Davis's call for change, which McCloy characterized as a "severe indictment." McCloy hoped to postpone discussion, but Davis would not let him. "It cannot be satisfactorily explained why one soldier can purchase an article at a post exchange and another soldier cannot purchase the same article in that exchange," Davis said. He also criticized the apparent acquiescence of the federal government in the segregation policies of the southern states. Davis questioned whether the states could be allowed to formulate policy for the United States government; he then cited a statement that some southern law-enforcement agencies "seek the opportunity to shoot down Negroes." He wondered whether the War Department could not protect soldiers against these people. "It is impossible," he said, "to cultivate in the colored soldier cheerful, willing obedience, and a desire to make, if necessary, the supreme sacrifice for a cause that does not guarantee to him the same privileges accorded to other men wearing the uniform issued to him." Finally, he brought up the issue of the segregation of blood plasma. Whatever the reason for this practice, Davis felt it was "most offensive and insulting to the colored people." All of these policies reduced the effectiveness of blacks in the military. Apparently McCloy did not like the statement, but it had the effect of moving the committee to take some action at its next meeting.[28]

Davis's catalog of complaints formed one of the focuses for the 29 February meeting of the Advisory Committee. First was the Red Cross's policy of segregating the blood of black donors. McCloy noted that a change would only draw attention to the issue, and this in turn would create a fuss. He felt it would be better to "let sleeping dogs lie." Davis responded by pointing out that these policies seriously affected the morale of the black soldiers. However, he backed off on some of his charges by saying, "I didn't mean to indict the committee." General Porter asked if Davis was withdrawing his proposals, but McCloy saved Davis's position by indicating that the committee would continue to consider the points that Davis had raised. In the end, the committee avoided responding to Davis's criticisms.[29]

At the same meeting, the committee was forced to address one grievance of the black community—the failure to use black troops in combat. Davis noted that if the army wanted to use blacks in combat, "it can do it." After a long discussion the committee adopted a resolution to the effect that the army should introduce blacks into combat as soon as possible, even if the service had to reorganize existing units. Stimson concurred with this recommendation, and the army began to make efforts to place black troops into combat.[30]

Although Davis attended a few more meetings of the Advisory

Committee that year, his major role was finished. During his two years on the committee, he had advocated the fair treatment of blacks, the utilization of blacks in combat, a halt to segregation on and off the bases, an end to the segregation of blood, and a more active role for the committee. Some of these suggestions were implemented, but most were not. When he really challenged the committee to take an active stance, he had to back down, but his request seemed to galvanize it into taking positive steps.

At the same time as Davis was active on the policy advisory level, he continued his work in the IG. He made a series of inspection trips to posts around the country, such as Camp Ellis, Illinois, and Fort Benning, Georgia. Although he received the usual quantity of anonymous requests for help, he continued to ignore these and to deal with more concrete problems. One of his most difficult situations occurred at Selfridge Field, Michigan. In late 1943, Davis and Gibson, at the request of the commanding officer of the First Air Force, visited the facility. Davis discovered no racial complaints and found morale to be good. Early in 1944, however, things began to change. The arrival of the 477th Bombardment Squadron started the chain of events. When the black officers of this unit tried to enter the Officers' Club, they were told by the base commander that they were not welcome. Then the army began to construct separate facilities for the black personnel, and discontent escalated. Davis and Col. Harvey Shoemaker, of the Inspector General's Corps, visited the post in March 1944. The investigators concluded that there had been discrimination at the club, which was certainly in violation of Michigan law. The two officers had an argument over what to include in the report; Davis was for a strong description of the actions by the post commander, and he was able to convince Shoemaker. In their report they noted that discrimination had occurred and that the post officers had been lax in enforcing the War Department's policies. Despite Davis's recommendation, the Army Air Forces transferred the 477th Squadron and halted the construction of the separate club, but it did reprimand the post commander.[31]

Davis's inspections also took him back to Fort Huachuca, where conditions had improved since his last visit. Housing for the officers had been integrated on the post. During an April 1944 inspection, Davis took part in a hole-in-one tournament, the first time he had played golf. Davis and Gibson attended a baseball game and watched a program at the service club. A number of pictures of the visit were taken by Homer Roberts of the Bureau of Public Relations. Davis thought that the troops of the Ninety-second Division were in good shape and that the "high morale" would be better maintained if the unit were sent overseas. He also recommended that Colonel Hardy be commended for having made efforts to develop good race relations between the post and nearby towns and for developing recreational facilities at the fort. Davis thought the situation had greatly improved since his earlier visits.[32]

Davis's assessment helped to convince the army to assign the Ninety-second Division to combat that year. The 370th Regimental Combat Team was sent to Italy and was followed shortly by the remaining elements of the division. For the next year and a half they engaged in heavy fighting against strong German positions in northwest Italy. Their success or failure, like that of the Ninety-ninth Fighter Squadron, has been judged differently by different observers. Their German opponents did not think very highly of them, finding them unimaginative. Gen. Mark W. Clark thought that the division did not do badly, given its lack of combat experience. In early 1945, Truman Gibson visited the Ninety-second and tried to evaluate some of the claims that the division had retreated in the face of enemy fire. His response was to raise questions about the attitudes of the white commanders. By the end of the war there was no clear-cut evaluation of the combat effectiveness of the black soldiers. The white commanders focused on examples of the inability of black soldiers and officers to perform well in combat in order to support their contention that blacks were not capable of participating in combat. Davis may have been overly optimistic in his assessment of the combat readiness of the unit in early 1944, but it was also clear that morale would begin to suffer if the unit did not go into combat shortly.[33]

In addition to participating in inspections and serving on the Advisory Committee, Davis also performed public-relations functions. In January 1944 he delivered an address on the black war effort to Crispus Attucks High School in Indianapolis, where he said: "I have been a soldier all my life, and the army is my life. I take pride in it and I like to see others filled with that same sense of pride. . . . Colored soldiers are honored members of the army." He ended with a ringing declaration, pointing to the American flag as he said: "Victory will be ours. We cannot fail. You may read it in these stars." In March of that year, he delivered the commencement address at Meharry Medical College, Nashville, Tennessee; and in June he was a guest of Buffalo, New York, during the celebration of Negro Day. The War Department took advantage of these appearances to enhance Davis's public image. Many civilians requested his picture. One individual indicated that he would put the Davis photo with that of the "big" generals, "so that we can have some of our people to talk about."[34]

In 1942 the army had decided to make an educational film about black soldiers. Marc Connelly, a white writer on black subjects, and Carlton Moss, a young black author, were in charge of the project. After visiting black soldiers around the country, they wrote a screenplay, which was set in a black church and focused on its congregation. Through Moss's portrayal of the preacher, it told the history of blacks in combat and what the black soldiers and officers were doing in the current conflict. Moss and Connelly were aware of discrimination, but they tried not to show it, because they thought everyone already knew about this aspect of black military life.[35]

A question was raised about the appropriate target audience. Originally the film had been made for distribution to black troops. Even before its official release, however, a number of individuals began to argue that it should have a wider audience. When Davis viewed the film in November 1943, he thought that the historical aspects of the film were good but that the modern events were "somewhat misrepresented." After much discussion, the film was modified. Some footage that showed black officers commanding blacks was eliminated, and a scene showing black service workers in World War I was added. In February 1944 the film became a part of the orientation program for all incoming white troops. It was well received by both black and white soldiers. Some suggested that it be made available to white and black civilian audiences, and in April 1944 the War Department agreed.[36]

The War Department believed that Davis could encourage film distributors to show the movie. In early March 1944, Davis had convinced the New York War Activities Committee to show the film. Gibson was impressed with this, and at the same time, he decided that Davis could assist Moss with the problems the latter was experiencing in Hollywood. In late March, Davis and Gibson joined Moss on the West Coast. Davis's job was to "sell them . . . on the importance of doing something affirmative" and to encourage the distributors to show the film.[37]

Davis's two-week stay in Los Angeles and Hollywood received a great deal of attention. One paper described him as a "silver haired, dignified gentleman of 66, whose eyes twinkle as brightly behind his rimless spectacles as the silver star on each shoulder." The presence of a black general was impressive, and it allowed Gibson and Moss to get a sympathetic hearing from the movie distributors. In the process, Davis met a number of celebrities. Being an avid moviegoer, he was enthralled with the people and places he saw. Instead of staying at the local black hotel, Davis was housed in the heart of Beverly Hills with Mr. and Mrs. Ira Gershwin, who hosted a party for him and took him to several dinners. After the film's premiere on 13 April, Davis mounted the stage and made a short speech. He pointed out that the film accurately portrayed the role of blacks in America's past wars and in the current fighting. He finished with another familiar theme: "All we ask of you is security—freedom from fear; no more, no less than you have guaranteed to us, and that in the enjoyment of being citizens of this great country." The next day

General Davis with Homer Roberts, Hattie McDaniel, and Lena Horne, probably in Hollywood in 1943 or 1944

a private showing was held for more distributors. Davis again emphasized the importance of the film.[38]

Davis's efforts generated a great deal of interest in distributing the film. When the film was distributed, however, only a small number of theaters decided to show it, possibly because of its length; so Gibson and Moss decided to edit it. While this was going on, Davis began asking Gibson when they could return to the West Coast. The civilian aide wrote to Moss: "General Davis is worrying hell out of me in getting out to California. I guess the only thing to do is to get him there to keep him quiet for a while." In late June the two returned to Los Angeles to meet with officials from RKO and MGM. Jack Warner found the shortened version of *The Negro Soldier* greatly improved. As a result, RKO and MGM really began to push its distribution, and it was shown at a great many theaters, including more than three hundred in New York alone. Even some southern theaters showed the film. It had a wide impact and was used as a race-relations teaching tool. Davis's second visit to Hollywood had produced positive results.[39]

The success of *The Negro Soldier* and Davis's role in its distribution led to another assignment: making a sequel. Some of the media experts wanted to show the role of blacks in the combat theaters. In their report to McCloy, Davis and Gibson pointed out that the film had helped to convince blacks that they were important to the war effort. However, whites still did not realize the extent of the black contribution, especially overseas. Gibson and Davis argued for a sequel to show this facet. They suggested a new organization to make combat films, using the crew that had made the original film. Gibson added an additional note: "I think General Davis should go along with them. He wants to do this and I think there are a lot of good reasons for ordering him out with the unit."[40]

In July 1944 the army decided in favor of the sequel. Carlton Moss was directed to go to Europe "as a writer and consultant to assist in properly selecting the material," and Moss requested that Davis be involved with the film unit. Because it might look strange to have a general heading a photographic unit, McCloy suggested that while they would all go over together, Davis would be officially on a "routine inspection of Negro units in the theater." As a result, in mid July 1944, Davis was ordered to Europe on ninety-day temporary duty.[41]

The assignment to the ETO brought an end to Davis's war work in the United States. By 1944 the Advisory Committee and public-relations functions began to dominate his schedule, and he ceased the inspections that had previously filled his schedule. Davis continued to call for an end to discrimination and unfair treatment and for the assignment of blacks to combat. His very presence was a media event that the War Department utilized. In addition, his visits to Hollywood helped to convince the motion picture industry that it should distribute the revised version of *The Negro Soldier.* He could see some successes, but there was always frustration that no real progress had been made in ending the quota system or in preventing the segregation of blood plasma. His request for a staff-level bureau to deal with the issues had been ignored. Again, the middle years of the war repeated the pattern that had been established earlier: some success, but no real headway against discrimination and segregation. Davis could ameliorate the impact of these policies at times, but he was less successful in convincing the army to take the necessary steps to abolish them.

7 | World War II—
The ETO: 1944–1945

THE FINAL YEARS of General Davis's World War II service took place in the European Theater of Operations. Working for General Lee and others, Davis was involved in the events that resulted in the first cracks in the longstanding walls of segregation.

By mid July 1944, Davis, Moss, and the film crew were in Europe and beginning to work. The differences in their ages, backgrounds, and philosophies were a source of conflict between the two men. Moss, then in his twenties, was the product of an artistic background. The sixty-seven-year-old Davis was Old Army, and he liked to talk to the officers about the old days, which caused delays and annoyed Moss. Davis, on the other hand, felt that he had gone to a lot of effort to set up a shooting situation, which Moss would then change. "I see no reason why his changes were not thought out before. I think he enjoys that method which is trying to me," Davis said. By early August the conflict came to a head. Moss complained to Gibson that Davis was not giving him enough support. After consulting with McCloy, Gibson wrote to Davis to encourage him to expedite the activities of the film crew. Eventually, Davis and Moss came to realize that each one had to tolerate the other's differences in order to work.[1]

Philosophical differences also influenced their leisure activities. When the soldiers whom the two encountered on their evening walks in London would not salute Davis, Moss would stop them and demand the respect due a general. Davis felt that Moss was hypersensitive, that he believed whites were always wrong, and that he saw discrimination everywhere.[2]

Members of the film crew spent approximately two months in England, on the Continent, and in the Mediterranean. In England they visited many installations where black troops were in training. Then they crossed the channel to Normandy and filmed a variety of black service units, taking pictures of black troops in the rear areas and as close to the front lines as they could go. Davis wrote home to his wife: "I have had a wonderful experience. . . . I have seen some prisoners and wounded brought in. I have been forward of our artillery positions and heard the projectiles going over." While the film crew continued its work, the effects of the generation gap began to resurface. One incident involved a black soldier who was accused of rape. Davis asked the soldier why he was making conditions hard for blacks, while he, Davis, was trying to show that blacks were decent people. Moss thought this episode was an example of Davis's accommodationist approach to race relations.[3]

After completing its work in France, the film detachment proceeded to the Mediterranean Theater, where it filmed some black service troops and some of the combat troops of the Ninety-second Division. One of the highlights of this part of the film work was a visit to Italy. Davis participated in an awards ceremony for several black aviators and was given the honor of pinning a Distinguished Flying Cross on his own son. He told reporters that it was "my happy privilege and good luck to be here for this grand occasion," and he commented to Sadie that he felt "very proud" during the ceremony. He remembered the long discussion on the McCloy Committee about the future of the unit and the efforts to eliminate black flyers. Davis also visited Pompeii, Rome, and Naples, which he commented "looks very dirty and poor."[4]

Davis was relieved of his assignment after filming in the Mediterranean had concluded, although Moss continued to work on the project for several more months. The footage taken in Europe was supplemented by stock footage from the major newsreel producers. When the finished product, the film *Teamwork*, was finally released in mid 1946, the war was over.[5]

The army's public-relations officers planned to keep news of Davis's visit to Europe quiet until he had been over to France. Then they intended to publicize his visits to the troops and their "important activities." They hoped that one of the highlights

General Davis pinning the DFC on his son in Italy, 1944

of this visit would be a speech that Davis would make on the radio describing his experiences.[6]

In early August the public-relations project went into high gear. In a press release issued on 10 August 1944, Davis was quoted as having said: "I'm thoroughly pleased with the performance and conditions under which Negro troops are operating here, especially the performance under fire." Press releases were issued about the film crew and its tour of the continent. The *Journal and Guide*, a black paper published in the United States, quoted Davis's statement that "there appears to be more harmony and lack of racial friction in the combat zone than is found behind the lines." This issue was also brought up at the press conference that Davis held for those members of the black press who were assigned to the ETO. Among the points Davis made was that he found no "racial unpleasantness," a change from the conditions of his previous visit. A more controversial topic involved relations between black troops and French women. When questioned about this, Davis replied that any group of people, white or black, who committed crimes against women or who forced their attentions on others "is not ready to enjoy the freedom of American citizenship." This statement bothered Truman Gibson, who felt it could easily be misconstrued. "The Southern dailies gave it a considerable spread." Davis's defense was that his words had been twisted. "I think you have known me long enough and you have been with me to understand my attitude." Davis commented to his wife that the reporter who kept pressing him on this issue told him afterwards that he did not like Davis's answer. Davis wondered why the reporter had brought up the question.[7]

In mid September 1944 the film crew returned to the United States, and General Lee seized this opportunity to add Davis to his own staff. In 1943, Lee had asked for Davis's assistance but had been told that Davis was not available. Some people in Eisenhower's headquarters felt that Davis's work in 1942 had not been very helpful. Despite the negative comments, General Lee was happy to welcome Davis to England in July 1944. The two spent some time together during this visit, and after some effort, Lee was successful in convincing Eisenhower to have Davis retained in the ETO.[8]

There was a growing racial problem in the ETO, and it involved the service troops in General Lee's command. By mid 1944 the majority of black soldiers were overseas, with most of them in the service branches of the armed forces. Although General Lee made every effort to ensure fairness in the treatment of individuals, the soldiers did not always perceive that this was the case. As new troops arrived in the ETO, they were told that it was official policy that all military personnel be dealt with equally. One of Davis's functions was to check on the compliance with Lee's orders and to try to find out what the black troops were thinking. In many ways it was similar to the job he had performed for General Peterson in the United States.[9]

Davis looked forward to working with Lee, because he thought the two of them were of one mind on the issue of racial equality. Davis believed that Lee was more interested in him than General

General Davis in France, 1944

Peterson had been back in Washington. As Davis commented to Sadie, "Your 'Ole Man' seems to be desired by some others besides you." However, he did have one problem with Lee: the latter's insistence upon church attendance. He was "as bad as Ma about church," Davis said. To avoid this, he tried to time his breakfasts to miss the church call, but he was not always successful.[10]

Davis set to work to try to reduce racial friction. He visited a number of units in France, including the 3920th QM Gas Supply Company, which had been relieved from its assignment because of poor performance. Davis inspected the company, talked with the men, viewed the facilities, and tried to gain an understanding of their problems. He concluded that the unit was "well on the road to rehabilitation." On another occasion while he was in France, Davis addressed a group of black soldiers and tried to impress upon them the importance of their conduct. "The German soldier has been taught to look down upon [black soldiers], and . . . the only way that they could impress the German soldier was by the display of superior soldierly conduct." Davis also stressed what a negative impact VD could have upon the lives of the soldiers. During a visit to the 1314th General Service Regiment, Davis reiterated another theme: the officers had to be alert and to supervise their men at all times. He emphasized that the soldiers had to be made "conscious of the fact that they are soldiers and not just laborers, mechanics, etc." Overall, Davis felt that the officers he met "welcome my criticisms and suggestions."[11]

Another familiar aspect of Davis's new job in Europe was handling complaints and requests that came through the mail. One serviceman who had endured a long training period asked for help in getting an assignment to a unit. Davis suggested patience: "Remember that he who waits in compliance with orders, also serves." Davis also received letters from officers with special problems. One officer, thinking about the postwar situation and asking Davis's help in trying to get an ROTC post, said, "By your brilliant record in the military field, I am trying to guide mine." Davis merely suggested that the officer keep track of War Department publications on the subject. Another officer, apparently the only black in a group of whites, asked Davis's help in obtaining a transfer. Davis had little sympathy with this request: "It is the duty of a member of the military service, especially an officer, to be able to adjust himself to his local surroundings."[12]

Davis's perspective on racial matters was made clear in his response to a letter from a Nisei—an American born of Japanese parents. This soldier did not understand why he could not get into the air corps. Davis responded that it was "the duty of every patriotic citizen who is inducted into the Military Service to accept the initial assignment given by those charged with the responsibility of prosecuting the war."[13]

Davis also continued to be active in public relations. In November 1944, at the request of Red Cross Commissioner H. D. Gibson, Davis addressed a group of black Red Cross workers in Bristol, England. He described the Red Cross policy of no overt discrimination but did note that some of the clubs, through their designation of the race of the staff, tried to suggest which race should attend which clubs. Using the same reasons that he had stressed to the Advisory Committee, Davis cautioned against the use of the term *Negro*. On another matter he said: "Our enemies back home emphasize these crimes [rape] to show justification for their denial of the things we most want—equality of American citizenship and all that goes with it." He worried that such crimes would make more impact on people's minds than the good deeds of the black soldiers. "Your mission is to use the facilities at your command to prevent this," he said. Davis also made a radio broadcast to the United States in which he explained the racial situation in England and on the Continent. It was his feeling that white civilians and military personnel related better to blacks who were in combat areas than to those in noncombat areas. He wrote home to Sadie: "I think I have not done badly in my speeches. General Lee is receiving many requests for me to make visits to troops."[14]

Davis's work began to receive recognition from the army. When he left for Europe, General Peterson nominated him for the Distinguished Service Medal because of his contributions "in the establishment of better understanding of the problems involved in effective employment of the Negro soldier." As a result of this recommendation, Davis was awarded the DSM in February 1945. He was very pleased by Peterson's recommendation: "In the performance of my duties I have always been influenced by what I deem to be the best interests of the United States, and at the same time, uninfluenced by any personal feelings." The presentation of the award was done by Gen. Ben Lear, in the presence of Gen. Charles H. Bonesteel and a group of staff officers. Davis was pleased with the award but said: "I would much rather have another star. Maybe that will come." It was an idea that he had been thinking about for a while, and he hoped the publicity about the DSM would bring Roosevelt to that same conclusion. It was a dream he held for some time.[15]

While Davis's work was being rewarded by the army, he was also receiving a different sort of recognition. *True Comics* created a story called, "Two of a Kind," which featured the two Davises. The story played up what they had done to help win the war and to "insure the perpetuation of our ideals of democracy and opportunity." By the time the comic book was issued in 1945, Davis had helped to take a giant step forward in that quest—an end to segregation.[16]

Davis's experiences in Europe had convinced him that the army's policy of segregation could not continue without more disturbances. The fraternization between black soldiers and English and French civilians, especially women, had been commented upon by many. Although there were problems associated with this, such as a high incidence of VD, the attitude of the civilians was much different than it had been in the United States. Davis believed that this experience would make it difficult for black soldiers to return to the racial status quo in America. In addition, blacks were becoming increasingly frustrated with their secondary roles. What forced a change was a factor beyond the control of either race—namely, manpower shortages caused by problems on the battlefield.[17]

By early December 1944 the normal sources of manpower replacements were close to exhaustion, and in November, Eisenhower had requested more men. The War Department sent a few more infantrymen; these were men who had nearly completed their training period. The department also suggested that a better source of manpower was already in Europe in the supply areas behind the front lines. Eisenhower partially accepted this suggestion, so the army began to retrain white troops from other arms and services for infantry. General Lee was in favor of this plan, even if it would cause him to lose troops. The process was accelerated by the German counterattack in the Ardennes in late December 1944, when battle casualties and nonbattle casualties for the month reached 77,700 and 56,700 respectively. As the need for replacements increased, the high command made the

Brig. Gen. Benjamin O. Davis, Sr., being awarded the DSM by Lt. Gen. Ben Lear, 1945

momentous decision to include black service personnel in the retraining program.[18]

General Lee, who had always been sympathetic to blacks, approached Davis in December 1944 with a suggestion that black service personnel be allowed to volunteer for the combat replacement program. Davis thought this was an excellent idea. Lee then asked Davis to draft the directive to be issued outlining the program. According to Lee, the volunteers were to be limited to the ranks of private and private first class and should have scored no lower than class-4 on the AGCT. Davis, who wrote the directive and helped argue for it with the staff, was very proud of his role in this process: "Yesterday I secured a decision from the High Command which I think is the greatest since the enactment of the Constitutional amendments following the emancipation." Lee, who was also quite proud of Davis's role in convincing the high command of the correctness of this decision, said: "A great presentation old man, and we have at last gotten through what you and I have been fighting for, for the last two years." It was one of Davis's greatest moments.[19]

Lee and Davis's replacement plan soon encountered opposition, however. Initially the plan had called for replacement blacks to be put into units on the basis of individual needs. This would have opened a major crack in the army's traditional policy of segregation. When the program reached Gen. Walter Bedell Smith, chief of staff at the Supreme Headquarters Allied Expeditionary Forces (SHAEF), he realized that this proposal would not be popular. Smith tried to convince General Lee to change his mind, but Lee would not do so. Smith claimed that he knew more about their policy on black soldiers than did Lee or Davis and suggested to Eisenhower that the War Department be consulted. Instead, Eisenhower rewrote the directive. Black replacements were to be grouped together into platoons and placed into white companies to fill manpower needs. Although this was not as far-reaching as the initial program, it nevertheless marked a breakthrough. Davis was disappointed, though he continued to advocate the original proposal. In the meantime he closely watched the progress of the black replacement units, for he realized how important their performance would be for the future.[20]

During the first months of 1945, Davis visited the units in their training camps and near the fighting front, and he wrote to Sadie: "We are doing some very drastic things over here. . . . The colored soldier has really justified my faith in him and the faith of the veteran officers who were present in former wars." At the Reinforcement Training Center at Compiègne, France,

Davis observed the activities of black replacements. He told them about the high command's interest in their progress, and he spoke about the history of black fighting men. He also pointed out that they might need to be diplomatic: "You are going to run into some who will doubt your ability to carry on and do a job as well as they think they are doing it." As he reported to John McCloy at the end of March, "Reports to date about the conduct of these units in battle have been encouraging." However, a number of people, including General Lear, opposed the program. Davis continued to follow the black replacements' progress during the next months, and in discussions about the future utilization of black manpower, he used the information generated by the performance of these soldiers.[21]

At the same time as Davis was overseeing a new beginning in racial policy, he was shifting around in the organizational structure. First, General Lee gave Davis a new title—special advisor to the theater commander on matters affecting colored troops. Then Davis was transferred to a new organization that grew out of General Eisenhower's concern about growing racial tension. Interviews with returning soldiers indicated that there was a variety of morale problems. General Marshall asked the theater commander to conduct an inquiry and then to provide a solution. After studying the ensuing report, Eisenhower asked General Bonesteel to head an agency to deal with the problems, which was called the General Inspectorate Section. Not accidentally, its initials (the GI Section) indicated the commands' concern for individual soldiers. In early January 1945, General Bonesteel conferred with General Davis to coordinate their efforts. Shortly thereafter, Davis was transferred into the GI Section.[22]

He became head of the Colored Troops Affairs division and also headed one of the GI Section's six field teams. The inspection teams were responsible for investigating a number of topics: morale, facilities, recreation, respect between the races, and discrimination. Each field team collected evidence, prepared reports, and recommended remedial action. Although similar to the IG, the GI Section would not conduct investigations into violent incidents; it dealt only with complaints affecting the morale of individual soldiers.[23]

Davis was particularly concerned about the black reinforcement platoons and their problems. One issue that came up during the inspections concerned black NCOs who had accepted a reduction in rank in order to join the reinforcement platoons. They were concerned about their pay and benefits. During Davis's February visit to Compiègne, this issue was raised, and he in turn discussed it with General Bonesteel, who took it up with his commander, General Lear. In April, Davis visited a number of black units in the First and Third armies. He was interested in how they were being used, "their efficiency, morale, and well-being." Davis talked to Gen. Omar Bradley about the conduct of the black personnel under the latter's command. This discussion was continued when, later in the day, Davis met with Gen. Courtney H. Hodges, commander of First Army. After these meetings, Davis visited with a number of small units that had black personnel. He found the officers and enlisted men enthusiastic. One group of blacks "expressed themselves as being very grateful for the privilege given them to participate in battle, and for the way in which they had been received by the other men of the company." Davis also talked with a number of unit officers, who were pleased with their black soldiers. Believing that there was no interracial friction, he suggested that "the original idea of feeding these men into the squads be followed." Conditions in the Seventh Army were somewhat different. Davis found that morale was at a lower level and that there was a less efficient use of the black replacement platoons. Although trained as platoons, they were often used together as companies. Davis explained that the problems that subsequently arose grew out of this lack of proper training. Overall, he found that the actions of the black replacements vindicated his faith in black fighting men.[24]

Other racial issues also occupied Davis's time at the GI Section. The high frequency of rape was a problem that particularly concerned him. As part of the campaign against it, he recommended a pamphlet that a black chaplain had prepared. This brief tract, he hoped, would "arouse in them [black soldiers] a consciousness of their responsibilities in upholding the good name of our Army, and their race." When speaking to a group of arriving black soldiers in Birmingham, England, in February 1945, he approached the same point from a different perspective: he cautioned the soldiers to forget the racism of America and to "meet the people of the United Kingdom with an open mind." This was one of the topics he discussed with Truman Gibson during the latter's inspection trip to Europe in March 1945. It would continue to concern Davis during the remainder of his stay in the ETO.[25]

Davis's work and travels with the GI Section did not change the way in which he filled his leisure time. During this period he lived in Paris at the Hotel George V and wrote to Sadie every few days. His chambermaid at the hotel washed and darned his socks, but he did his own handkerchiefs. He paid the maid with cigarettes, which she preferred to money. In his many letters to Sadie he tried to keep her abreast of his activities, without really divulging great details about his work. She told him about her daily life, and both of them frequently discussed the future. At times he felt discouraged that his efforts were not achieving results. As the GI Section work drew to a close, his next assignment was unclear; and this bothered him: "I don't like just going from day to day without a plan." Yet the successes that he had achieved cheered him up, and he communicated this in his letters to Sadie. When enlisted men told him that his work was successful, "I feel happy that they think so." He believed that as long as he could accomplish something, "I think I ought to stay." However, this question of the future began to loom larger as the war came to an end in Europe.[26]

The military thought highly of Davis's work. After a March 1945 visit to the ETO, Truman Gibson noted that Davis had given him a great deal of help and that several field commanders had commented on the valuable practical advice that Davis had offered. Finally, General Bonesteel, Davis's immediate superior, gave him a very high rating in his May 1945 evaluation: "He has backed up the War Department many times to the detriment of his own standing with members of his race." Bonesteel wrote that although Davis had slowed down somewhat because of his age, "his judgement is sound and fair." He noted that Davis was emotionally stable, "except when confronted with proof of unjust discrimination against the colored soldier." Overall, Bonesteel found Davis a good officer. The French government was also pleased with Davis's work. They awarded him the Croix de Guerre with Palms.[27]

While Davis was pleased with these comments and awards, he wanted a job that would allow him to do something positive, rather than merely conducting investigations as he had done while in the United States. When Gibson came over for his inspection tour, Davis talked with him about some possibilities. Davis hoped that Gibson could involve him in "developing the future military policies regarding colored troops." Gibson suggested a continuation of the type of service that Davis had been performing with the GI Section, only now for the process of demobilization. For several weeks, Davis kept up his hopes, but by the beginning of May he realized that an early recall to Washington was not in the works for him.[28]

In May 1945 the GI Section was dissolved, and General Bonesteel and his staff were reassigned. Bonesteel was appointed acting inspector general, and the GI Section was made the nucleus of the Office of the IG in Europe. Davis continued on Bonesteel's staff, where his work was described as "the conduct of special inspections of colored troops, and investigations concerning inter-racial incidents which may occur from time to time." He was to continue working for General Bonesteel in this capacity for several more months.[29]

In early July 1945, Davis was recalled to the United States, and while he was there, he discussed his future with officials in the War Department. These discussions included Gibson, McCloy, and Maj. Gen. Stephen Henry, G-1. Davis mentioned the racial problems that he had encountered in Europe and his efforts to improve them. Davis reminded the others about the racial problems that had disturbed American society during demobilization in 1919. He hoped that the armed forces would make some effort to prevent a repetition of them, and he suggested that he could aid in this program. General Henry mentioned the possibility of sending Davis to the Pacific Theater. Because current planning was envisioning another year in order to defeat Japan, this sounded feasible. As a result, when Davis returned to Europe in late July, he thought he would soon be on his way to the Pacific; but the end of the war in August changed these plans. Then Davis asked General Bonesteel when he thought Davis could be relieved. This date, Davis thought, should be communicated to the War Department G-1. He was also motivated by thoughts of Sadie, home life, and possible retirement. These were eliminated when General Bonesteel told Davis that he would be transferred to General Lee's command again. Davis was happy. He thought that Bonesteel had meant to be fair but that he could not see blacks and whites as equal. Davis perceived Lee as much more sympathetic; he had always believed they could work well together.[30]

With this new assignment, Davis began to dream more about a promotion and less about retirement. His thoughts on this issue varied. When he was feeling depressed about the racial situation or his own usefulness, he despaired of a second star. In other situations, his views changed. Late in August, General Lee told Davis that he had Davis's promotion all arranged but that the war had come to an end, and as a result, all promotions had been frozen. Therefore, the dream of a second star was never fulfilled.[31]

Lee tried to arrange an active-duty command for Davis. In early October 1945, Lee suggested to Davis that Lee might ask the army if Davis could command the Ninety-second Division. The SOS commander believed that the army would accept Davis in this position since the war was over. Several weeks later, Lee had another idea: he wanted to place Davis in charge of the American forces remaining in the Cherbourg area. Davis asked the SOS commander if he had cleared the idea with Eisenhower. When Lee informed Davis that he had not, the black officer suggested that Lee be cautious in his moves. Davis was then ordered to Washington for several weeks of duty. Lee requested that Davis be returned within thirty days "in order that he may be given a command assignment." Upon Davis's return, Lee officially offered him the command of the Cherbourg region. Gen. Egmont F. Koenig, the commander of Channel Base Section, had agreed to this move. Lee noted that both officers hoped that the appointment would "be enjoyable to you as well as successful in accomplishing the mission of redeployment." However, the command would have placed Davis under the authority of an officer with less seniority than his, so Davis reluctantly turned it down.[32]

While these discussions were going on, Davis continued with his duties for General Lee. Knowing the violence that blacks faced in 1919 when they returned from overseas, Davis suggested a program of education to try to prevent a repetition. He wanted a series of orientation lectures to acquaint white troops with the problems that blacks faced, and his program was adopted. Among the source materials used were the pamphlets that Davis had worked on while he was a member of the McCloy Committee. It was his feeling that the historical data included would increase the respect that whites had for blacks. After a month of operation, Davis thought the program was working to decrease racial animosity. He hoped that it would lead to better conditions in the United States. In a sense he was successful. While there were no major race riots, the situation for blacks in and out of the service was still difficult.[33]

In addition to this program of education, Davis had to deal with a variety of problems generated by the process of demobilization in Europe. A number of replacement soldiers had been reassigned to service units, and they especially resented this. In August, Davis met some of these men during his inspection of Camp Herbert Tarreyton near Le Havre, France. They explained that they had already served in combat and then had been pulled out and reassigned to service units. The men had expected that combat would open up new opportunities for them. But, Davis noted, "while they were considered good enough to fight with these divisions during the war, they were not good enough to accompany them back home." Davis talked to the men and told them that disobedience to orders was not a way to get a redress of their grievances. Then he argued their case in his inspection report: "The colored soldier does not feel that he fought for a continuance of discrimination and segregation as applied to him in certain parts of the country." Davis recommended that the men be reassigned to their infantry units, and many of them were. On another inspection tour, Davis visited the Army University Center at Shrivenham Barracks, England. Out of the thirty-three hundred students, ninety were black. Davis questioned them as to whether they thought they were encountering discrimination, but they responded that they were getting along well. These problems were simple compared to those at other camps. On one occasion near Le Havre, a group of blacks was threatening to stage a sit-down strike. Davis talked to them and calmed them down. It was Davis's feeling that the soldiers respected him, and he tried to keep their confidence through his handling of their legitimate complaints. On another occasion in August 1945, he quieted a group of men who wanted to mutiny, again because of being transferred from the combat to the service branches. Davis talked them out of any violent act, and some officers commented that only Davis could have resolved the situation.[34]

During this period, Davis also tried to help shape postwar policy. In early 1945 the army began to study the progress of the black replacement units, and Davis contributed his observations to this process. He tried to convince the army that only those officers who had blacks in their commands were appropriate sources of information. War Department G-3 studied the situation as well. Based on interviews of many black and white participants in the experiment, as well as higher-ranking officers, it reported that the blacks' performance was generally good. The department's recommendation was that in the future, integration be continued on the same basis—by placing black platoons in white companies. Gibson found the report interesting and recommended it to Davis: "It conclusively proves the correctness of yours and General Lee's position."[35]

As the result of many requests, including that of Gibson, the army created a committee to investigate and make proposals on future policy in regard to black manpower. Secretary of War Robert Patterson appointed the committee, which was headed by Gen. Alvan C. Gillem, Jr., and it began to hold hearings in October 1945. During the next four months the board listened to the testimony of many witnesses, both military and civilian; in addition, it examined previous studies that the military had done on the utilization of black manpower. Among the witnesses were Gen. Benjamin Davis, Sr., and Col. Benjamin Davis, Jr. At the request of the board, General Davis was ordered to the United States on temporary duty in mid October. He remained in Washington for fourteen days and testified before the board on two different occasions. In his view, blacks had consistently been misassigned because of the army's adherence to the policy of segregation. His recent experiences with the replacement platoons indicated to him that integration could work. He also criticized the obsession with segregation before military effectiveness. He commented that "American Negroes were not accepted in clubs in Europe while African Negroes, with fezzes were accepted." His solution was integration, for which whites could be prepared through a policy of education. After Davis had returned to Paris, he continued to gather material to send to the committee, including his annotated version of the G-3 investigation of attitudes about the replacement program. He underlined sections that indicated a change in white attitudes after close contact with blacks. He also noted: "Segregation fosters intolerance, suspicion, and friction." Board members viewed this testimony, along with that of other blacks, with a great deal of skepticism. Gen. Aln D. Warnock thought that Truman Gibson had coordinated the testimony of the blacks. The board's attitude was that full integration was impracticable and that the time was not ripe for such a change. The board was in favor of a greater utilization of black manpower but vague on how or when this was to be accomplished. It seemed to support the continuation of most aspects of segregation for the present. In the postwar army, Davis was to be involved in the problems of implementing their suggested changes.[36]

Despite his successes in Europe, Davis was becoming increasingly concerned about race relations and his own future. After his visit to the United States in July, he commented to Sadie that discrimination was more noticeable after living abroad for a year and not having to put up with different treatment because of his race. Several months later he told her that he thought it was impossible that whites could be fair and just to nonwhites. He sounded discouraged when he wrote, "I hope I'll soon be freed from this mess." He tried to relax by reading mystery stories or by having a drink in the evening with his aide and Sadie's cousin John Overton. On other evenings, Davis would go for a walk and try to practice his French during these strolls. His duty assignments did not seem to generate as much interest as they had, and he kept talking about returning home. By early October he was thinking about finishing up his work for Lee and returning to the United States by Christmastime.[37]

Davis was concerned about his future, and sometimes he talked about retirement: "I feel like I would enjoy being retired from trying to bring about harmony." When he declined the offer of the command at Cherbourg, this set in motion his final return to the United States. He notified the War Department that he was available for reassignment, and it ordered him home for a forty-five day rest. He wrote to Sadie: "If after forty five days of rest we decide that I don't stay on we can be retired." Even before he returned, he thought about what he could do after his rest. One possibility he suggested to Gibson was that he might work in the War Department in charge of developing future racial policies, but the creation of the Gillem Board prevented this. He then envisioned working in the Veterans Bureau or "as a member of the board to be recommended by the Gillem Board to supervise assignments, employments, etc., of colored troops in the postwar period." He also thought about the possibility of writing a book. All of this receded from his mind when he returned home in November 1945. He spent several weeks getting back into the old home routine: reading the papers, resting, and winding clocks. He also had a number of personal business matters to attend to. His brother Louis had died in August 1945, and Benjamin had to help straighten out Louis's affairs. Henrietta, then ninety years old, who had been living with Louis, now came to live with Sadie and Benjamin. "While she is very well considering her advanced age, it means that we do not like to leave her alone." In early January 1946, after some thought, Benjamin decided to remain on duty. His new assignment was with the IG in Washington.[38]

Davis's return to Washington in November 1945 brought an end to his service in the European Theater. He had helped deal with the problems of segregation, assignment, and promotion; he had facilitated the assemblage of the footage for *Teamwork;* he had worked well with General Lee; and he had contributed to the first real breakthrough in the color line—the replacement program. On the other hand, he had been frustrated by a number of things, including the discrimination that he had encountered, the War Department's refusal to follow through on the original proposal for manpower utilization, his personal failure to be promoted or to receive a real troop command, and his feeling at times that his work was not having a significant impact. The tasks that he had performed in Europe were similar to those he had done in the United States, but during this period he had gotten close to the front lines and had been instrumental in a breakthrough. What the future would hold for a sixty-eight-year-old brigadier general during a period of postwar retrenchment was quite unclear. He wanted to continue to serve, but only if he thought he could accomplish something useful.

8 | A Career Closes: 1946–1970

AFTER HAVING BEEN involved in many important duties during World War II, General Davis spent the last years of his life far removed from such power. He remained in the army until 1948; then he retired, but continued to serve his fellow citizens for as long as his physical abilities would allow.

After a brief period of readjustment in late 1945 and early 1946, Davis was soon back at work at some familiar tasks. He resumed his assignment as assistant inspector general, under the command of Gen. Dan I. Sultan, the new inspector general. Davis's duties were "the same as before my departure from Washington."[1]

Davis was on the periphery of the army's decisions involving the utilization of black manpower. The Gillem Board issued its report in March 1946, which recommended that the army's goal should be to eliminate, as quickly as possible, any "special consideration based on race." Davis, who was present at the press conference at which the Gillem Report was made public, thought that the event "marked the dawn of a new day for the colored soldier." He believed that these words meant that segregation "was going to be gradually dropped and that the tendency would be to begin working toward the integration of colored soldiers into all units." This probably was wishful thinking, but it was an idea that he had long fought for. At the end of the press conference, the finished version of *Teamwork* was shown. Davis and others hoped that these new policies would lead to genuine teamwork in the army.[2]

Although the Gillem Board's recommendations were never really put into practice, Davis tried to exert some pressure toward this end. In August 1946 he spoke in Columbus, Ohio, at the national convention of the Frontiers Club. He attacked the notion that separation implied equality: "There is no such animal."

He called upon whites and blacks to work together to fight segregation and prejudice. In 1947, at the convention of the United Negro and Allied Veterans of America, he reiterated the same theme: "I feel that the time is now more opportune than heretofore for the integration of the colored veteran and the colored people as a whole into all of the activities of our American government and society." These public statements constituted but one facet of his effort to encourage integration.[3]

In his activities inside the War Department, Davis tried to convince officials that they must implement the spirit and the meaning of the Gillem Report. He informed the army that black public opinion was turning against it because of the continuation of segregation. The black press, said Davis, reflected the view that "little has been done." The army's response was to try to convince Davis that it was moving forward to implement the Gillem Report. Davis did not think that this was the case, and he sought to use recent events to show the army that it was out of step with society. He pointed out that President Harry Truman's Commission on Civil Rights had condemned segregation in the armed forces. Davis also suggested that Truman's actions indicated that he was "deeply interested in bettering the conditions under which our colored people live." Finally he suggested: "Now is an opportune time for the War Department to take some action that will emphasize that efforts are being made to conform" to the Gillem Board's policy. But nothing was done.[4]

The discussion of Universal Military Training (UMT) provided another forum for the debate over segregation in the armed forces. Based on the experiences of World War II, planning for a future conflict included the establishment of large ground armies. To provide the manpower for them, a number of military leaders proposed UMT. At the insistence of the army, the legislative proposal for this program did not contain a clause prohibiting segregation. Blacks focused on this point. Davis had been aware of the problem even before the proposal had reached Congress. In mid 1946 he had written: "Colored people will not whole heartedly support universal military training as long as the army adheres to its old policy." In 1947, Davis again informed the army that segregation was the cause for the vocal opposition of black groups to UMT. In 1948, A. Philip Randolph went so far as to threaten civil disobedience if Jim Crow continued. He failed to convince enough congressmen, however; so the 1948 Selective Service Act did not ban segregation.[5]

Davis also attacked army segregation on other fronts. In early 1947 he encouraged Gen. William Kelley, chief of staff of the New York National Guard, to push forward with a program of integration. Davis justified this view with his often-stated views about segregation, and he also cited the impact of segregation on non-white groups around the world and at the United Nations. "Their observations of the treatment of the colored people in the United States will, in my opinion, greatly influence their estimate of the advantages of our democracy." In general, the army opposed these integration efforts by states.[6]

Davis's field work brought home to him the evils that existed in the army: "I have learned [more] about the evils of racial prejudices during this period than I knew about it all the years of my life before. . . . I have been astounded by hearing expressions of hate from both races." It reinforced his longstanding opposition to all forms of segregation and discrimination, but he was uncertain if he would ever see an end to the evil.[7]

Another of Davis's functions was to make awards and give speeches. In June 1946 he went to New York to present Selective Service Medals to the members of nine selective-service boards. The ceremony was held at a site familiar to Davis, the 369th Infantry Armory. Davis's speechmaking was not confined to awards ceremonies. Early in 1946 he was Boston's guest for Negro History Week and was honored during a program on blacks in American wars. In April 1946 he spoke at Prairie View College in Texas and, in May, at Memorial Day exercises at Tuskegee Hospital. He ended the year by being the featured speaker at the Armistice Day celebrations held by the 369th Regiment.[8]

During his last years of army service, Davis again had the opportunity to be with his wife and family. With his army salary, he was able to live a comfortable life. In the evenings he would relax on the porch of his Washington house, take walks, or go to see a movie. One particular film that caught his attention was *Rhapsody in Blue*. As he wrote to Mr. and Mrs. Ira Gershwin, it brought back memories of his visit to Hollywood: "I have thought of you both many times and I always carry with me pleasant memories of the great contribution you made to my comfort and pleasure during my stay with you." Elnora and James McLendon moved to Chicago in 1946, but they continued to visit Benjamin and Sadie on a regular basis. A Christmas get-together became a tradition, as did a spring visit. Benjamin and Sadie went to Chicago during the summer, and these visits continued for many years afterwards.[9]

By 1947, Davis had been on active duty for forty-nine years and was, as far as the army was concerned, seventy years old. Early in that year, Maj. Gen. Willard S. Paul, director of personnel, suggested that all retired officers who were then in the service be relieved from duty. After a physical examination found that Davis was in good health, the army decided to keep him on duty. He was pleased that "they still think I am worth something on active duty." He received a new title, special assistant to the secretary of the army; and his duties were approximately the same as when he had been with the IG. Gen. Ira T. Wyche, the IG, kept Davis informed about the IG's activities, and Davis helped Wyche whenever the IG requested. This continuing career, Davis hoped, "inspired some of our younger colored men." He did not have much time to think of this at the time, however, because in mid 1947 he was given a very special assignment, which took him back to Liberia.[10]

Because the United States was one of Liberia's closest allies, the State Department gave careful thought to how the United States would participate in the 1947 celebration of Liberia's centennial. The Navy Department indicated that it might be able to send one or more ships for a brief visit. The Liberian government, early on, suggested that the United States consider appointing Davis as the American representative for the event. In March 1947 the United States government received formal notification of the celebration. Shortly afterwards it decided to participate and to make Davis head of the delegation. Assistant Secretary of State Dean Acheson justified United States participation because of the "close historical relationship" between the two countries and "the active interest of American Negroes in Liberia." Acheson also noted that a number of nations were sending representatives with the rank of ambassador. In justification for his suggestion of a representative, he noted that Liberia's President Tubman had already informally asked for Davis. Acheson recommended that Davis "be designated as your [Truman's] representative with the personal rank of Ambassador at the centennial celebration." This proposal was passed on to Secretary of State Marshall, who approved, and then to President Truman, who gave his assent on 22 May 1947.[11]

Numerous details had to be settled before the delegation could depart. Benjamin O. Davis, Jr., was added to the diplomatic party, and the navy agreed to send a small task force, including the carrier USS *Palau*. With the travel arrangements made, the State Department began to brief Davis and prepare him for his diplomatic mission. In early June he met with Andrew G. Lynch, of the State Department, to begin his preparations. The current state of American-Liberian relations and all the factors that affected them were included in the discussion. Lynch then talked with Davis about the speech that Davis was to make and what the State Department was putting into it. He also told Davis what topics to avoid while in Liberia. Finally, Lynch gave Davis a manuscript that described the economic role of the United States in Liberia.[12]

Davis's return to Liberia began when the USS *Palau* left the United States on 5 July 1947. He was quite impressed with the integrated crews on his vessel and on the accompanying destroyers. All the racial groups participated together in the ceremonies that took place when they crossed the equator on 15 July. At that time "King Neptune" visited the ship. The "shellbacks"—that is, men who had not crossed the equator before—were initiated. Benjamin Davis, Jr., was included in that company; he had to carry a sandwich board proclaiming that men should reenlist in the navy and that the army backed such a policy. He was also beaten with a paddle and dumped in some water. After these events, the cruise continued. Davis was kept busy with last-minute preparations for his ambassadorial debut. The speech he was to deliver had been approved before his departure, but it was refined during the trip over. The carrier's band director, Ens. Gabriel Petre, decided that it would be appropriate for the band to be playing the Liberian National Anthem as the ship arrived at Monrovia. Petre asked General Davis if he had brought the appropriate music with him. When Davis replied that he had not, Petre asked if Davis could sing the anthem. Davis said he could, and he sang it several times while one of the musicians transcribed it. Considering that Davis had not been in Liberia for more than thirty years, the feat of recalling the anthem was quite extraordinary. With this preparation the *Palau*'s band was able to join in the ceremonies when the Americans arrived.[13]

During the week that Davis was in Liberia he was very busy with a variety of official functions in connection with the centennial celebration. On the day of the Americans' arrival they were met by President Tubman and were entertained by him at a private party. The two Davises stayed at a villa outside of Monrovia, and on the next day, Davis gave a luncheon on the ship for the Liberians. A demonstration of flying was put on by one hundred American planes. That evening, Davis hosted a dinner for Tubman and ranking governmental officials at the American Legation. The highlight of the visit for Davis occurred on Saturday, 26 July 1947, when he gave the official United States address honoring the Liberian centennial.[14]

When the Liberian government had learned earlier that Davis was to give an address on Liberian–United States relations, Tubman had requested that the address be delivered publicly on Centennial Day. The speech was heard by a large audience and was given a great deal of attention because it was recognized as a major statement by the United States government. Davis began by citing his longstanding interest in Liberia, tracing it back to his first visit in 1910. He continued by explaining the deep United States concern about Liberia, and he offered assurances that the United States would extend aid to assist Liberia, depending on what the Liberians did to help themselves. Davis was interrupted by applause eighteen times during the thirty-seven minutes it took him to deliver the speech. President Tubman and Secretary of State Dennis initially seemed to be pleased with the talk. Some of the foreigners who were present thought the speech contained too much boasting about American accomplishments, but they all wanted copies to send to their governments. President Tubman soon changed his mind about the address and attacked it as "boasting, haughty and bad taste." He suggested that it might better have been given in private. The government encouraged press reactions, including attacks on the speech. Tubman probably realized that he should not have let the United States have the advantage of making an address on such a public occasion, and he probably generated the unfavorable publicity as a way of correcting his mistake. After a brief storm, however, the furor died down, and Davis's visit continued uneventfully.[15]

During the remaining few days of his stay, Davis toured parts of Liberia and listened to more speeches. He visited a Firestone rubber plantation and toured the Booker T. Washington Institute. He viewed the facilities of the U.S. Public Health mission and hosted a reception at the American Legation for prominent Liberians and Americans. He probably had a chance to talk over the old days with Secretary of State Dennis, who had been one of Olive's playmates back in 1910-1911. In a speech on Executive Day, President Tubman, in a partial turnabout, made a point of specifically welcoming the return of Davis to Liberia. The government also presented Davis with the award that it had given him in 1943, the Order of the Star of Africa. The United States representatives left Liberia on 31 July. After a two-week voyage, including a stop at Dakar, they returned home to Norfolk, Virginia, on 16 August. Despite all the ceremonies and attention, Davis drew his own conclusions about the country: "While I enjoyed my visit, I would not care to reside there for any great length of time."[16]

After his return to the United States, Davis received commendations for his performance. Robert Lovett, acting secretary of state, wrote that Davis had discharged his duties "with unfailing tact, energy and resourcefulness." Davis's response was to suggest that he might be able to help the State Department "in its dealings with the governments of non-white people."[17]

In 1948 the question of Davis's retirement was again brought up. Early in the year, Davis was interviewed by the press on his retirement plans. He told reporters that he did not have any; as far as he knew, the army was going to keep him on. Rumors persisted, however. Some people asked the NAACP to lobby for Davis's promotion to the rank of major general. Roy Wilkins, assistant executive secretary of the NAACP, argued that the NAACP's general opposition to segregation would not allow it to push a request based solely on race. However, Senator Clyde R. Hoey introduced a bill in June 1948 to raise Davis to the permanent rank of brigadier general on the retired list. His justification for this special consideration was Davis's long service for the country. The bill was referred to committee but died there. Shortly thereafter, Congress passed another piece of legislation that achieved the same result, but for a larger number of officers.[18]

At the same time there was some truth to the rumors that Davis might be appointed as ambassador to Liberia. Beginning in April 1948, the State Department had considered the idea. Finally, Secretary of State Marshall recommended the appointment to Truman. The State Department argued that Liberia would regard Davis as ambassador quite favorably. In addition, because of Davis's "wide experience along military lines, it is believed [he] would contribute much in assisting the Liberian government in strengthening their defense." Unstated was the fact that it was an election year and that such an appointment would help win black votes. If Truman approved, Marshall said that he would discuss the matter with Davis. In late April, Truman gave his assent. At the end of the month, Loy Henderson, director for Near Eastern and African affairs, and Joseph Palmer II, acting chief of the Division of African Affairs, talked with Davis. They explained all the considerations that had gone into the decision to offer him the appointment. Davis said that he was deeply appreciative of the offer and that he wanted to continue to serve the government but that he needed several days to discuss the matter with Sadie and to think it over. He remembered his feelings during his tour in 1910-1911 and his recent visit. On the other hand, it was a chance for a new career. After a great deal of thought, Davis declined the offer. The key reason was his mother, Henrietta, who was "too old to travel." If he had gone to Liberia, it would have meant leaving Sadie to take care of Henrietta. Sadie offered to do this, but Davis "did not feel that I could leave Mrs. Davis for a mission like that." After Davis had explained the situation to the State Department, it accepted his reasons for declining the position. He made it clear that he hoped the department would ask him again in the future.[19]

During these negotiations, the Department of the Army proceeded with its own plans for Davis's future. In May the army decided that Davis should be retired as of 30 June 1948. Several days later the chief of personnel called Davis and asked him why he had not informed the army that this retirement date would prevent him from serving fifty years. Davis responded that the army had not asked him and that the whole process had taken him by surprise. The chief of personnel asked Davis if he would be willing to remain on duty until 14 July so that he would complete fifty years of service. Davis responded positively. Under pressure from the black community for its opposition to any integration, the army saw an opportunity to act positively toward a black military man by having a public retirement ceremony in which Davis would be awarded a scroll signed by President Truman, Secretary of the Army Kenneth C. Royall, and Chief of Staff Omar Bradley.[20]

The event took place on Tuesday, 20 July 1948, in the office of President Truman, who told Davis that he had always wanted to see what a man who had served in the army for fifty years looked like. Among the guests were Sadie, Benjamin, Jr., and Agatha, Elnora and James McLendon, and Mr. and Mrs. Perry Howard. Olive and George Streator were not there because she had just given birth to a son. Various other officials were present, including Campbell Johnson from the Selective Service and James Evans, civilian aide to the secretary of the army. Before Truman presented Davis with the special scroll, he talked briefly

President Harry S. Truman, General Davis, and Sadie Davis at Davis's retirement ceremony in 1948

about Davis's career and the changes that had occurred during it. Truman noted that when General Davis had started in the army, there had only been one black officer in the service, and now there were many, even more than there had been during the war. Truman also handed Davis a letter which informed him that he had reached the permanent retired rank of brigadier general. When they left the White House that day, the active military career of Benjamin O. Davis was over.[21]

Davis received many notes of congratulations on his retirement. His old friend General Lee wrote one of them. Chief of Staff Omar Bradley noted: "Your record will remain an inspiration to those who must take up tasks which you, in your time, have borne so well." The black press also congratulated Davis on his retirement, wished him well, and suggested that now Davis would have the opportunity to write about his many experiences. This was one of the varied new possibilities that were open to Davis as his active-duty career came to an end.[22]

Davis now began a whole new stage in his life, a career outside of the army. After fifty years of service, he now had to rearrange his daily routine. Davis thought he was in good physical shape: "My physicians tell me I am as physically fit as men 20 years younger that myself." He did not want for money, since he retired on 75 percent of his active-duty pay, or almost $6,000 a year. His retirement pay continued to rise as Congress made adjustments. By the 1960s he was receiving almost $800 a month. He did not spend money lavishly, however. The Davis's did not have any household help, even when they were both old. When they went grocery shopping, they did not have the items delivered; instead, Benjamin brought them home himself. More of an issue was what to do with leisure time. One possible opportunity that he considered was getting involved with an ROTC program or another type of teaching job. He continued to think about governmental service, especially in connection with Liberia. However, jobs that might take him outside Washington would have to be deferred as long as his mother was still alive and living with them.[23]

Sadie believed that the more activities there were, the more they would retard the problems of loss of sight and memory for Benjamin. In the afternoon and evening there were many card groups. Sadie had been a member for years, but now Benjamin joined them. Often he was the only man present, and although he complained about this in the beginning, after a while he got used to it. He also began work on an autobiography, but he found this difficult. He was able to write about the years before he received his commission in 1901, but then he put the project aside and never resumed it. Benjamin and Sadie were able to travel. They often went to New York City for a day or two to see some shows and to visit with Olive, George, and their son. Sadie traveled to the Caribbean for a period with a lady friend. The Davises had to make their plans around Henrietta, who lived with them until her death in December 1950, at the age of ninety-five.[24]

After Henrietta's death, Benjamin began to feel that he could undertake a new assignment. He hoped that his good friend Gen. John Lee, with whom Davis had maintained a correspondence, might be able to help. Davis wrote to Lee a number of times during the late 1940s and in the 1950s. They discussed two major topics: a new position for Davis and the developing racial situation. During the early part of the decade, Davis had suggested that he would be willing to go back to work for Lee in a position similar to that which he had held in 1944-1945. Lee was enthusiastic in his response: "Should I be called to take a service command, I'd be delighted to have you again as an associate." Davis kept Lee apprised of his activities, including a trip to Liberia in 1951. He told Lee about his daily schedule and cited Henry W. Longfellow's poem "The Village Blacksmith," to explain his feelings about his life:

> Each morning sees some task begun,
> Each evening sees its close
> Something attempted something done
> To earn a night's repose.

Davis looked with favor on Eisenhower's election campaign in 1952, although he believed that the candidate had not worked strongly enough for integration back in 1945. Davis thought that Lee's plan "would not only have worked successfully then but, at this time, there would be little doubt of his [Eisenhower's] receiving a larger share of the colored votes on November 4."[25]

As the decade wore on, the two commented on the growing civil-rights movement. Lee made a speech in early 1956 in Richmond, Virginia, in which he quoted Davis. Lee told the white audience that Davis's advice had been, not to push the racial issue, "but to continue taking appropriate time in working out all problems." In 1957, Davis indicated to Lee that he believed there was something wrong in giving a great deal of attention to suffering Hungarians while ignoring the problems of American blacks. Nothing was being done to help "our colored citizens who without violence are trying to enjoy the privileges resulting from the decisions of the highest court in the land." Lee agreed with these sentiments: "My heart goes out to our fellow Americans in the South in their efforts to do right against continuing odds." Davis continued to follow the course of events, including those in Montgomery, Alabama, and he still believed that he had something to offer: "While I may be considered 'A worn out tire' I believe I still have some good mileage left. (I can dream, can't I?)." The racial disturbances that accompanied attempts to integrate the Little Rock schools in 1957 depressed Davis.[26]

Davis also kept in touch with the racial situation in the armed forces themselves. Six days after Davis retired, Truman had issued an executive order ending racial discrimination in the armed forces. With Executive Order 9981, President Truman pushed the armed forces along the road to integration. By early 1950 the process had begun in the army, but quite slowly. Davis kept watch over this. He was asked for his advice on how to deal with a racial situation at an isolated Air Force base that had few black personnel. Thomas White, deputy for personnel in the Fourth Air Force, asked Davis to visit the Moses Lake Air Force base and give the Air Force the benefit of his views. He turned down the invitation, probably because he thought there was little he could contribute that was not already being done. Another request that he rejected was one from the Department of the Army in 1951 to "orient you [Davis] on current Army matters." Davis was pleased that the army was finally moving to eliminate the segregation that he had always hated, yet he did not think that he could contribute much new in this area.[27]

Davis's ties with Liberia continued throughout this period, and he hoped that this might lead to a renewed offer of an ambassadorship. In October 1951, Liberian Secretary of State Dennis invited Benjamin and Sadie to come to Liberia to attend the inaugural ceremonies for President Tubman's second term. The Liberian government offered to pay their travel expenses to and from Liberia, so Davis accepted. The Davises remained in Liberia for a month and stayed at the executive mansion during the inaugural ceremonies. After his return to the United States in early 1952, Davis did not forget Liberia or the Liberians, however. Later in the year he wrote to Tubman that he was keeping current on

Liberia's activities and had been to the library to obtain a few books on the subject. Davis also offered his services to help develop the military forces of Liberia, but his offer was turned down. Davis continued to think along these lines, however, and the election of Eisenhower in late 1952 renewed his hopes for another offer of the position as ambassador to Liberia.[28]

Davis viewed his good friend General Lee and his other old military associates as possible levers to convince Eisenhower to give Davis a new assignment. Shortly after the election the seventy-four-year-old retired general wrote to Lee: "I wish there was some way in which I could help him. . . . However, I shall not curry him with an application or requests." Davis then told Lee about the offer to serve in Liberia in 1948 and why he had to turn it down. Davis also noted that the State Department had had high praise for his performance as the United States representative at the Liberian centennial celebration. Lee took the hint and shortly afterwards wrote to Secretary-of-State-Designate John Foster Dulles. Lee told Dulles about Truman's 1948 offer to Davis and why Davis had had to turn it down. Lee also indicated that Davis wanted to serve the country again. According to Lee, Davis "would render loyal, devoted service representing our country in any capacity for which he regarded himself as qualified. And I believe him uniquely qualified for State Department duty." Although nothing came of this effort for a diplomatic position, Davis was not deterred. Another person whom he approached was Howard Snyder, Eisenhower's personal physician. Davis had known Snyder for many years, going back to service at Fort D. A. Russell in 1912 and continuing through the war years, when they both worked for the IG. Writing to Snyder in early 1953, Davis gave an outline of his qualifications, including his knowledge of French and Spanish. This failed campaign did not stop Davis, for he continued to try to gain a position in the national government. Several months later he noticed that James Evans, civilian advisor to the secretary of defense, was retiring. Davis hinted to Lee that he would be interested in this job, but again nothing happened.[29]

Two years later, in 1955, the Liberian ambassadorship became a live issue again. Davis's efforts were triggered by events that occurred during President Tubman's visit to the United States. Davis and his wife were invited to the Liberian Embassy for dinner, along with President and Mrs. Eisenhower. Ike remembered Davis quite well, and this renewed Davis's hopes. Several weeks later, Davis went to the State Department and visited the Division of West African Affairs to see if he knew any of the staff. After Davis met one of the officers who remembered him, "I offered my services to the department through him." Davis suggested that he "might be used in connection with Liberian affairs." Davis recounted this visit and included a broad hint in a letter to Lee. Davis had revived the idea because the United States ambassador to Liberia had just died. Davis also told the foreign-service officer that he was still in good physical condition, an important point to make because Davis was in his seventies at that time. Lee took the hint and again recommended Davis to be ambassador. Davis's response was: "Perhaps I am all wet, but I feel better for having mentioned it to you and your recommending me to the State Department." The administration again disappointed Davis by appointing someone else.[30]

Despite the failure of his efforts to return to Liberia, Davis did find opportunities to serve society. In March 1952 the commissioners of the District of Columbia set up an advisory committee to study the public-works program for the District. Davis was appointed as a member of the Water, Sewer, and Aqueducts Subcommittee. He regarded the invitation "as a duty," and he served on the subcommittee, even though it was involved in a subject that was outside his own area of expertise. After several months of study, the subcommittee proposed a program of rebuilding the sewer system and improvements to the water system of the District.[31]

In the following month he received another job offer, this time as a member of the Citizens' Advisory Council, a panel of nine citizens who advised the commissioners on public matters in the District. Davis served on the panel until June 1953 but was not reappointed. However, he was not really disturbed because he had received yet another public office by that time, as a member of the American Battle Monuments Commission (ABMC).[32]

The ABMC had been established after World War I and had been placed in charge of the cemeteries in Europe where American soldiers were buried. It also had been given the responsibility of supervising the construction of several chapels at the cemeteries. After World War II the ABMC performed a similar task. In the process it selected sites and approved architecture and artworks for those cemeteries. The ABMC was made up of eleven appointed members and a permanent staff. Apparently the requests by General Lee for a position for Davis helped bring Davis to the attention of the Eisenhower administration. In June 1953, Davis received a letter from Sherman Adams, Eisenhower's assistant, asking Davis if he would be willing to serve on the ABMC. Davis agreed and began his new job in July 1953.[33]

The commission usually met twice a year. Davis's first meeting, in September, was also the first for a number of other new members, including Adm. Thomas Kinkaid, Mrs. Wendell Willkie, Mrs. Theodore Roosevelt, Jr., and Congressman John Phillips. At that meeting, the commission discussed the general activities of the ABMC and the European tour that the new members would take to visit the sites of the construction projects. It was a strenuous trip, and Sadie and Mrs. Kinkaid did not try to visit all of the sites with their husbands. Mrs. Roosevelt, whom Davis described as a "wiry little lady," was a hard worker, and they "found lots to talk about." The members reported to the whole ABMC that they had visited all of the official and some private American World War II cemeteries, as well as those of some of our allies. The commission members found some of the projects that were already under way, such as the one at Hamm, to be inappropriate and some of the artworks, such as the ones proposed for Cambridge, "completely unsuitable." Apparently the conservative tastes of the visitors were offended by the more modern ideas of the contributing artists, which was a consistent problem for the committee. This report became the subject of discussion at the next ABMC meeting, in December 1953.[34]

This first substantive ABMC meeting that Davis attended set

General Davis after his retirement

the tone for the others during the next seven years of his work on the commission. The meeting began with a discussion of the trip to Europe. The travelers repeated their comments about the faults that they had found in the Hamm Memorial. The entire ABMC decided to ask the architect to respond in writing to its complaints. The next topic was a mosaic at the Cambridge Memorial: the touring party had objected to the colors in it. The

ABMC decided to ask for comments from the artist who was responsible for the mosaic. The last major topic involved the cemetery at St. Avold. Sculptor Michael Lantz came to talk to the commission about the details of the sculpture. Members of the group had a number of comments about the design, such as the fact that they thought one of the pieces looked like a bearded prophet, rather than like Saint Michael. Lantz indicated that he would try to incorporate their comments into his design changes. Close supervision of these projects, such as the St. Avold Memorial, continued for years. The questions that were raised at the December 1953 meeting were typical of the ABMC meetings: issues concerning large and small aspects of the memorials. The ABMC, whose meetings Davis characterized as "in the nature of a reunion with old friends and comrades," told professional architects and sculptors how to do their work.[35]

Although the ABMC only met a few times each year, the work continued. The permanent staff kept in touch with the members by mail. The staff would often send out ballots so that members could vote on questions. At times these were accompanied by charts or pictures to help the members decide. Before the next meeting, in mid March 1954, there were three such votes. One concerned the Hamm Memorial. The issue was whether to discharge the architect or to try to convince him to make changes. All eleven voted to get a new architect, for as Davis noted, there was little chance that the old architect would agree to make any revisions in the plans. The next month the members had to deal with the St. Avold Memorial and its sculpture; and they voted on the themes for the artwork. Shortly before the March meeting, the members were sent a list of subjects for discussion and photographs of the proposed work. During that March meeting, the members voted to inform one sculptor that he should "avoid the modernistic or freakish." This clearly reflected their taste.[36]

Davis's work on the commission was not taxing, so he had time for a variety of activities. Agatha and Benjamin, Jr., saw his parents whenever Benjamin, Jr.'s, duty assignments permitted. The younger couple took the parents to dances and movies on occasion, or listened to Benjamin, Sr., play a variety of piano pieces, including some by Victor Herbert. Elnora and Jim continued to visit in the spring, and Benjamin and Sadie reciprocated during the summer. George, Olive, and their son visited occasionally. Several days after one such visit, Olive called to tell her parents that George had suddenly died of a heart attack. In 1957, Sadie went to the hospital with complaints about indigestion, but the doctors found that she had a heart problem. She was put to bed, where she remained for a month before they let her out. It was November before she was allowed to go home. Sadie's sister, Lawrence, came to take care of Benjamin during this period, when he visited Sadie in the hospital every day. He found home a very empty place: "The home atmosphere left when Sadie left." By November she was much better and was soon back to her old self. Davis himself had eye surgery in 1958 and 1959 for cataracts, and he had some difficulty seeing after the second operation. In August 1958, Benjamin's long-term close friend John Lee died of a heart attack at the age of seventy-one. Lee was buried in Arlington Cemetery. Despite these evidences of aging, however, Davis remained on the ABMC, and Benjamin and Sadie made several trips to Europe during the 1950s.[37]

Throughout the 1950s the ABMC continued to review the construction of the memorials and various design details. In 1956 a number of the commission members journeyed to Europe for the dedication of six cemeteries and the inspection of work on several more. They went to Cambridge, England; Normandy, Brittany, Epinal, and the Rhone Valley in France; and the Sicily-Rome Memorial. Davis took part in all the dedications and laid a memorial wreath at both Epinal and Cambridge. The visits to the cemeteries had an impact on him: "I wonder sometimes if those who shape policy and legislate us into wars would hesitate to take such a step if they saw these many crosses marking the last resting places of the 'Flower of our young manhood.' "[38]

In June 1961, Davis received a letter from Kenneth O'Donnell, an assistant to President John Kennedy, asking that Davis, along with the other appointees on the commission, submit their resignations so that the president would have the option of appointing new people. Davis complied and was replaced on the commission. This marked the end of his public-service career.[39]

By the early 1960s, Benjamin's and Sadie's health had begun to deteriorate, which limited their activities. As his eyesight became worse, driving became more difficult for him, but he would not stop until he had an accident that resulted in some bruised ribs for Sadie. Benjamin continued to go for walks, but this, too, came to an end when the police asked him to stop. They told him the neighborhood had changed and that it was no longer safe for him to take those walks. In early 1960, Davis received an invitation to speak at Armed Forces Day celebrations at Tuskegee, but he had to turn the invitation down because he was going to Walter Reed for observation and did not know when he would be finished. Despite all of these physical problems, Sadie and Benjamin continued together quite happily: "Just two old people both still very much in love with each other and each trying to contribute to the happiness of each other." In 1966 Sadie was taken to the hospital with what was thought to be kidney trouble. Instead, it was a ruptured appendix. The doctors wanted to operate, but she delayed before finally giving them permission. Lawrence again came to Washington to look after her brother-in-law. Elnora was also there to help her father. The two took him to the hospital for daily visits. In October, Sadie had another heart attack, and she died on 25 October 1966. After forty-seven years of marriage to Sadie, Benjamin was alone again.[40]

Elnora convinced her father that he could not stay in Washington by himself and that he should move in with Jim and her. The house on S Street was sold, and all of the family items were moved to Chicago. It was a difficult time, for Benjamin's mind was not as sharp as it once had been. He remembered the past quite well, but information about the present soon escaped him. He often thought about Henrietta and talked a lot about her. He still kept his military bearing and looked like an old soldier. Elnora tried to arrange a routine for Benjamin, to help him adjust to his new home. He got a newspaper in the afternoon, and then he watched television in the evening. She tried to play cards with her father, but he would forget what he had in his hand. In November 1970, at the age of ninety-three, Davis was admitted to Great Lakes Naval Hospital. With Elnora present, he died on Thanksgiving Day, 26 November 1970. The cause of death was listed as acute leukemia.[41]

Four days later, Davis received a soldier's funeral at Arlington Cemetery. His coffin was carried on a caisson drawn by six white horses. It was followed by a riderless black horse, with the boots in the stirrups turned backwards. Among those who were present were Secretary of Transportation John Volpe and a former director of Selective Service, Lt. Gen. Lewis Hershey, who had received his promotion to brigadier general at the same time as Davis. Liberia's Ambassador Edward Peal also attended. There were a number of black officers, including several colonels, such as West A. Hamilton. All three of the Davis children were there. The chaplain from Fort Myer, James Hayes, read the Twenty-third Psalm and talked about Davis's work in bringing about integration. Thirteen volleys of rifle fire saluted the general, and a soldier played taps. The flag that draped the coffin was handed to Elnora. The grave site was only a few hundred feet from that of President John F. Kennedy.[42]

Benjamin Davis lived a long and fruitful life, which included more than fifty years of service to his country. During the immediate postwar period he had moved further away from the centers of power. He spoke out against racism in the army, but this did not seem to have much impact. For the last two years of his active-duty career he continued to perform inspections, make speeches, and serve as special minister to the Liberian Centennial celebration. After his retirement in 1948 he sought continued public service and did do so in a variety of forums. Before his health began to fail, he always thought that he could do more than he was asked to do. Finally, death claimed this hard-working American citizen.

9 | Conclusion

ALTHOUGH A NUMBER of people have already made assessments of the career of Benjamin O. Davis, Sr., one must understand his unique situation in order to fully comprehend his achievements. Two years after his father's death, Benjamin Davis, Jr., commented that his father had been a great man, a good storyteller, and above all, a man who had filled his life with the United States Army. Although the elder Davis was totally committed to improving the quality of life for the black soldier, he did not share his experiences or reactions to specific events with his son. Carlton Moss, who had known Davis for only a short period, felt differently. He saw Davis as an accommodationist and a strait-laced "pleasant man, who would not allow himself to direct any hostility." William Miles, in his television documentary about black officers, dismissed Davis as a man who was merely serving his time. Davis, Jr., was obviously quite close to the subject, while Moss and Miles knew relatively little about the man and what he really had done.[1]

At the time of Davis's death, a number of editorial writers commented about his life and its impact. Charles Loeb, of the *Cleveland Call and Post*, noted that Davis had made progress but that the military still reflected the discrimination in American life. A Middletown, Ohio, editor commented that Davis's career mirrored a mixed bag of changes, including progress on a small scale, but still "his promotion can scarcely be said to have touched off a trend." Other papers took the view that positive changes had occurred. One noted that rising from the rank of private to general would probably never occur again. For the most part, the press thought that Davis had accomplished much and had made "significant contributions to the cause of equality." However, many of these people did not understand the military and only used Davis's life to support their particular editorial positions.[2]

The first step toward an evaluation of Davis should be an understanding of the world in which he grew up. There were few opportunities for blacks to advance in Washington, D.C.; however, the Davis family had already begun to take advantage of every chance they received or made. By the time Benjamin was born, his father had risen into the ranks of the small black middle class. His government job provided him with a good income, and unlike most blacks, the Davis family owned its own home. Benjamin grew up in relative wealth, but his family's career aspirations for him were limited. For middle-class blacks, government jobs, teaching, or the clergy were highly esteemed occupations; the military was not. When, in 1898, Benjamin Davis entered the army with the idea of making it a career, he was stepping outside the current patterns in his social group: he was making himself even more of a minority.

As a member of an institution that was dominated by whites, Davis often had to cope with some form of prejudice or discrimination. His father provided an example of what to do. Louis Davis had to do a good job but at the same time show the proper deference to whites. This experience shaped Benjamin's philosophy on his career. As he himself said, his career was an effort "to show that I could make my way if I knew my job." By proving to the military community that he could do a job as well or better than a white man, he hoped that it would come to regard him as an equal and treat him that way. Furthermore, he would serve as an example of the capabilities of blacks and thereby would shape how the whites viewed and treated all black men.[3]

Davis's behavior when dealing with whites was reinforced by the army's protocol—deference to authority was a desirable trait for enlisted men and officers as well. One usually advanced in the military hierarchy by working within the system. Davis understood that active protest, such as that espoused by the Niagara Movement in 1905, never would have worked in the military. From the beginning he was willing to work through channels to remedy what he perceived as wrongs. An examination of his career at Wilberforce University or his attempts to reform the Liberian army are indicative of his character.

Another key element in his life was his isolation. Only when he was an enlisted man did he have a significant group of peers, and even here his educational attainments distinguished him from his fellows. Once he became an officer, he was isolated. Even after his marriage in the early twentieth century, the situation hardly changed. There were few black civilians in the rural areas where he served his first assignments. When he arrived at Wilberforce, he found more blacks, but his constant conflicts with the school's administrators made this association difficult. He could hardly establish roots because, like most army officers, he was soon assigned to another, distant post. Often his social group was limited to his own family, and he was quite lonely when they were not there, as was true during his second Philippine Island tour. As he gained more wealth through longevity, promotions, and frugality, the number of his black peers decreased. Friendships were difficult to maintain because of the relatively brief period he remained at any one site. While life in Cleveland and New York was quite varied, life in rural Ohio and Alabama, where he spent much of his time after 1920, was very restricted. Thus, racially, geographically, and socially, Benjamin Davis was often quite isolated.

Despite all this, the army provided a good life for this black man. He was encouraged by his fairly rapid advancement from lieutenant to major between 1901 and 1917. By the time the promotions slowed down, during the 1920s and 1930s, and it became clear that they were being influenced by nonobjective factors, Davis still felt that the army was his best career choice. The military provided a nice standard of living for Davis and his family. By the 1920s, Davis's income and way of life were far better than those of most black Americans, including his parents and siblings. During the ensuing depression this was even more the case. Few Americans were able to travel to Europe or to own their homes or an automobile; all this the Davis family did. The Davises were also able to provide their children with an excellent education. Davis believed that his career choice was a good one, whatever the consequent degree of isolation from black America.

There was also an element of luck in Davis's career development. As an enlisted man, Davis was fortunate to be assigned to the same post as the only black officer in the army, Charles Young. Young provided a role model and gave Davis assistance then and later in his career. The fact that John Green resigned in 1929 made Davis the only possible choice when the government went ahead with the Gold Star Mothers' Pilgrimages in the early 1930s. Governor Herbert Lehman's need to win black votes led to the assignment of Davis to the New York National Guard. Franklin Roosevelt's similar concerns in 1940 clearly led to Davis's promotion and the start of a new aspect of his career. In all of these instances, Davis's abilities allowed him to make the most of the opportunities that chance had provided him.

Benjamin Davis was a minority within a minority. As a black man, he was a member of the small middle class. Unlike many of them, he worked in an institution that was almost universally white. For many periods of his life he was physically separated from his black peer group, the middle class. As an officer, he was also isolated. Davis was excluded from the army's system of postgraduate education. This meant that he had little chance of obtaining a large-scale command. The army insisted that black officers should command only black troops and that they should never give orders to white officers. By the 1920s this meant that Lieutenant Colonel Davis would have to serve away from his cavalry unit. He knew from firsthand experience that racial equality did not exist in the army.

Background, occupation, economic status, race, and American life all helped to shape the man and officer that was Gen. Benjamin O. Davis. He knew what he could and could not do within the military system. He developed a certain way of coping with it, based on his own background, his personality, and the military structure itself. While outsiders viewed this behavior as deferential or even derogatorily as acquiescent, Davis realized that it was most suited to him and his situation.

Benjamin Davis made a number of contributions during his lifetime. In his early career he provided a role model for the black soldiers who served under him. Like Charles Young and John

Green, he showed the enlisted men that during a period of intense discrimination, some blacks could still succeed. He was the first military attaché to Liberia, and he continued the program of military education at Wilberforce and Tuskegee. During the 1920s and 1930s he made small contributions, although to the institutions he was involved in, these were important. The black community in Ohio had long sought a black National Guard unit, and the federal government's need to assign Davis to some position helped make this possible. The black Gold Star Mothers appreciated his assistance on the ocean voyages that were part of their pilgrimages. The New York black community was proud to have a black Regular Army officer commanding and instructing the 369th Infantry. However, if these had been the only accomplishments of Benjamin O. Davis's career, one would be correct in saying that he had done little.

The most significant part of Benjamin Davis's service occurred between 1941 and 1945. With his appointment as brigadier general, he showed that blacks could rise to high positions of authority and responsibility. His role in the Office of the Inspector General was significant. When he conducted an inspection or investigation, black soldiers and officers thought that his was a sympathetic ear and that they could speak frankly. Privately he tried to ameliorate the problems facing black soldiers and officers, and he worked with William Hastie and Truman Gibson to achieve an end to discrimination. In an indirect way the civilian aides and Davis reinforced one another. Davis was a quiet voice working from within the military hierarchy. The civilian aides, who were viewed as outsiders, were more vocal in their objections. In this situation, Davis and his views were seen as more acceptable, and they carried more weight with the army. From a long-term perspective, Davis helped to begin the erosion in the wall of segregation. Change, such as the partial integration experiment in the ETO at the end of the war or the wide distribution of *The Negro Soldier*, came about in some measure because of the activities of Benjamin Davis. It is unlikely that all the things that Davis accomplished could have been done without him. By example and effort, Davis did help to make World War II somewhat easier for the black people of the United States.[4]

It might be argued that Davis did not do as much as he could have done to fight the army's discriminatory policies. At times on the McCloy Committee he avoided confrontations, even after he had raised crucial issues. Yet not only would challenging the leadership have been out of character, given his background and experiences; it probably would also have been counterproductive. One only has to look at the career of William Hastie as a civilian aide to see the limited effectiveness of active protest. At that time in American history, there was little white support for civil rights. What Davis did was to help to lay the foundation for the integration of the armed forces, the first major break in the wall of segregated America. He would not have accomplished what he did by being a radical protester such as A. Philip Randolph.[5]

Davis's postwar contributions were limited by his advancing age and retirement, although his presence and comments kept the issue of segregation before the army. He served, in his small way, to help his hometown and the nation's war dead by his committee work. His desire for an ambassadorship to Liberia was not fulfilled, but he did show American concern during his visit in 1947.

Benjamin Davis was a unique individual. As a member of two minorities, he worked most of his life in isolation. In his own mind he was first of all an army officer, and then a black man. For the black community, he was first of all a black. These different viewpoints led to different approaches to problems, and Davis at times took positions that did not please other blacks. To the army, Davis was also a minority, and his points of view were ones that few other officers espoused. Davis's career followed a pattern different from that of most army officers of his generation. Despite the isolation, however, Davis persevered in his chosen occupation: he was proud to be an officer of the United States Army.

Benjamin O. Davis, Sr., did more than merely spend fifty years in the army and become the first black general. He served his country, and he accomplished things for America and for its black community. In doing his duty, he helped to improve the United States Army. Despite his isolation, he achieved a measure of success. The life of Benjamin O. Davis did prove that one could advance and achieve success by doing one's job to the best of one's ability.

Notes

ACRONYMS USED IN THE NOTES

ACP   Appointment, Commission and Promotion
AGO   Adjutant General's Office
ASD   Agatha S. Davis
BOD   Benjamin Oliver Davis
LC   Library of Congress
MID   Military Intelligence Division
NA   National Archives, Washington, D.C.
NAMP   National Archives Microfilm Publication
NYNG   New York National Guard
NYT   *New York Times*
OAG   Ohio Adjutant General
RG   Record Group
SD   Sadie Davis
WCRC   War College Record Card
WNRC   Washington National Records Center, Suitland, Md.

PROLOGUE: A MINORITY OF ONE

1. E. Franklin Frazier, *Black Bourgeoisie* (Chicago, Ill.: Free Press, 1957), pp. 195–212.
2. Ibid., pp. 213–228.
3. Morris Janowitz, *The Professional Soldier: A Social and Political Portrait* (New York: Free Press, 1960), pp. 79–123.
4. Ibid., pp. 125–149.

CHAPTER 1. THE EARLY YEARS: 1880–1898

1. United States, *Fifth Census: or, Enumeration of the Inhabitants of the United States, 1830* (Washington, D.C.: D. Green, 1832), p. 85; Benjamin O. Davis, "The Family Tree and Early Life," n.d., Benjamin O. Davis Papers (hereinafter cited as "Family Tree," which is a series

of unnumbered typewritten pages describing his life up to 1900); the Davis Papers are in the possession of Elnora Davis McLendon; interview, Elnora Davis McLendon with author, 2 May 1981 (hereinafter cited as McLendon 1981 interview); United States Census, 1860, District of Columbia, Georgetown, ward 4, p. 173, records of the Bureau of the Census, RG 29, NAMP M653 (hereinafter cited as 1860 Census); notification of Alexandria County Court, 25 June 1849, Davis Papers; interview, Benjamin O. Davis, Jr., and Agatha S. Davis with author, 23 May 1981 (hereinafter cited as BOD, Jr.–ASD 23 May 1981 interview); 1860 Census, District of Columbia, 1st ward, p. 176; William H. Boyd, comp., *Boyd's Directory of the District of Columbia* (Washington, D.C.: W. H. Boyd, 1858; hereinafter cited as Boyd, followed by the relevant dates); ibid., 1860–1871; 1860 Census, District of Columbia, Georgetown, ward 4, p. 173.

2. Statement by Addison Carter, 31 Jan. 1908, Addison Carter pension file, records of the Veterans Administration, RG 15, NA; Davis, "Family Tree;" United States Census, 1850, slave schedule, Virginia, Northumberland County, p. 359, RG 29, NAMP M432; David Carter, compiled military service record, records of the Adjutant General's Office, 1780s–1917, RG 94, NA; Addison Carter statement, 16 Mar. 1915, Addison Carter pension file; David Carter, compiled military service record; Addison Carter, compiled military service record, RG 94, NA; Hezekiah Carter, compiled military service record, RG 94, NA; Frederick H. Dyer, *A Compendium of the War of the Rebellion*, vol. 3: *Regimental Histories* (Des Moines, Iowa: Dyer Publishing Co., 1908), p. 1723; Hezekiah Carter, general affidavit, 1 May 1893, Hezekiah Carter pension file; and Addison Carter pension file; Daniel Stewart statement, 7 Sept. 1916, RG 15, NA.

3. Davis, "Family Tree;" United States Census, 1870, District of Columbia, ward 3, p. 141, RG 29, NAMP M593 (hereinafter cited as 1870 census); United States Census, 1880, District of Columbia, vol. 1, enumeration district 4, p. 21, RG 29, NAMP T9 (hereinafter cited as 1880 Census); United States Census, 1900, District of Columbia, enumeration district 63, p. 17, RG 29, NAMP T623 (hereinafter cited as 1900 Census); BOD, Jr.–ASD 23 May 1981 interview; Davis, "Family Tree;" Boyd, 1866–1870; Deposition of Charlotte Stewart, 8 Sept. 1916, Addison Carter pension file; 1870 Census, District of Columbia, 3d ward, p. 141, and 2d ward, p. 38.

4. Constance M. Green, *The Secret City: A History of Race Relations in the Nation's Capital* (Princeton, N.J.: Princeton University Press, 1967), pp. 58–60; James H. Whyte, *The Uncivil War: Washington during the Reconstruction, 1865–1878* (New York: Twayne Publishers, 1958), p. 31.

5. Green, *Secret City*, pp. 60–74; Whyte, *Uncivil War*, pp. 32–34, 49–57.

6. Green, *Secret City*, pp. 84–85, 87, 89.

7. Mrs. John A. Logan, *Reminiscences of a Soldier's Wife: An Autobiography* (New York: Charles Scribner's Sons, 1913), p. 322; Green B. Rarum to John A. Logan, 28 May 1880, John A. Logan Papers, Manuscript Division, LC; *Official Register of the United States, 1881* (Washington, D.C.: Government Printing Office, 1881).

8. McLendon 1981 interview; Davis, "Family Tree;" 1880 Census, District of Columbia, vol. 1, enumeration district 4, p. 21; Boyd, 1872–1880; return of live birth, District of Columbia, no. 23066.

9. 1880 Census, District of Columbia, vol. 1, enumeration district 4, p. 21; McLendon 1981 interview; *Official Register of the United States, 1883* (Washington, D.C.: Government Printing Office, 1883); Boyd, 1880–1897; interview, Elnora Davis McLendon with author, 3 Nov. 1973 (hereinafter cited as McLendon 1973 interview); 1900 Census, District of Columbia, enumeration district 50, p. 2; Davis, "Family Tree."

10. Green, *Secret City*, pp. 119–134.

11. Ibid., pp. 135–154; *Washington Post*, 13 Apr. 1981, sec. B, p. 3.

12. Davis, speech, Washington, D.C., 21 Feb. 1942, Davis Papers.

13. Davis, "Family Tree;" McLendon 1973 interview.

14. McLendon 1973 interview; Davis, "Family Tree."

15. Davis, "Family Tree."

16. Ibid.

17. Ibid.; Green, *Secret City*, p. 137; *Washington Post*, 13 Apr. 1981, sec. B, p. 3.

18. Davis, "Family Tree."

19. Ibid.

20. Ibid.; Davis to Adjutant General, 13 Feb. 1901, AGO document no. 368520, document file, 1890–1917, RG 94, NA.

21. Davis, "Family Tree;" Davis, speech, 21 Feb. 1942, Davis Papers; *Evening Star* (Washington, D.C.), 2 Apr. 1898.

22. Interview, Benjamin O. Davis, Sr., with author and Edward M. Coffman, 2 June 1968 (hereinafter cited as BOD, Sr., interview); McLendon 1981 interview.

23. Davis, "Family Tree."

24. Ibid.; *Evening Star*, 26 Mar. 1898.

25. *Evening Star*, 25 Apr. 1898; Davis, "Family Tree."

CHAPTER 2. A CAREER BEGINS: 1898–1901

1. Marvin Fletcher, "The Black Volunteers in the Spanish-American War," *Military Affairs* 38, 2 (Apr. 1974): 48–49.

2. Ibid., p. 39; Adjutant General to Eli Huggins, 31 May 1898, AGO.

3. Davis, "Family Tree;" physical examination, Benjamin Davis, 14

June 1898, and Adjutant General to Benjamin Davis, 27 June 1898, AGO no. 92823; Davis, "Family Tree."

4. Adjutant General to Huggins, 31 May 1898, muster roll, Eighth United States Volunteer Infantry, muster rolls of volunteer organizations: Spanish-American War, RG 94, NA (hereinafter records of the Eighth USVI in this group will be cited as 8th RR); Huggins to Adjutant General, 24 June and 2 July 1898, 8th RR; Davis, speech, 21 Feb. 1942, Davis Papers; Davis, "Family Tree;" Eighth USVI, muster in roll, 8th RR; Huggins to Adjutant General, 12 July 1898, AGO no. 123058. When Davis submitted his oath of allegiance, he changed his birthdate from 1880 to 1877, which would remain with him for the remainder of his career. Davis to Adjutant General, 21 July 1898, AGO no. 104913; McLendon 1981 interview; BOD, Sr., interview.

5. Huggins to Assistant Adjutant General, 10 July 1898, 8th RR.

6. Davis speech, 21 Feb. 1942, Davis Papers; Davis, "Family Tree."

7. Davis, "Family Tree."

8. Ibid.

9. Regimental special order no. 36, 26 Aug. 1898, and James Hepburn to Huggins, 25 Aug. 1898, 8th RR; Davis, "Family Tree."

10. General order no. 153, 1898, orders and circulars, RG 94, NA; Huggins to Adjutant General, 10 Nov. 1898, 8th RR; Huggins to Adjutant General, 11 Nov. 1898, AGO; Davis, "Family Tree."

11. Davis, "Family Tree."

12. Huggins to Adjutant General, 19 Oct. 1898, 8th RR; Davis, "Family Tree."

13. Nelson A. Miles to Adjutant General, 20 Feb. 1899, record and pension document file no. 614449, document file, 1889–1904, records of the Record and Pension Office, RG 94, NA (hereinafter cited as RP no. AGO).

14. Davis, "Family Tree;" Adjutant General to Huggins, 20 Feb. 1899, RP no. 614449 AGO; William Hughes to Adjutant General, 7 Mar. 1899; Secretary of War to Attorney General, 9 Mar. 1899, RP no. 614449 AGO.

15. Davis, "Family Tree;" Huggins to Cushman Davis, 7 Feb. 1899, AGO appointment no. 1812 ACP 79; William Hughes to Adjutant General, 7 Mar. 1899, AGO.

16. *Washington Bee*, 25 Mar. 1899; Davis, "Family Tree."

17. Davis to Adjutant General, 28 Mar. 1899, AGO no. 235363; Shelby Cullom to Adjutant General, 5 May 1899, AGO no. 234082; Mrs. John A. Logan to William McKinley, 9 June 1899, AGO no. 368520.

18. Davis, "Family Tree." Proctor's residence in Washington was about twenty blocks from that of Davis. Muster out papers, 8th USVI, AGO no. 293145.

19. Sumner to Adjutant General, 30 Jan. 1899, AGO; "Case of John C. Proctor and Benjamin O. Davis," 12 June 1899, AGO no. 244608.

20. Davis, "Family Tree."

21. Ibid.; the description of the post was taken from plans found in records of the Office of the Chief of Engineers, RG 77, NA.

22. Ninth Cavalry return, Sept. 1899, returns from Regular Army cavalry regiments, 1833–1916, RG 94, NAMP M744 (hereinafter cited by using the number of the regiment and the date of the return). There were four black units in the army at this time: Ninth Cavalry, Tenth Cavalry, Twenty-fourth Infantry, and Twenty-fifth Infantry. With one exception, all of the officers were white, and all of the enlisted men were black. The exception was Charles Young, a black officer.; Ninth Cavalry return, Dec. 1899 and July 1900.

23. Davis, "Family Tree;" Davis, speech to 369th Infantry officers, NYNG, 26 Sept. 1940, Davis Papers.

24. Davis, "Family Tree."

25. Ibid.; BOD, Sr., interview.

26. Davis, "Family Tree;" Mrs. John Logan to Capt. John Guilfoyle, 14 June 1899, Davis Papers; BOD, Sr., interview; James F. Cave to Benjamin O. Davis, Jr., 21 July 1945, ETO 1945 correspondence file, Davis Papers (these are labeled file folders included in the Davis Papers; hereinafter they are cited as Davis files).

27. Cave to Benjamin O. Davis, Jr., 21 July 1945, ETO 1945 correspondence file, Davis files; Davis, "Family Tree;" Charles Young to Adjutant General, 10 May 1900, AGO.

28. Mrs. John A. Logan to Col. Thomas McGregor, 14 June 1899, Davis Papers; Davis to Adjutant General, 13 Feb. 1901, AGO no. 368520; Huggins to Adjutant General, 30 Aug. 1899, AGO no. 271666; Davis to Adjutant General, 26 Aug. 1899, no. 271225; Davis to Mrs. Logan, 17 Sept. 1899, Davis Papers; Mrs. Logan to Col. Duvall, n.d., Davis Papers. It should be noted that in "Family Tree," Davis wrote that he did not apply for a volunteer commission.

29. Davis, "Family Tree;" BOD, Sr., interview. During this interview, Davis repeatedly stated that the soldiers had told him that blacks should not apply for a commission.

30. Marvin E. Fletcher, *The Black Soldier and Officer in the United States Army, 1891–1917* (Columbia: University of Missouri Press, 1974), pp. 72–74; Bruce J. Dinges, "Court-Martial of Lieutenant Henry O. Flipper," *American West* 9, 1 (Jan. 1972): 13–17, 59–60.

31. Charles Young to Davis, 28 Aug. 1905, Davis Papers; Davis to Maj. Gen. Orlando Ward, 31 Aug. 1950, speech file, Davis files.

32. Martin Hughes to Adjutant General, 8 Feb. 1901, AGO no. 368520; Charles Young letter, 26 Jan. 1901, and Davis to Louis Davis, 9 Feb. 1901, Davis Papers; for an example of a letter of recommendation see Walter F. Halleck to Adjutant General, 25 Feb. 1901, AGO no. 364455.

33. Davis, "Family Tree;" Jesse M. Lee to Adjutant General, 16 Mar. 1901, AGO no. 368516.

34. Davis's competitive examination for second lieutenant, 25 Feb.-12 Mar. 1901, AGO no. 368520.

35. Ibid.; Davis, "Family Tree."

36. Davis, competitive examination, 1901, AGO no. 368520; Lee to Adjutant General, 16 Mar. 1901, AGO no. 368516; Davis, "Family Tree."

37. *Washington Bee*, 30 Mar. and 6 Apr. 1901; BOD, Sr., interview; Davis, "Family Tree."

38. Fletcher, *Black Soldier*, pp. 74-75.

39. General order no. 90, series of 1900, AGO; Davis, "Family Tree."

40. Davis, "Family Tree;" Ninth Cavalry return, May 1901; Davis to Adjutant General, 19 May 1901, AGO no. 379726.

CHAPTER 3. TRIUMPHS AND TRAGEDIES: 1901-1920

1. Davis, "Family Tree;" BOD, Sr., interview; Davis, report of expedition to Villa Real and Tolalora, Samar, 31 May 1901, file no. 10759, Department of Visayas, general correspondence, Jan.-Nov. 1901, records of U.S. Army overseas operations and commands, 1898-1942, RG 395, NA.

2. Davis, physical examination, 18 Apr. 1947, Benjamin O. Davis, Sr., 201 file, National Personnel Records Center, St. Louis, Mo. (hereinafter cited as Davis 201 file).

3. Davis, "Family Tree."

4. Benjamin Davis, efficiency report, 1901-1902, AGO; U.S., Congress, House of Representatives, House Document no. 2, vol. 9: *Report of the Lieutenant-General Commanding the Army and Department Commanders, 1902*, 57th Cong., 2d sess., 1902-1903, pp. 386-387; Benjamin Davis, individual service report, 1900-1901, AGO; Tenth Cavalry return, Aug. and Sept. 1901; Davis to Adjutant General, Fifth Separate Brigade, 28 Feb. 1902, file no. 960, Department of Visayas, general correspondence, Dec. 1901-Sept. 1902, RG 395, NA (hereinafter cited as Visayas 1902); Tenth Cavalry return, Dec. 1901 and Mar. 1902.

5. AGO to Quartermaster, 12 May 1905, AGO no. 981227.

6. Tenth Cavalry return, Aug. 1902; Fort Washakie return, Aug. and Dec. 1902.

7. Fort Washakie return, Apr. 1904 and Sept. 1902.

8. BOD, Sr., interview; Fort Washakie return, Oct. 1903; Tenth Cavalry return, Oct. 1903 and Nov. 1902.

9. *Washington Bee*, 18 Oct. 1902; McLendon 1973 interview.

10. 1880 Census, District of Columbia, vol. 4, enumeration district

30, p. 122; Boyd, 1871–1897; 1877 tax book, District of Columbia, records of the government of the District of Columbia, RG 351, NA; BOD, Jr.–ASD 23 May 1981 interview.

11. Benjamin Davis to Adjutant General, 1 Aug. 1902, AGO no. 448823; the adjutant general's response is the seventh endorsement, 21 Aug. 1902, AGO no. 448823; Adjutant General to Secretary of War Taft, Jan. 1905, AGO no. 967143.

12. Thomas Carson to Adjutant General, 1903, AGO no. 480328; Fort Washakie return, Sept. 1903; Benjamin Davis, individual service report, 1903–1904, AGO; Benjamin Davis, efficiency report, 1904, AGO.

13. Thomas Carson to Commanding Officer, Fort Robinson, 7 May 1904, AGO no. 533040; Davis, individual service report, July 1904–June 1906, AGO; Thomas Carson to Adjutant General, 18 May 1903, AGO no. 487775.

14. Special order no. 108, Department of Colorado, general orders, special orders, and circulars, records of U.S. Army Continental Commands, 1821–1920, RG 393, NA (hereinafter records from this group are cited by the name of the command); Davis, "Family Tree;" general order no. 27, 25 July 1903, Department of Colorado.

15. Proceedings of a board of officers convened at Fort Robinson, Nebr., 13 May 1904, AGO no. 533040; Adjutant General to Thomas Carson, 24 Feb. 1905, AGO no. 979736; proceedings of a board of officers convened at Fort Washakie, 21 and 28 Feb. 1905, AGO no. 992510.

16. Davis to Adjutant General, 17 Mar. 1905, AGO no. 995948; memo, Adjutant General, 3 Apr. 1905, AGO no. 996953; Fort Robinson return, Apr. and Aug. 1905.

17. William Scarborough, "Wilberforce University in the Army," n.d., in Scarborough Papers, Wilberforce University Archives (hereinafter cited as Scarborough Papers); for examples of Wilberforce's attempt to obtain Davis see Horace Talbert to Adjutant General, 16 Dec. 1903, AGO no. 512339; Adjutant General to Talbert, 18 Dec. 1903, and Talbert to Adjutant General, 22 Dec. 1903, AGO no. 512339; Talbert to Adjutant General, 26 June 1905, AGO no. 1031313.

18. BOD, Sr., interview; McLendon 1973 interview; Charles Young to Davis, 5 May and 28 Aug. 1905, Davis Papers.

19. Charles Young to Davis, 5 May and 28 Aug. 1905; Benjamin Davis to Adjutant General, 17 Aug. 1908; and goods leaving from Wilberforce, July 1909––all in Davis Papers.

20. Davis to Military Secretary, 3 Oct. 1906, Davis Papers; Davis to Adjutant General, 3 Apr. 1908, AGO no. 1298176; Davis, efficiency report, 1906, AGO; Davis, individual service report, July 1907–June 1908, AGO; Davis, individual service report, July 1904–June 1906, AGO.

21. Davis to Adjutant General, 3 Oct. 1906, AGO no. 1171020; Adjutant General to Davis, 9 Oct. 1906, AGO.

22. Davis to Adjutant General, 16 Oct. 1906, Davis Papers; Chief of Staff memo to Secretary of War, 20 Oct. 1906, Adjutant General to Davis, 24 Oct. 1906, Adjutant General to Joshua Jones, 24 Oct. 1906, and Joshua Jones to Secretary of War, 26 Oct. 1906—all in AGO no. 1171020; Davis to Adjutant General, 3 Apr. 1908, AGO no. 1298176.

23. *Cleveland Gazette*, 30 June 1906; BOD, Sr., interview.

24. Secretary of War to Davis, 12 Dec. 1908, Davis Papers; Davis, efficiency report, 1909, AGO; Davis, individual service report, July 1906–June 1907, AGO; Davis, paper "Military Training in Civil Schools," Davis Papers.

25. BOD, Sr., interview; *Cleveland Gazette*, 11 May 1907, 22 and 29 June 1907.

26. Davis to Adjutant General, 5 June 1906, AGO no. 1136220; Chief of Staff to Davis, 9 July 1906, AGO no. 1145941; instruction circular no. 4, Camp Roosevelt, Aug. 1906, Davis Papers; Davis to Adjutant General, 6 Aug. 1906, AGO no. 1154557; Commanding General, District of Columbia Militia, to Adjutant General, 2 June 1908, AGO no. 1386889; Davis to Adjutant General, 20 Aug. 1908, AGO no. 1416833; Davis, individual service report, July 1908–June 1909, AGO; Davis to Adjutant General, 11 May 1909, AGO no. 1522513; Commanding General, District of Columbia Militia, to Adjutant General, 29 May 1909, AGO no. 1529732; Davis to Adjutant General, 4 Nov. 1909, Davis Papers; Ernest Harris to Adjutant General, 26 Aug. 1909, AGO no. 1559663.

27. Davis to Adjutant General, 15 Apr. 1908, and Joshua Jones to Adjutant General, 23 April 1908, AGO no. 1368436.

28. Davis to William Scarborough, 15 Jan. 1909, Davis Papers; BOD, Sr., interview; Scarborough to Secretary of War, 20 Jan. 1909, and Scarborough to Adjutant General, 26 Jan. 1909, AGO no. 1478800.

29. Ninth Cavalry return, Dec. 1909.

30. Fletcher, *Black Soldiers*, p. 92; newspaper clipping, Apr. 1909, sent by Emmett J. Scott to William H. Taft, William H. Taft Papers, Manuscript Division, LC; Ernest Lyon to Secretary of War, 20 Nov. 1909, AGO no. 92823; Ernest Lyon to Benjamin Davis, 20 Nov. 1909, Davis Papers; Davis to Adjutant General, 2d endorsement, Lyon to Secretary of War, 25 Nov. 1909, AGO no. 92823.

31. Davis to Lester Walton, 20 Feb. 1937, 121.5482/21, State Department decimal file, 1930–1939, general records of the Department of State, RG 59, NA (hereinafter cited as State decimal file, 1930–1939); memo from J. Franklin Bell to Adjutant General, 29 Nov. 1909, AGO no. 92823.

32. Matthew Hanna to Davis, 13 Dec. 1909, Davis Papers; Henry D. Todd, Jr., to Davis, 23 Dec. 1909, file no. 5797, War College Division,

general correspondence, 1903-1919, RG 165, NA (hereinafter cited as War College correspondence); Secretary of State to Secretary of War, 11 Jan. 1910, 1729/131, numerical and minor files of the Department of State, 1906-1910, RG 59, NAMP M862; Davis, individual service report, July 1909-June 1910, AGO no. 92823; Davis to War Department, 25 Apr. 1910, Davis Papers.

33. Davis to Andrew G. Lynch, 2 June 1947, Liberia 1947 file, Davis files; Davis to Quartermaster General, 27 Dec. 1909, record card no. 5816, record cards to the correspondence of the War College Division and related General Staff and Adjutant General Offices, 1902-1919, records of the War Department General and Special Staffs, RG 165, NAMP M1023 (hereinafter cited as WCRC with number); Davis to Quartermaster General, 27 Dec. 1909 and 7 Jan. 1910, WCRC no. 5816; Davis to War Department, July 1910, WCRC no. 5815; Davis to Quartermaster General, 15 Feb. 1911, and Quartermaster General to Davis, 11 Mar. 1911, WCRC no. 5816; Davis to War Department, 25 Nov. 1910, and War Department to Davis, 29 Dec. 1910, WCRC no. 5815.

34. McLendon 1973 interview; Davis to War Department General Staff, 23 Jan. 1911, Liberia file, Davis files.

35. Davis, efficiency report, 1911, AGO no. 92823; Davis to War Department, June 1910, WCRC no. 6041; Davis to War Department, 8 Nov. 1910, WCRC no. 5797; Davis to War Department, 31 Dec. 1910 and 20 Feb. 1915, and Davis, "The Military Forces of Liberia," report, 12 Oct. 1911, War College correspondence; W. B. Fletcher to Davis, 8 May 1910, Liberia file, Davis files; Davis to American Minister, 11 May 1910, WCRC no. 5796; Ernest Lyon to Davis, 6 Sept. 1910, AGO no. 92823.

36. Davis to Secretary of State, Liberia, 13 Feb. 1911, F. E. R. Johnson to Davis, 5 Apr. 1911, and Davis to Secretary of State, Liberia, 6 Apr. 1911, Liberia file, Davis files; Davis to War College Division, 6 Apr. 1911, 121.5/193, State Department decimal file, 1910-1929, RG 59, NA (hereinafter cited as State decimal file, 1910-1929); Philander Knox to Crum, 25 May 1911, 882.20/-, records of Department of State relating to internal affairs of Liberia, 1910-1929, RG 59, NAMP M613 (hereinafter cited as Liberia 1910-1929); memo, Leonard Wood to Secretary of War, 18 May 1911, AGO no. 1783949.

37. Davis to War Department, 14 July 1911, WCRC no. 5787; J. D. Leith to Davis, 16 Aug. 1911, and Davis to Secretary of State, Liberia, 12 Sept. 1911, Liberia file, Davis files; War Department to Davis, 13 Oct. 1911, WCRC no. 5787; R. O. Bailey to Adjutant General, 16 Nov. 1911, AGO no. 1850170; Davis to War Department, 16 Oct. 1911, WCRC no. 5787.

38. Davis, physical examination, 1912, AGO no. 1449814; War Department to Davis, 28 Dec. 1911, WCRC no. 5787; Davis to Adjutant General,

26 Dec. 1911, AGO no. 1858681; Charles Young to Davis, 4 Jan. 1912, Liberia file, Davis files; Davis to Matthew Hanna, 21 Dec. 1911, Davis Papers; S. J. Steinmetz to Adjutant General, 18 Dec. 1916, AGO no. 92823; Davis to Hanna, 21 Dec. 1911, Davis Papers; Davis to F. H. Holland, 20 Oct. 1942, miscellaneous file, Davis files.

39. Ninth Cavalry return, Dec. 1911 and Jan. 1912; Fort D. A. Russell return, Jan. 1912.

40. Ninth Cavalry return, Feb. and Mar. 1912; Davis physical examinations, 1912 and 1913, AGO no. 1449814.

41. Fletcher, *Black Soldier*, p. 53; Davis, efficiency report, 1913, AGO no. 92823.

42. For examples see Ninth Cavalry returns, Dec. 1912 and Feb., May, and June 1913.

43. Davis to Thomas E. White, 20 May 1950, speech file, Davis files; notes to statement of 1948 on postwar army, secret file, Davis files; Harry Wheeler to Adjutant General, 2 Oct. 1912, AGO.

44. Davis to Norman Witkin, 9 Jan. 1948, Davis Papers; Davis to Adjutant General, 27 Jan. 1919, Philippine Islands 1917–1920 file, Davis files.

45. Davis, efficiency reports, 1914 and 1915, AGO no. 92823; "Proceedings of a Board of Officers, Convened at Douglas, Arizona, 1915, in the case of 1st Lieutenant Benjamin O. Davis," AGO no. 2263390.

46. Scarborough to Woodrow Wilson, 23 May 1914, War Department to Scarborough, 22 May 1914, and Secretary of War to Simon D. Fess, 25 July 1914, AGO no. 2168314; Scarborough to Chief of Staff, 31 July 1914, AGO no. 2194339.

47. Davis to Adjutant General, 2 Mar. 1916, AGO no. 2374347; *Cleveland Gazette*, 20 Mar. 1915; Davis, efficiency report, 1916, AGO no. 92828.

48. Davis to Chief of Cavalry, 10 Oct. 1920, miscellaneous file, Davis files; McLendon 1973 interview.

49. McLendon 1973 interview; 1880 Census, Mississippi, Noxubee County, vol. 16, enumeration district 31, p. 73; Buford Satcher, "Blacks in Mississippi Politics, 1865–1900" (Ph.D. diss., Oklahoma State University, 1976), p. 260; 1900 Census, Mississippi, Noxubee County, vol. 38, enumeration district 67, p. 18; Sadie Davis, application for teaching certificate in Ohio, Davis Papers; Benjamin O. Davis, Jr.–Agatha S. Davis, interview, 30 May 1981 (hereinafter cited as BOD, Jr.–ASD 30 May 1981 interview).

50. Davis to Adjutant General, 22 Jan. 1917, and W. H. Simons to Commanding General, Central Department, 11 Feb. 1917, AGO no. 2524659.

51. William Scarborough to Adjutant General, 28 Feb. 1917; Scarborough, complaint against Capt. B. O. Davis, n.d.; W. H. Simons to Adjutant General, 8th endorsement, 5 Mar. 1917; Adjutant General to Chief of Staff, 10th endorsement, 14 Mar. 1917—all in AGO no. 2524659.

52. Bernard C. Nalty, *Strength for the Fight: A History of Black Americans in the Military* (New York: Free Press, 1986), pp. 102–106.

53. R. Evans to Adjutant General, 26 Sept. 1917, Davis 201 file; Adjutant General to Evans, 9 Nov. 1917, Scarborough Papers; Commander, Department of the Philippines, to Adjutant General, 8 July 1918, 3d endorsement, Davis to Commander, Department of the Philippines, 29 June 1918, Davis 201 file; Eli Huggins to Adjutant General, 4 Mar. 1918, miscellaneous correspondence file, Davis files.

54. Ninth Cavalry, military histories of officers, 1898–1919, records of the U.S. Regular Army mobile units, 1821–1942, RG 391, NA (hereinafter cited as Ninth Cavalry histories); general orders no. 19, Headquarters Ninth Cavalry, 11 May 1919, and Davis to Commanding Officer, Ninth Cavalry, 18 Jan. 1918, Philippine Islands 1917–1920 file, Davis files; Davis to Howard Snyder, 11 Jan. 1953, speech file, Davis files; Davis, efficiency report, 1917, AGO no. 92823.

55. Davis, "Cavalry in the Present War," Davis Papers; memo, Davis to Commanding Officer, Ninth Cavalry, 31 Aug. 1918, Philippine Islands 1917–1920 file, Davis files.

56. Davis to Maj. Daniel Day, 22 Jan. 1947, and Davis to Sadie Overton, 12 July 1919, Davis Papers.

57. Davis to Sadie Overton, 12, 17, and 18 July 1919, Davis Papers; Davis to Quartermaster General, 5 Aug. 1919, Philippine Islands 1917–1920 file, Davis files.

58. Davis to Sadie Overton, 26 June 1919, Davis Papers; interview, Benjamin O. Davis, Jr., with author, 8 Aug. 1972 (hereinafter cited as BOD, Jr., 1972 interview); Davis, efficiency report, 1920, Davis 201 file; Davis to Sadie Overton, 15 July and 29 June 1919, Davis Papers.

59. Department Adjutant to Commanding Officer, Camp Stotsenburg, 2 Dec. 1919, Ninth Cavalry histories; Department Adjutant to Davis, 18 Feb. 1920, and Davis to Commanding Officer, Department of the Philippines, 16 Feb. 1920, Davis Papers; Davis to Commanding Officer, Department of the Philippines, 21 Sept. 1919, miscellaneous correspondence file, Davis files; special orders no. 74, Department of the Philippines, 29 Mar. 1920, Ninth Cavalry histories; Davis to Sylvester W. Booker, 22 Oct. 1946, 1946 file, Davis files.

60. BOD, Jr.–ASD 23 May 1981 interview.

CHAPTER 4. A HOLDING PATTERN: 1920-1940

1. National Defense Act of 1920, secs. 40 and 55c; memo, Assistant Director, War Plans Division to Adjutant General, file 062.12 ROTC, central decimal file, 1917-1925, records of the Adjutant General's Office, 1917-, RG 407, NA (files in this group are hereinafter cited by number, followed by AGO 1917-1925); memo for Chief of Staff: commissioned personnel for duty with the Reserve Officers' Training Corps, 10 Nov. 1923, file 000.862 ROTC, AGO 1917-1925; "Course of Instruction and Training for Junior Units of the Reserve Officers' Training Corps Established in Schools and Preparatory Departments Other Than Essentially Military Schools," Davis Papers; circular 65, 10 Dec. 1920, Fourth Corps Area, general correspondence, file 000.7, records of U.S. Army Continental Commands, 1920-1942, RG 394, WNRC; "Courses of Study in the Infantry Units of the Reserve Officers' Training Corps," file 000.862 6-2-23-II, AGO 1917-1925.

2. Davis to Robert R. Moton, 3 Aug. 1920, Robert R. Moton Papers, Tuskegee Institute Archives; Davis to Moton, 19 and 6 Aug. 1920, Davis Papers; *Tuskegee Student*, 8 Oct. 1921; McLendon 1973 interview.

3. Davis, "Outlook for the ROTC," *Tuskegee Student*, 27 Nov. 1920; Regulation of ROTC, 192__, and Davis to Commandant of Cadets, 16 Nov. 1920, Moton Papers.

4. David Shanks to Davis, 17 Apr. 1923, Moton Papers; *Tuskegee Student*, 15 May 1923; Shanks to Moton, 24 May 1923, Moton Papers.

5. Moton to Davis, 17 Jan. 1921, Davis Papers; Moton to Davis, 22 Jan. 1921, Moton Papers; report, 1921 inspection, Tuskegee file, Davis files; report, 1920-1921 inspection, 14 Feb. 1921, file 000.862 Tuskegee, AGO 1917-1925.

6. *Tuskegee Student*, 27 Nov. and 25 Dec. 1920.

7. McLendon 1973 interview; BOD, Jr.-ASD 30 May 1981 interview; McLendon 1973 interview; BOD, Jr., 1972 interview; McLendon 1973 interview.

8. BOD, Jr., 1972 interview; McLendon 1973 interview.

9. BOD, Jr., 1972 interview; McLendon 1973 interview.

10. McLendon 1973 interview; *Tuskegee Student*, 17 Dec. 1921 and 15 May 1923.

11. Davis to Moton, 12 Apr. 1922, Moton Papers; Davis, physical examination for promotion, 5 Jan. 1920, and physical examination, May 1923, Davis 201 file; BOD, Jr., 1972 interview; R. B. Parrott to Davis, 12 Mar. 1924, miscellaneous correspondence file, Davis files; McLendon 1973 interview; Davis, physical examination, 1924, Davis 201 file.

12. Pete Daniel, "Black Power in the 1920s: The Case of the Tuskegee

Veterans Hospital," *Journal of Southern History* 36 (Aug. 1970): 368–388; BOD, Jr.–ASD 23 May 1981 interview.

13. Davis to Adjutant General, 22 Feb. 1922, miscellaneous file, Davis files; Moton to R. B. Parrott, Fourth Corps, 27 Apr. 1922, Davis Papers.

14. Garnet Wilkinson to Davis, 28 June 1922, Davis Papers; Davis to Harrison Hall, 2 July 1922, and H. G. Bishop to Moton, 10 July 1922, miscellaneous file, Davis files.

15. Wilkinson to Davis, 1 Sept. 1922, Emmett Scott to Davis, 14 Sept. 1922, and Wilkinson to Davis, 2 Oct. 1922, miscellaneous file, Davis files.

16. Moton to Shanks, 28 May 1923, and sixth endorsement, M. H. McRae, 25 June 1923, file 000.862 Tuskegee, AGO 1917–1925.

17. Davis to Edward Burr, 27 June 1923, miscellaneous file, Davis files; handwritten note on W. R. Smedberg, Jr., memo for Assistant Chief of Staff, G-1, 5 July 1923, file 000.862 Tuskegee, AGO 1917–1925.

18. Wall to Baltzell, 11 Jan. 1924, Weeks to Slemp, 22 Jan. 1924, and Sixth Corps to Adjutant General, 24 Jan. 1924, Davis 201 file; see also Fifth Corps to Adjutant General, 26 Jan. 1924, and David Shanks to Adjutant General, 31 Jan. 1924, ibid.; Whipple to M. Romer, 1 Feb. 1924, ibid.

19. Wilkinson to Adjutant General, 11 Feb. 1924, Liberia 1947 file, Davis files; Adjutant General to Wilkinson, 14 Feb. 1924, Davis Papers; Wilkinson to Davis, 19 Feb. 1924, Liberia 1947 file, Davis files; Moton to Slemp, 24 Feb. 1924, John Weeks to Slemp, 6 Mar. 1924, and Robert Davis to Secretary of War, 6 June 1924, Davis 201 file.

20. Lowell D. Black, *The Negro Volunteer Militia Units of the Ohio National Guard, 1870-1954: The Struggle for Military Recognition and Equality in the State of Ohio* (Manhattan, Kans.: Military Affairs/Aerospace Historian Publishing, 1976), pp. 269, 280, 289, 307; John Weeks to James W. Johnson, 2 June 1921, NAACP Papers; *Gazette*, 5 Apr. 1924; Elijah Reynolds, "The Negro and Preparedness," NAACP Papers; Ohio National Guard, 1924, records of the National Guard Bureau, RG 168, WNRC (hereinafter cited as NG records).

21. *National Guard Regulation Number 40*, 1 Apr. 1927, sec. 6, Publications of the U.S. Government, RG 287, WNRC; BOD, Jr.–ASD 23 May 1981 interview; memo, relationship of federal government and its agencies to the National Guard, 13 May 1925, file 325.5, AGO 1917–1925; special course of instruction for officers detailed for duty as instructors of the National Guard, file 210.651, AGO 1917–1925.

22. *Gazette*, 2 Nov. 1924; McLendon 1973 interview; BOD, Jr.–ASD 30 May 1981 interview; Kenneth L. Kusmer, *A Ghetto Takes Shape: Black Cleveland, 1870-1930* (Urbana: University of Illinois Press, 1976), p. 183; letters from Elnora McLendon to author, 11 Aug. 1981 and 11 May 1982.

23. McLendon 1973 interview; Kusmer, *Ghetto Takes Shape*, pp. 149–151; McLendon 1973 interview.

24. BOD, Jr.–ASD 23 May 1981 interview; Davis to W. P. Dabney, 4 Mar. 1947, Davis Papers; Robert L. Daugherty, "Citizen Soldiers in Peace: The Ohio National Guard, 1919–1940" (Ph.D. diss., Ohio State University, 1974), p. 127; BOD, Jr.–ASD 23 May 1981 interview; general orders no. 10, 4 May 1925, and no. 12, 10 May 1925, and special order no. 142, 8 June 1925, records of the Ohio Adjutant General, Ohio Historical Society, Columbus (hereinafter cited as OAG); *Gazette*, 11 July 1925.

25. *Gazette*, 22 Nov. 1924; Secretary of War to Wilkinson, 10 July 1925, and Wilkinson to Secretary of War, 21 Apr. 1925 and 16 Mar. 1926, Davis 201 file.

26. Gilbert to OAG, 30 June 1928, and Davis to Frank Henderson, 13 July 1928, miscellaneous file, Davis files; OAG to Militia Bureau, 30 June 1928, and 3d endorsement, Adjutant General, Gilbert to OAG, 30 June 1928, Davis 201 file.

27. Davis to Adjutant General, 13 Mar. 1929, and Adjutant General to Commander, Fifth Corps Area, 1929, Davis 201 file; Moton to Herbert Hoover, 6 June 1929, and Secretary of War to Moton, 20 June 1929, file 000.862 Tuskegee, central decimal file, 1926–1939, RG 407, NA (hereinafter files in this group are cited by the number, followed by AGO 1926–1939).

28. *Historical Statistics of the United States, Colonial Times to 1970* (Washington, D.C.: Government Printing Office, 1975), p. 299; McLendon 1973 interview.

29. BOD, Jr.–ASD 30 May 1981 interview; McLendon 1973 interview.

30. *Forcean, 1929*, p. 70, Wilberforce Archives; Benjamin Davis to Sadie Davis, 31 Mar. 1945, Davis Papers (hereinafter similar letters in the Davis papers will be cited as BOD to SD, followed by the date); Davis to Moton, 17 Mar. 1930, Moton Papers; Robert Whitehead to Adjutant General, 23 May 1930, file 000.8 ROTC (5-23-30), AGO 1926–1939; report of 1930, historical reports, general administrative file, 1921–1932, file 319.1, Fifth Corps Area, RG 394, WNRC; *Defender* (Chicago), 7 Dec. 1929; *New York Times*, 1 Mar. 1930 (hereinafter cited as *NYT*); *Defender*, 15 Mar. 1930. For another comment see *Gazette*, 8 Mar. 1930.

31. For an example see U.S., Congress, Senate, *A Bill to Enable the Mothers and Unmarried Widows of the Deceased Soldiers, Sailors, and Marines of the American Forces Interred in the Cemeteries of Europe to Make a Pilgrimage to These Cemeteries*, S. 5332, 70th Cong., 2d sess., 1928–1929; Public Law 952, 70th Cong.

32. Oscar DePriest to Hoover, 16 Apr. 1930, file 516, Pilgrimage Gold Star, records of the Office of Quartermaster General, RG 92, WNRC (hereinafter cited as pilgrimage file); *Defender*, 7 June 1930; *New York*

Amsterdam News, 11 June 1930 (hereinafter cited as *Amsterdam News*);
DeWitt to Diary, 29 Apr. 1930, pilgrimage file.

33. Report of the Quartermaster General—pilgrimage of mothers and
widows to the cemeteries in Europe, 2 Mar. 1929 and 30 June 1931, pilgrimage file, p. 38; Chief of Cavalry to Adjutant General, 27 Feb. 1930,
file 516, AGO 1926–1939; Davis to Moton, 17 Mar. 1930, Moton Papers;
Moton to Hurley, 28 Mar. 1930, pilgrimage file; Davis to Moton, 20 Apr.
1930, Moton Papers.

34. Davis to A. E. Williams, 12 May 1930, and Williams to Davis,
15 May 1930, Davis 201 file, miscellaneous file 1922–1936, RG 92,
WNRC (hereinafter cited as misc. file).

35. *Cleveland Gazette*, 5 July 1930; *New York Herald Tribune*, 12 July
1930, quoted in pilgrimage file.

36. BOD, Jr.-ASD 23 May 1981 interview; supervisor, Suresnes Cemetery, file 032.2 U.S. Senators, misc. file; report on the activities in Europe
of the American pilgrimage, Gold Star mothers and widows, 1930, file
319.1, reports of conducting officers, misc. file; *Amsterdam News*, 13
Aug. 1930.

37. *Amsterdam News*, 13 Aug. 1930; *Cleveland Gazette*, 23 Aug. 1930;
special order no. 88, pilgrimage file.

38. Rodney A. Ross, "Black Americans and Haiti, Liberia, the Virgin
Islands, and Ethiopia, 1929–1936 (Ph.D. diss., University of Chicago,
1975), pp. 96–97; memo, R. C. Foy to Gilbert, 21 Apr. 1930, file 121.5482/6,
and memo, 24 Apr. 1930, file 121.5482/7, Liberian military attaché, main
decimal file, 1930–1939; memo, Arthur Walsh to Military Attaché and
Foreign Liaison Section, 25 Apr. 1930, file 2257-zz-103, Military Intelligence Division, 1920s–1930s, RG 165, NA (hereinafter cited as MID);
memo, Gilbert to Carr, 6 May 1930, file 121.5432/4, main decimal file,
1930–1939.

39. Stimson to Hurley, 21 May 1930, file 121.5482/4a, main decimal
file, 1930–1939.

40. Memorandum, 6 June 1930, file 121.5482/4a, main decimal file,
1930–1939; Davis to Kroner, 30 Sept. 1930, miscellaneous file, Davis
files; Moton to Secretary of War, 1 Oct. 1930, Moton to Hoover, 18 Oct.
1930, Moton to Newton, 7 Nov. 1930, Hurley to Newton, 15 Nov. 1930,
and Newton to Hurley, 22 Nov. 1930, file 000.862 Tuskegee, AGO 1926–
1939; Payne to Secretary of State, 6 Dec. 1930, file 121.5482/13, main
decimal file, 1930–1939.

41. BOD, Jr., 1972 interview; McLendon 1973 interview; *Defender*,
18 Jan. 1930; *NYT*, 22 Nov. 1930; telephone interview, Benjamin O.
Davis, Jr., with author, 24 Nov. 1987 (hereinafter cited as BOD, Jr., 1987
interview).

42. Davis to Moton, 17 Dec. 1930, Moton Papers.

43. DePriest to Hurley, 3 Mar. 1931, Spencer Dickerson to National Guard Bureau, 13 Feb. 1931, and Hurley to DePriest, 9 Mar. 1931, Davis 201 file; Davis to F. H. Pope, 10 Apr. 1931, Davis 201 file, misc. file.

44. Mary E. Williams to Pope, 28 July 1931, file 513, misc. file.

45. McLendon 1973 interview; Davis to Moton, 2 July 1931, Moton Papers; McLendon 1981 interview.

46. Davis to Pope, 23 Jan. 1933, Davis 201 file, misc. file.

47. Interview, John Krouse with author, 17 July 1980 (hereinafter cited as Krouse interview); interview, Prentice H. Polk with author, 18 July 1980 (hereinafter cited as Polk interview); *Collegiana—The Cub's Bible, 1935,* Tuskegee Institute Archives.

48. Consolidated report of inspection of ROTC units of the Fourth Corps Area, section 55c schools, 1933, file 000.8 ROTC (7-15-33), AGO 1926–1939 (hereinafter similar inspection reports are cited by the year made and the file date); 1934 report, file 000.8 ROTC (7-7-34); 1935 report, file 000.8 ROTC (6-7-35); 1936 report, file 000.8 ROTC (6-19-36); 1937 report, file 000.8 ROTC (5-28-37).

49. Guy V. Henry to Davis, 15 Aug. 1933, Gold Star Mothers file, Davis files; Davis memorandum to accompany statement of preferences 1933–1934, 1 Oct. 1933, and Summers to Summerall, 13 July 1934, Davis 201 file. The citation 55c refers to the section in the National Defense Act of 1920 that created a course of military instruction at schools that wanted to provide military instruction even though they did not have a Reserve Officers Training Corps unit. They had to have at least one hundred students to receive an officer-instructor.

50. Davis to Moton, 30 May 1934, and Moton to Mordecai W. Johnson, 8 June 1934, Moton Papers; memorandum, 4 June 1934, file 882.01/839, Davis to Walton, 20 Feb. 1937, file 121.5482/21, Walton to H. A. McBride, 18 Mar. 1937, and memo, Hugh Cumming, 12 May 1937, main decimal file, 1930–1939.

51. Summary of efficiency reports for consideration of elimination, 20 June 1934, Davis 201 file.

52. Charles Houston to MacArthur, 29 Aug. 1934, as quoted in Morris J. MacGregor, Jr., and Bernard Nalty, *Blacks in the United States Armed Forces, Basic Documents* (Wilmington, Del.: Scholarly Resources, 1977), vol. 4, pp. 447–448 (hereinafter cited as *Basic Documents*); MacArthur note on Houston to MacArthur, ibid.; Davis to Moton, 30 May 1934, and Moton to Mordecai Johnson, 8 June 1934, Moton Papers; Moton to Franklin Roosevelt, 14 June 1936, and Edwin Watson to Moton, 12 July 1937, official file 2369, Franklin D. Roosevelt Library.

53. BOD, Jr.–ASD 30 May 1981 interview; letter, Elnora McLendon to author, 11 Aug. 1981; McLendon 1973 interview; interview, Elnora

Davis McLendon with author, 23 Oct. 1982 (hereinafter cited as Mc-Lendon 1982 interview).

54. BOD, Jr.-ASD 23 May 1981 interview.

55. Memo, Chief of Cavalry to Adjutant General, 28 Jan. 1936, file 210.64 (10-1-35); memo, Chief of Cavalry to Adjutant General, 29 Jan. 1937, file 210.64 (10-1-36); Adjutant General to Commander, Fifth Corps, 4 June 1937, file 210.64 ROTC (10-1-36); Ormonde Walker to Adjutant General, 5 June 1937, ibid.; Chief of Cavalry to Adjutant General, 10 June 1937, ibid.; and Adjutant General to Chief of Staff, 21 July 1937, ibid.—all in AGO 1926-1939.

56. Telephone interview, Hondon Hargrove with author, 8 July 1981 (hereinafter cited as Hargrove interview); telephone interview, Aaron Fisher with author, 14 July 1981 (hereinafter cited as Fisher interview); Hargrove interview.

57. *Bulletin of Wilberforce University, Annual Catalog, 1937–38,* Wilberforce University Archives; Fisher interview; Hargrove interview.

58. *Pittsburgh Courier,* 5 Mar. 1938; R. M. Levy to Fifth Corps, 21 May 1938, file 210.64 ROTC (10-1-37), AGO 1926-1939; BOD, Jr., 1972 interview; *Amsterdam News,* 30 Apr. and 7 May 1938; *Pittsburgh Courier,* 7 May 1938.

59. *National Guard Regulations under the Constitution and the Laws of the United States, 1922,* secs. 390, 397–403, RG 282, WNRC; Ernest Burt, JAGD, to G-1, General Staff, n.d., file no. 15279, G-1, secret-classified general correspondence, 1920–1942, RG 165, NA (hereinafter cited as G-1 correspondence).

60. *Cleveland Gazette,* 4 June 1938; *Amsterdam News,* 11 June 1938; - *Pittsburgh Courier,* 11 June 1938; *Amsterdam News,* 17 Sept. 1938.

61. McLendon 1973 interview; Davis, 6 Feb. and 9 July 1940, five-year diary, Davis Papers (hereinafter cited as diary).

62. BOD, Jr.-ASD 30 May 1981 interview; diary, 15 Aug. 1939; for an example of drill as a social event see *Amsterdam News,* 11 Mar. 1939.

63. McLendon 1981 interview; Davis, speech to meeting, 26 Sept. 1940, 369th NYNG file, Davis files.

64. Henry Woodring to Herbert Lehman, 5 Oct. 1939, file National Guard, no. 1194, general correspondence, Secretary of War, 1932–1942, records of the Office of the Secretary of War, RG 107, NA (hereinafter cited as general correspondence); memo, George V. Strong to Adjutant General, 11 Jan. 1939, file 325, AGO 1926-1939; Adjutant General to Chief of National Guard Bureau, 17 June 1940, file 210.651 New York, central file, 1940–1942, RG 407, NA (hereinafter files in this group are referred to by the number, followed by AGO 1940–1942); memo, Chief of Staff to Chief of Coast Artillery, 10 Apr. 1940, ibid.; Brigadier General

Gasser to W. H. Haskell, 11 Apr. 1940, ibid.; memo, Marshall to Chief of Coast Artillery, file no. 19308-4, secret correspondence, 1932–1942, RG 107, NA [hereinafter cited as secret correspondence]; *Amsterdam News*, 22 June 1940; diary, 26 and 27 Aug. 1940; *New York Age*, 7 Sept. 1940.

65. *Pittsburgh Courier*, 14 May 1938; Arthur Hayes to Walter White, 16 May 1940, NAACP Papers; *Washington Post*, 28 Sept. 1940; *New York Age*, 5 Oct. 1940.

66. *Amsterdam News*, 12 and 19 Oct. 1940; Adjutant General to Representative A. G. Schiffler, 14 Oct. 1940, and Adjutant General to Edward D. Tolbert, 14 Oct. 1940, Davis 201 file.

67. Walter White, *A Man Called White: The Autobiography of Walter White* (New York: Viking Press, 1948), p. 188; *Amsterdam News*, 19 Oct. 1940; *Afro-American* (Baltimore, Md.), 19 Oct. 1940, as cited by Richard M. Dalfiume in "Military Segregation and the 1940 Presidential Election," *Phylon* 30, 1 (Spring 1969): 52; White, *Man Called White*, p. 188; Dalfiume, "Military Segregation," p. 53; *Washington Post*, 18 Oct. 1940.

68. Henry Lewis Stimson diaries, 22, 23, and 25 Oct. 1940, vol. 31, pp. 71–72, 74, 80, 82–83 (microfilm edition, reel 6), Manuscripts and Archives, Yale University Library, New Haven, Conn.; Nancy J. Weiss, *Farewell to the Party of Lincoln: Black Politics in the Age of FDR* (Princeton, N.J.: Princeton University Press, 1983), pp. 278–282.

69. McLendon 1973 interview; diary, 25 and 30 Oct. 1940, *Amsterdam News*, 2 Nov. 1940, *New York Age*, 2 Nov. 1940. For examples of favorable comments see M. F. Whittacker to FDR, 28 Oct. 1940, and Lewis Jackson to FDR, 30 Oct. 1940, Davis 201 file. For political reaction see R. R. Wright, Jr., to National Democratic Headquarters, 30 Oct. 1940, official file 2369, Roosevelt Library; and *Evening Star*, 26 Oct. 1940. For negative comments see Parker Smith to Senator Morris Shepard, 26 Oct. 1940, Davis 201 file; and Oswald G. Villard, *Christian Century*, 18 Dec. 1940, p. 1584. For white-press reaction see *Evening Star*, 25 Oct. 1940, for a generally favorable coverage, and *Washington Post*, 26 Oct. 1940, for how the story could be buried.

70. Edward M. Coffman and Peter F. Herrly, "The American Regular Army Officer Corps between the World Wars: A Collective Biography," *Armed Forces and Society* 4 (Nov. 1977): 64–68; *Historical Statistics*, p. 299.

71. *Amsterdam News*, 21 and 28 Dec. 1940.

CHAPTER 5. WORLD WAR II–
INSPECTOR GENERAL: 1941–1942

1. Memo, Chief of Staff to William D. Hassett, 22 Oct. 1940, file 322.97, AGO 1940–1942; Ulysses Lee, *The Employment of Negro Troops*

(Washington, D.C.: Government Printing Office, 1966), pp. 107–108, 125.

2. Terry Allen to Chief of Staff, 13 May 1941, as quoted by MacGregor and Nalty in *Basic Documents*, vol. 5; diary, 21 May and 17 June 1941.

3. Davis to Maj. Gen. W. Bryden, 19 Dec. 1940, and Bryden to Davis, 2 Jan. 1941, Davis 201 file.

4. *Defender*, 22 Feb. 1941; BOD, Jr.-ASD 30 May 1981 interview; BOD, Jr.-ASD 23 May 1981 interview; diary, 10 Apr. 1941.

5. *Defender*, 22 Feb. 1941; Davis to Adjutant General, 26 May 1941, Davis 201 file.

6. Louis R. Lautier to Ulysses S. Geyer, 6 June 1941, Emmett Scott to Guyer, 6 June 1941, and Emmett Scott to Louis R. Lautier, 4 June 1941, Davis files; U.S., Congress, Senate, *A Bill to Authorize the Secretary of War to Retain Brigadier General Benjamin O. Davis, United States Army, on Active Duty with Combat Troops*, S. 1656, 77th Cong., 1st sess., 1941 (HR 5006, introduced at the same time by Congressman Guyer, had the same title).

7. Adams to Robert Reynolds, 24 June 1941, William Bryden to Harold Smith, 12 July 1941, and Smith to Stimson, 19 July 1941, Davis 201 file; Stimson to Andrew J. May, 25 July 1941, file no. 18861-103, secret correspondence.

8. Marshall to Bryden, n.d., Davis 201 file; Marshall to Davis, 5 June 1941, file no. 18861-97, secret correspondence; diary, 6 June 1941; Bryden to Adjutant General, 12 June 1941, file no. 18861-97, general correspondence. For examples of letters see Jesse A. Graham, executive secretary of Arlington Civil League, to Franklin Roosevelt, 24 June 1941, Davis 201 file; see also Harold O. Howard to Roosevelt, 23 June 1941, ibid.; *New York Age*, 21 June 1941.

9. BOD, Jr.-ASD 30 May 1981 interview; McLendon 1973 interview.

10. Miscellaneous file; "The Negro in the Army: A Pamphlet Especially Prepared for the Conference of Negro Editors and Publishers, Washington, D.C., Dec. 8–9, 1941," T. Gibson file; and "History of Special Section, Office of the Inspector General, 29 June 1941 to 16 Nov. 1944" (hereinafter cited as Hist. Spec. Sec.)—all in Davis files.

11. H. S. Clarkson to Peterson, 13 June 1941, Davis 201 file; McLendon 1982 interview.

12. Hist. Spec. Sec.; for views in the black community toward segregation in the army see Phillip McGuire, "Desegregation of the Armed Forces: Black Leadership, Protest and World War II," *Journal of Negro History* 68, 2 (Spring 1983): 152–154.

13. Noel Parish to Davis, n.d., and report of inspection, Tuskegee, 4–7 Aug. 1941, Tuskegee file, Davis files.

14. C. C. Albaugh to author, 28 Nov. 1980; *Pittsburgh Courier*, 29 Nov. 1941; *Chicago Defender*, 29 Nov. 1941.

15. Hist. Spec. Sec.; BOD to SD, 1 Sept. 1941, Davis Papers; *Defender,* 27 Sept. 1941.

16. Diary, 17 and 14 Oct. 1941; memo, Davis to Chief of Staff, 24 Nov. 1941, speech file, Davis files.

17. Lee, *Employment,* pp. 137–139; memo for Secretary of War from Chief of Staff, 1 Dec. 1941, file no. 15640-120, G-1 correspondence.

18. A. D. Surles to Inspector General, 1 Dec. 1941, committee file, Davis files; Conference of Negro Newspaper Representatives—8 Dec. 1941 file, subject file, Assistant Secretary of War, Civilian Aide to the Secretary, RG 107, NA (hereinafter cited as Civilian Aide subject file).

19. "Program for the Conference of Negro Newspaper Representatives, War Department—Munitions Building, 8 Dec. 1941, 9:00 A.M.," race relations file, Davis files; Benjamin Davis, transcript of remarks, Conference of Negro Newspaper Representatives—8 Dec. 1941 file, Civilian Aide subject file.

20. *Chicago Defender,* 1 Nov. 1941; diary, 21 and 22 Dec. 1941.

21. BOD, Sr., interview; BOD to SD, 13 Jan. 1942, and special inspection of colored troops, Camp Livingston, La., 7 Feb. 1942, Davis Papers.

22. For an example see Gibson to Davis, 24 Feb. 1942, Aberdeen Proving Ground file, Civilian Aide subject file; inspection notes on Aberdeen Proving Ground, Md., 24 Feb. 1942, and special inspection, colored troops, MacDill Field, Tampa, Fla., 1 Apr. 1942, Davis files.

23. *Journal and Guide* (Norfolk, Va.), 25 Apr. 1942.

24. Ibid., 18 Apr. 1942.

25. Memo to Executive Officer, 24 Apr. 1944, and medical record, Davis 201 file.

26. For information on these trips see BOD to SD, 2 and 5 June 1942, Davis Papers; Lee, *Employment,* pp. 126–128, 335–336; diary, 22 June 1942.

27. "Inspection of Post by General Davis, July 21–29, 1942;" memo, "Subject: Complaints, Colored Officers, 93rd Division;" memo, "Subject: Complaints, Enlisted Men, 93rd Division, 28 July 1942;" memo, Col. Edwin Hardy to Davis, 28 July 1942; and memo, Inspector General to Chief of Staff, 6 Aug. 1942—all in Fort Huachuca, Ariz., file, Davis files.

28. BOD to SD, 13 Jan. 1942, Davis Papers; McLendon 1982 interview; diary, 27 May 1942.

29. Davis to Executive Division, 8 Sept. 1942, and Peterson to Assistant Chief of Staff, G-3, 11 Sept. 1942, file 291.2 conference correspondence miscellaneous (6-17-42); for an example see Somervell to SOS, 12 Aug. 1942, file no. 291.2 miscellaneous (6-25-42). Both files are in records of the Office of the Inspector General, RG 159, WNRC (hereinafter cited as IG files).

30. Davis 201 file.

31. John McCloy to Hastie, 2 July 1942, file no. 291.2 negro troops, Assistant Secretary of War files, RG 107, NA (hereinafter cited as ASW files); Lee, *Employment*, pp. 157–160.

32. Ulysses Lee, "Employment of Negro Troops," chap. 7, pp. 51–52, Office of the Chief of Military History files, records of the Army Staff, RG 319, NA (hereinafter cited as Lee ms., followed by chapter and page number). This is a typescript of what became Ulysses Lee's book. Some material here was excised from the book.

33. SOS to General Staff, 24 Sept. 1942, file no. 322.97 (9-24-42), and telegram, 6 Aug. 1942, file no. 210.31 (8-6-42) Great Britain, Operations Division Files, RG 165, NA (hereinafter cited as OPD files); diary, 10 and 28 Aug. 1942; orders, 5 Sept. 1942, Davis 201 file, OPD files.

34. BOD to SD, 20 Sept. 1942, Davis Papers; diary, 25 Sept. 1942.

35. Diary, 26 Sept. 1942; BOD to SD, 26 Sept. 1942, Davis Papers; diary, 27 and 28 Sept. and 2 Oct. 1942. For another account of Davis and his activities in Great Britain see Graham Smith, *When Jim Crow Met John Bull: Black American Soldiers in World War II Britain* (New York: St. Martin's Press, 1988), pp. 153–157.

36. Diary, 5 and 6 Oct. 1942; *Journal and Guide*, 3 and 10 Oct. 1942; letter, Farrell D. Lowe to author, 12 Nov. 1980; diary, 10 Oct. 1942; BOD to SD, 11 Oct. 1942, Davis Papers.

37. Diary, 13 Oct. 1942; BOD to SD, 26 Oct. 1942, Davis Papers; *Times* (London), 14 Oct. and 7 Nov. 1942; *Journal and Guide*, 26 Dec. 1942; BOD to SD, 31 Oct. 1942, Davis Papers.

38. Hist. Spec. Sec.; diary, 29 Oct. 1942.

39. BOD to SD, 26 Oct. 1942, Davis Papers; diary, 27 Oct. 1942; BOD to Elnora Davis, 25 Oct. 1942, and BOD to SD, 23 Oct. 1942, Davis Papers; Marshall to Eisenhower, 24 Oct. 1942, Davis 201 file, OPD files.

40. Davis to Commanding General, ETO, 25 Oct. 1942, miscellaneous file, Davis files; Lee ms., chap. 23, pp. 77–78; Lee to Eisenhower, 1st Ind., 26 Oct. 1942, Davis to Commanding General, ETO, file no. 291.2, AGO misc. records, ETOUSA, records of U.S. Army Commands, 1942–, RG 338, WNRC.

41. *Afro-American*, 24 Oct. 1942. For another type of criticism, in a news story, see *Chicago Defender*, 7 Nov. 1942; Joseph Julian, "Jim Crow Goes Abroad," *Nation*, 5 Dec. 1942, pp. 610–612; *Journal and Guide*, 24 Oct. 1942; BOD to SD, 23 Oct. 1942, Davis Papers.

42. Lee to Davis, 4 Nov. 1942, Davis to Lee, 7 Nov. 1942, and Lee to Davis, 1 Aug. 1943, Lt. Gen. John Lee file, Davis files; J. L. Parkison to Colonel Clarkson, 23 Nov. 1942, Adjutant General file, Davis files.

43. Davis to IG, 24 Dec. 1942, Chief of Staff file, Davis files; BOD to SD, 30 Nov. 1942, Davis Papers.

CHAPTER 6. WORLD WAR II—
NEW DIRECTIONS: 1943–1944

1. Richard M. Dalfiume, *Desegregation of the U.S. Armed Forces: Fighting on Two Fronts, 1939–1953* (Columbia: University of Missouri Press, 1968), pp. 77–87; Morris J. MacGregor, Jr., *Integration of the Armed Forces, 1940–1965* (Washington, D.C.: Government Printing Office, 1981), pp. 37–41.

2. Memo, Davis to IG, subject: survey relative conditions affecting racial incidents at Fort Clark, Tex., 10 Aug. 1943, Davis files.

3. Davis to Ernest Pachon, 8 Apr. 1943, speech file, Davis files. For samples of Davis's comments on morale see report to IG, subject: investigation of morale and alleged mistreatment of colored soldiers, and of the transfer of two colored chaplains, 2d Cavalry Division, Fort Clark, Tex., 6 May 1943, Chief of Staff file, ibid.; and Davis to IG, memo, 13 Oct. 1943, file: attitudes of negro soldiers, Civilian Aide subject file.

4. Davis to IG, memo, subject: attitudes of negro soldiers, Fort Devens, Mass., 9 Sept. 1943, file: attitudes of negro soldiers, Civilian Aide subject file; BOD to SD, 20 Apr. 1943, Davis Papers.

5. Interview, Charles Brown with author, 26 Apr. 1981 (hereinafter cited as Brown interview).

6. BOD to SD, 16 July 1943, Davis Papers; diary, 18 July 1943; Davis to IG, memo, subject: survey relative conditions affecting racial attitude at Fort Huachuca, Ariz., 7 Aug. 1942, Fort Huachuca file, Davis files; Brown interview.

7. Davis to IG, memo, special inspection of colored troops at Fort Huachuca, Ariz., 2 Aug. 1943, Fort Huachuca file, Civilian Aide subject file; draft memo to IG, 4 and 5 Aug. 1943, Fort Huachuca file, Davis files.

8. Gibson to Dan Burley, 21 Sept. 1943, Fort Huachuca file, Civilian Aide subject file; Davis to McCloy, 7 Oct. 1943, Gibson file, Davis files.

9. Dalfiume, *Desegregation*, pp. 82–86; Davis to Hastie, 10 Jan. 1943, Hastie to Davis, 22 Jan. 1943, and John McCloy to Davis, 13 Jan. 1943, Gibson file, Davis files.

10. Gibson to McCloy, 3 Feb. 1943, file 291.2 Negro Troop Committee, ASW files; Davis, memo to Advisory Committee, subject: elimination of racial friction, 2 Jan. 1943, and minutes, Advisory Committee, 22 Feb. 1943, committee file, Davis files.

11. Lee, *Employment*, pp. 238–260; memo, Idwal Edwards to Committee, 17 Feb. 1943, file 291.2 Misc. Committee meeting (2:1743), IG files; Davis, "Notes in re the Committee," 19 Feb. 1943, committee file, Davis files; Lee, *Employment*, pp. 260–261.

12. Minutes, Advisory Committee meeting, 22 Mar. 1943, file 291.2

NTC, ASW files; memo, Davis to Leonard, 30 Mar. 1943, committee file, Davis files.

13. Minutes, Advisory Committee, 2 Apr. 1943, committee file, Davis files.

14. Leonard to McCloy, memo, 24 June 1943, file 291.2 NTC, ASW files.

15. Minutes, Advisory Committee, 28 June 1943, file 291.2 NTC, ASW files.

16. Gibson to Davis, memo, 30 June 1943, Gibson file, Davis files; memo, Leonard to Davis, 30 June 1943, committee file, Davis files; Lee ms., chap. 15, p. 4.

17. Minutes, Advisory Committee, 2 July 1943, file 291.2 NTC, and memo for Chief of Staff, subject: negro troops, 3 July 1943, file 291.2 Negro Troops—both ASW files; Lee, *Employment*, pp. 381-383.

18. Lee ms., chap. 14, pp. 71-73; minutes, Advisory Committee, 14 Aug. 1943, file 291.2 NTC, ASW files; Lee, *Employment*, pp. 389-391.

19. Alan M. Osur, *Blacks in the Army Air Forces during World War II* (Washington, D.C.: Government Printing Office, 1977), pp. 24-25, 45-50; minutes, Advisory Committee, 13 Oct. 1943, committee file, Davis files; BOD, Jr., 1987 interview; Osur, *Blacks in the Army Air Forces*, pp. 50-51.

20. Davis to McCloy, 10 Nov. 1943, committee file, Davis files; memo, John Hall to J. Leonard, 14 Nov. 1943, file 291.2, ASW files.

21. Cordell Hull to Henry Stimson, 3 May 1943, and Stimson to Hull, 14 May 1943, file 210.6 military aide (5-3-43), central file, 1943-1945, RG 407, NA; memo, Chief of Staff to Davis, 7 May 1943, Davis 201 file, Office of Chief of Staff 201 files, RG 165, NA (hereinafter cited as C/S 201 file); diary, 26 May 1943; *Washington Post*, 27 May 1943; *Afro-American* (Baltimore, Md.), 5 June 1943; diary, 26 May 1943; *Washington Post*, 28 May 1943; *Evening Star*, 28 May 1943; diary, 27 May 1943; *Afro-American*, 5 June 1943; diary, 28 May 1943; *Evening Star*, 29 May 1943; diary, 29 and 30 May 1943.

22. Diary, 1 June 1943; Afro-American, 12 June 1943; diary, 1 June 1943; *Afro-American*, 12 June 1943; John O'Hanley to Fitch, 24 June 1943, file 882.001 Barclay, Edwin/80, and Walter Walker to Cordell Hull, 8 May 1944, file 093.822/20, main decimal file, 1940-1944, RG 59, NA.

23. Lee, *Employment*, pp. 382-383; memo, subject: radio broadcast—negro in the army no. 2 (1042), file radio broadcast, ASW files; Davis, endorsement no. 3, 20 Apr. 1943, IG file 322.99—foreign service, race relations file, Davis files; Gibson to Assistant Secretary of War, 29 Apr. 1943, and William Scobey to Inspector General, 29 Apr. 1943, file 291.2 Negro Troops, ASW files; *Defender*, 22 May 1943; Gibson to Assistant Secretary of War, 14 May 1943, file 291.2 Negro Troops, ASW files; diary, late Mar. 1943.

24. *Journal and Guide*, 18 Sept. 1943; McLendon 1982 interview; *Journal and Guide*, 8 Jan. 1944; diary, 24 Oct. and 23 Aug. 1943.

25. Hardy to Adjutant General, 2 Aug. 1943, Davis 201 file; *Amsterdam News*, 2 Oct. 1943; Peterson to Adjutant General, 30 July 1943, and Rufus E. Clement to Adjutant General, 11 May 1943, Davis 201 file.

26. Minutes, Advisory Committee, 4 Jan. 1944, committee file, Davis files; minutes, Advisory Committee, 4 Jan. 1944, and pamphlet "The Command of Negro Troops," 8 Jan. 1944, file 291.2 NTC, ASW files.

27. Memo, Leonard to Advisory Committee, 6 Jan. 1944, committee file, Davis files; memo: suggested draft of a directive to be issued by the adjutant general, 22 Jan. 1944, file: McCloy Committee, Civilian Aide subject file.

28. Minutes, Advisory Committee, 11 Jan. 1944, and notes of General Davis, remarks made at 11 Jan. 1944 Advisory Committee meeting, committee file, Davis files; diary, 11 Jan. 1944.

29. Minutes, Advisory Committee, 29 Feb. 1944, committee file, Davis files.

30. Lee, *Employment*, pp. 474–481; McCloy to Stimson, 2 Mar. 1944, file 291.2, ASW files.

31. Davis to IG, 18 Oct. 1943, Selfridge Field file, Davis files; BOD to SD, 3 Mar. 1944, Davis Papers; Osur, *Blacks in the Army Air Forces*, pp. 52–55; BOD to SD, 12 Mar. 1944, Davis Papers; Osur, *Blacks in the Army Air Forces*, pp. 56–57.

32. McLendon 1982 interview; narrative notes on inspection by General Davis at Fort Huachuca, 15 Apr. through 21 Apr., report of special inspection of colored troops at Fort Huachuca, Ariz., 19 May 1944, and memo, Davis to IG, 20 May 1944, Fort Huachuca file, Davis files.

33. Lee, *Employment*, pp. 536–590.

34. *Congressional Record*, House of Representatives, 78th Cong., 2d sess., 1944, app., pp. A694–A695; Hist. Spec. Sec.; Claude S. Miller to Sir, 24 Oct. 1944, Bureau Public Relations 1942 file, Civilian Aide subject file.

35. Thomas Cripps, *Black Film as Genre* (Bloomington: Indiana University Press, 1979), pp. 108–109; interview, Carlton Moss with Barbara Reed, Aug. 1980 (hereinafter cited as Moss interview); Cripps, *Black Film*, pp. 109–113; Moss interview.

36. Thomas Cripps and David Culbert, "The Negro Soldier (1944): Film Propaganda in Black and White," *American Quarterly* 31, 5 (Winter 1979): 628–629; diary, 3 Nov. 1943; Cripps and Culbert, "Negro Soldier," pp. 629–630; Lee, *Employment*, pp. 388–89.

37. Gibson to IG, 10 Mar. 1944, file: negro soldier, Civilian Aide subject file; Moss interview; Gibson to Moss, 30 Mar. 1944, file: negro soldier, Civilian Aide subject file.

38. *Daily News* (Los Angeles), 7 Apr. 1944, in committee file, Davis files; Moss interview; diary, 7–10 Apr. 1944, Davis Papers; *Daily News*, 14 Apr. 1944; *Journal and Guide*, 22 Apr. 1944; memo, Davis and Gibson to McCloy, subject: Los Angeles trip, 25 Apr. 1944, committee file, Davis files.

39. Moss interview; Cripps and Culbert, "Negro Soldier," p. 632; Gibson to Moss, 14 June 1944, and Jack Warner to movie distributors, 29 June 1944, file: negro soldier, Civilian Aide subject file; *Journal and Guide*, 22 July 1944; Thomas Cripps, "Movies, Race, and World War II: *Tennessee Johnson* as an Anticipation of the Strategies of the Civil Rights Movement," *Prologue* 14, 2 (Summer 1982): 67; Moss interview.

40. Memo, Davis and Gibson to McCloy, subject: Los Angeles trip, 25 Apr. 1944, committee file, Davis files; Gibson to McCloy, 26 Apr. 1944, file: field trips, Civilian Aide subject file.

41. Hist. Spec. Sec.; Carlton Moss to Truman Gibson, 20 Mar. 1944, file: "The Negro Soldier," Civilian Aide subject file; McCloy to Lee, 26 May 1944, and message, OPD to CO ETO and NATO Air Force, 15 June 1944, file 291.2 negro troops publicity, ASW files.

CHAPTER 7. WORLD WAR II—
THE ETO: 1944–1945

1. Moss interview; Davis to Gibson, 19 July 1944, file: personal, and Moss to Gibson, 24 July 1944, file: ETO racial relations, Civilian Aide subject file, Davis files; BOD to SD, 8 Aug. 1944, Davis Papers; Gibson to Davis, 16 Aug. 1944, file: ETO racial relations, Civilian Aide subject file; Davis to Gibson, 24 Aug. 1944, Gibson file, Davis files.

2. Moss interview; BOD to SD, 23 Sept. 1944, Davis Papers.

3. Hist. Spec. Sec.; BOD to SD, 8 Aug. 1944, Davis Papers; Moss interview.

4. Hist. Spec. Sec.; diary, 29 Aug. 1944; *Journal and Guide*, 16 Sept. 1944; BOD to SD, 11 Sept. 1944, Davis Papers; diary, 30 Aug. and 18 Sept. 1944; BOD to SD, 4 Sept. 1944, Davis Papers.

5. Memo, Charles Dollard to Ralph Nelson, 18 Jan. 1945, file OF 14, orientation film production case files, records of the Office of the Chief Signal Officer, RG 111, NA. Other information about the production of *Teamwork* can be found in this file.

6. Memo, R. Ernest Dupuy to Deputy, 9 July 1944, Public Relations Bureau, and memo, Public Relations Office, ETOUSA, to Deputy Chief of Staff, subject: proposed visit to theater of General Davis, 7 July 1944, SHAEF records, records of Allied Operational and Occupation Headquarters, World War II, RG 331, NA (hereinafter records from this group are cited as SHAEF records).

7. Press release, 10 Aug. 1944, file 291.2-1 negroes, Public Relations Bureau, SHAEF records; *Evening Star*, 10 Aug. 1944, quoted in Lee ms.; *Journal and Guide*, 19 Aug. 1944; Davis to Gibson, 24 Aug. 1944, Gibson file, Davis files; Gibson to Moss, 16 Aug. 1944, and Gibson to Davis, file: ETO racial relations, Civilian Aide subject file; Davis to Gibson, 24 Aug. 1944, Gibson file, Davis files; BOD to SD, 23 Aug. 1944, Davis Papers.

8. First endorsement, 13 July 1943, on F. M. Edwards, Chief of Staff, ETO, to Commanding General, SOS, 12 July 1943, and memo, PBR to CG, ETO, 3 Oct. 1943, file 291.2 N, European Theater of Operations records, RG 332, WNRC (hereinafter records in this group are cited as ETO records); Lee to Davis, 12 July 1944, Davis Papers; Assistant Chief of Staff, G-1, memo, 14 Nov. 1944, Davis 201 file, C/S 201 file.

9. Lee, *Employment*, pp. 622–630.

10. BOD to SD, 17 Oct., 12 and 19 Nov. 1944, Davis Papers.

11. Inspection report, special inspection of certain colored units, Third United States Army, 26 Oct. 1944, and inspection report, special inspection colored units, advanced section, 11 Nov. 1944, file 333.1, Adjutant General's Section, records of U.S. Army Commands, 1942–, RG 338, WNRC (hereinafter records in this group are cited as AG Section); inspection of colored troops in the Normandy Base Section, 5 Dec. 1944, SHAEF file, Davis files; BOD to SD, 27 Nov. 1944, Davis Papers.

12. Davis to Charles Rice, 25 Aug. 1944, Francis A. Chunn to Davis, 10 Aug. 1944, Davis to Chunn, 3 Oct. 1944, and Davis to Leslie Polk, 26 Apr. 1945—all in correspondence—July–Dec. 1944 file, Davis files.

13. Joseph Toi to Davis, 28 July 1944, and Davis to Toi, 4 Oct. 1944, correspondence—July–Dec. 1944 file, Davis files.

14. Speech, 8 Nov. 1944, enclosed in Davis to H. D. Gibson, 13 Nov. 1944, file 333.1, AG Section; Davis to Waldron J. Cheyney, 4 Oct. 1944, correspondence—July–Dec. 1944 file, Davis files; Davis to Gibson, 7 Jan. 1945, Gibson file, ibid.; memo, Davis to Roy Grower, Brittany Base Section, 7 Jan. 1945, Brittany Base Section file, ibid.; BOD to SD, 24 Oct. 1944, Davis Papers.

15. Peterson to Davis, 9 Jan. 1945, and Davis to Peterson, 22 Jan. 1945, Davis 201 file; citation, DSM, Davis Papers; diary, 24 Feb. 1945; BOD to SD, 21 and 13 Feb. 1945, 19 Nov. 1944, and 27 Feb. 1945, Davis Papers.

16. Davis to Harold Field, 15 May 1945, ETO 1945 correspondence file, Davis files.

17. Davis to Dr. Emory Ross, 24 Feb. 1947, and BOD to SD, 30 Nov. 1944, Davis Papers.

18. Russell F. Weigley, *Eisenhower's Lieutenants: The Campaign of France and Germany 1944-1945* (Bloomington: Indiana University Press, 1981), pp. 567–568; Lee, *Employment*, p. 688.

19. Hist. Spec. Sec.; BOD to SD, 26 Dec. 1944, Davis Papers.

20. Lee, *Employment*, pp. 688-693; BOD to SD, 8 Feb. 1945, Davis Papers; Hist. Spec. Sec.

21. BOD to SD, 7 Jan. 1945, Davis Papers; speech, 16th Reinforcement Depot, Compiègne, France, 20 Jan. 1945, and Davis to McCloy, 30 Mar. 1945, ETO 1945 correspondence file, Davis files.

22. Memo, Davis to Lee, 7 Dec. 1944, correspondence—July-Dec. 1944 file, Davis files; "Chronological Outline of Activation and Operation of the General Inspectorate Section, European Theater of Operations, from: 25 November 1944 to: 15 May 1945," pp. 1-2, IG files, miscellany, ETO records (hereinafter this report is cited as chronological outline); Roland G. Ruppenthal, *Logistical Support of the Armies*, 2 vols. (Washington, D.C.: Government Printing Office, 1959), 2:384; Lee ms., chap. 20, p. 94; memo, R. B. Lovett, AG, to CO, ETOUSA, 22 Dec. 1944, as quoted in chronological outline, app. A; ibid., p. 11.

23. Chronological outline, pp. 14-15; memo no. 2, 4 Jan. 1945, app. E, ibid.; memo no. 1, 24 Dec. 1944, ibid.

24. Davis to CO, 4055 QM Service Company, 23 Apr. 1945, ETO 1945 correspondence file, Davis files; report no. 62, 25 Apr. 1945, G.I. Section, IG files, miscellany, ETO records; Hist. Spec. Sec.; Lee, *Employment*, pp. 699-701; chronological outline, pp. 31-32; BOD to SD, 30 Apr. 1945, Davis Papers.

25. Davis to Theater Chaplain, 23 Jan. 1945, ETO 1945 correspondence file, Davis files; speech, 13 Feb. 1945, Davis Papers; Gibson to Lee, subject: report of visit to European Theater of Operations, 31 Mar. 1945, file AG 291.2, ETO records (hereinafter cited as Gibson report memo).

26. BOD to SD, 7 Jan., 4 and 24 Apr., and 1 Mar. 1945, Davis Papers.

27. Gibson report memo; C. H. Bonesteel, general rating of general officers, 9 May 1945, Davis 201 file; BOD to SD, 17 Sept. 1945, Davis Papers.

28. BOD to SD, 1 and 17 Mar. 1945, Davis Papers; memo, Gibson to Lee, 31 Mar. 1945, Lt. Gen. John Lee file, Davis files; BOD to SD, 4 Apr. 1945, Davis Papers.

29. Ruppenthal, *Logistical Support*, 2:389; memo, R. B. Lovett to CO, ETOUSA, 4 May 1945, in chronological outline, app. B; memo, C. H. Bonesteel to Davis, 28 May 1945, ETO 1945 correspondence file, Davis files.

30. BOD to SD, 19 Aug. 1945, Davis Papers; Davis to Gibson, 27 Aug. 1945, Gibson file, Davis files; Davis to Bonesteel, 28 July 1945, ETO 1945 correspondence file, ibid.; BOD to SD, 25 July 1945, Davis Papers; diary, 27 and 31 July 1945; BOD to SD, 8 Sept. 1945, Davis Papers.

31. BOD to SD, 20 July and 30 Aug. 1945, Davis Papers.

32. Diary, 5 Oct. 1945; BOD to SD, 15 Oct. 1945, Davis Papers; communication, CG, US Forces, ETO, Rear, to War Department, 18 Oct. 1945, Davis 201 file, OPD files; Lee to Davis, 29 Oct. 1945, Lee correspondence file, Davis files; BOD to SD, 31 Oct. 1945, Davis Papers; Davis to Gibson, 31 Oct. 1945, Gibson file, Davis files.

33. Davis to Commanding General, HQ, TSFET, 18 Aug. 1945, ETO 1945 correspondence file, Davis files; Davis to Gibson, 27 Aug. 1945, Gibson file, ibid.; BOD to SD, 18 Aug. and 22 Sept. 1945, Davis Papers.

34. Report to CO, HQ, TSFET, subject: inspection of Camp Herbert Tarreyton, 16 Aug. 1945, Tarreyton file, Davis files; report, subject: special visit to the Army University Center no. 1, Shrivenham Barracks, Eng., 2 Oct. 1945, Shrivenham file, ibid.; BOD to SD, 16 and 30 Aug. 1945, Davis Papers.

35. Memo, Davis to Bonesteel, 24 Feb. 1945, and report no. E-118, "The Utilization of Negro Infantry Platoons in White Companies," Research Branch, Information and Education Division, HQ, ETO, June 1945, G-3 report file, Davis files; Gibson to Davis, 20 July 1945, Gibson file, Davis files.

36. Dalfiume, *Desegregation*, pp. 148–50; memo of telephone conversation, 13 Oct. 1945, Major Needham to USF, ETO, Rear, Davis 201 file, OPD files; Alan L. Gropman, *The Air Force Integrates, 1945–1964* (Washington, D.C.: Government Printing Office, 1978), p. 52; Bell Wiley, "Reflections after Reading Record of Testimony before Gillem Committee," Lee ms.; BOD to SD, 1 Nov. 1945, Davis Papers; Davis to Gillem, 6 Nov. 1945, Lee ms.; Davis, notes on pamphlet "Utilization of Negro Infantry Platoons in White Companies," ibid.; Wiley, "Reflections," ibid.; Dalfiume, *Desegregation*, p. 150.

37. BOD to SD, 14 July, 2 Sept., 1, 9, and 25 Aug., and 5 Oct. 1945, Davis Papers.

38. BOD to SD, 13 Aug. 1945, Davis Papers; diary, 31 Oct. 1945; BOD to SD, 15 Nov. 1945, Davis Papers; Gibson to Davis, 25 Sept. 1945, ETO 1945 correspondence file, Davis files; Davis to Gibson, 31 Oct. 1945, Gibson file, ibid.; Davis to C. A. Franklin, 3 Oct. 1945, and Davis to Daniel Sultan, IG, 15 Nov. 1945, ETO 1945 correspondence file, Davis files; diary, 2 Dec. 1945; Davis to Ira Eaker, 8 Jan. 1946, 1946 file, Davis files; memo for Chief of Staff, 8 Nov. 1945, C/S 201 file.

CHAPTER 8. A CAREER CLOSES: 1946–1970

1. Davis to Ira Eaker, 8 Jan. 1946, 1946 file, Davis files.

2. Dalfiume, *Desegregation*, pp. 150–151; Davis to William H. Draper, Jr., 24 Nov. 1947, secret file, Davis files.

3. Dalfiume, *Desegregation*, pp. 152–153; *Pittsburgh Courier*, 31 Aug. 1946; Davis to United Negro and Allied Veterans of America Convention, 8 May 1947, Davis Papers.

4. Davis to William H. Draper, 24 Nov. 1947, Draper to Davis, 26 Nov. 1947, and Davis to Draper, n.d., secret file, Davis files.

5. Dalfiume, *Desegregation*, pp. 154–155; Davis to Colonel H. R. Hallock, 23 Apr. 1946, 1946 file, Davis files; Davis to William Draper, Jr., n.d., secret file, Davis files; Dalfiume, *Desegregation*, pp. 164–167.

6. Davis to William H. Kelley, 21 Jan. 1946, Davis Papers; MacGregor, *Integration*, pp. 210–212.

7. Davis to Margaret Halsey, 3 Dec. 1946, Davis Papers; BOD, Jr., 1987 interview.

8. Davis to Capt. Theodore Thompson, 10 June 1946, 1946 file, Davis files; *NYT*, 13 June 1946; program: "The Negro in the Wars of America," 1946 file, Davis files; lecture assignments, 1946, and Frank Wallace to IG, 18 Nov. 1946, Davis 201 file; Frank Wallace to Chief, Speakers Bureau, 18 Nov. 1946, 1946 file, Davis files.

9. BOD, Jr., 1972 interview; Davis to C. A. Franklin, 7 Jan. 1946, and Davis to Mr. and Mrs. Ira Gershwin, 28 Jan. 1946, 1946 file, Davis files; McLendon 1982 interview.

10. Memorandum, W. S. Paul to Davis, 25 Mar. 1947, and medical examination, Apr. 1947, Davis 201 file; Davis to Brig. Gen. William H. Hobson, 23 June 1947, Davis Papers; Davis to Hobson, 31 Dec. 1947, and Davis to Melvin Jackson, 31 Dec. 1947, personnel file, Davis files.

11. James Forrestal to Donald Russell, 18 Dec. 1946, 882.607/12-1846; Lanier to Secretary of State, 13 Mar. 1947, 882.607/3-1327; Gabriel Dennis to Marshall, 18 Mar. 1947, 882.607 Monrovia/3-1847; Acheson to Truman, 18 Mar. 1947—all in main decimal file, 1945–1949, RG 59, NA (hereinafter cited as main decimal file, 1945–1949).

12. Secretary of State to Secretary of the Navy, 6 May 1947, 882.607 Monrovia/4-1147, main decimal file, 1945–1949; report of the United States Delegation to the centenary celebration of the Republic of Liberia, 24–31 July 1947 (hereinafter cited as Liberia 1947 report); note of phone call, Andrew Lynch to Davis, 28 May 1947, memo, ? to Lynch, 18 June 1947, Lynch to Davis, 21 June 1947, and memo, ? to Davis, 26 June 1947—all in Liberia 1947 file, Davis files.

13. Davis to Draper, n.d., secret file, Davis files; *The Summer Cruise of the U.S.S. Palau (CVE-122)*, Liberia 1947 file, ibid.; BOD, Jr.–ASD 30 May 1981 interview; Liberia 1947 report, Davis files; letter, Gabriel Petre to author, 12 Nov. 1980; *The Summer Cruise of the U.S.S. Palau*.

14. Liberia 1947 report, Davis files; BOD, Jr.–ASD 30 May 1981 interview; *The Summer Cruise of the U.S.S. Palau*.

15. Speech, Liberia 1947 file, Davis files; Lanier to Marshall, 29 July

1947, 882.607 Monrovia/7-2947; Lanier to Marshall, 3 Aug. 1947, 882.607 Monrovia/8-347; Lanier to Marshall, 15 Aug. 1947, 882.607 Monrovia/8-1547; Lanier to Marshall, 21 Aug. 1947,.711.82/8-2147; and American Legation, Monrovia, to Secretary of State, 22 Aug. 1947, 882.607 Monrovia/8-2247—all in main decimal file, 1945–1949.

16. Liberia 1947 report, app. B, Davis files; Marshall to American Legation, Monrovia, 11 July 1947, 093.822/6-2847, main decimal file, 1945–1949; Davis to Chester Franklin, 1948, Davis Papers.

17. Loy Henderson to Robert Lovett, Oct. 1947, 884.607 Monrovia/8-1847, main decimal file, 1945–1949; Lovett to Secretary of the Army, 16 Oct. 1947, Liberia 1947 file, Davis files; Davis to Sidney de la Rue, 31 Dec. 1947, Davis Papers.

18. *Afro-American*, 14 Feb. 1948; David Blake, Jr., to Walter White, 31 Mar. 1948, and Wilkins to Blake, 5 Apr. 1948, NAACP Papers; U.S., Congress, Senate, *A Bill to Authorize the Advancement on the Retired List of Colonel Benjamin Oliver Davis to the Grade of Brigadier General*, S. 2826, 80th Cong., 2d sess., 1948.

19. *Afro-American*, 5 May 1948; memorandum for President, 27 Apr. 1948, subject: proposed appointment of Brigadier General Benjamin Oliver Davis, USA (Ret.), as minister to Liberia, 123 Davis, Benjamin Oliver, and memorandum of conversation, 30 Apr. 1948, subject: possible appointment of General Davis as minister to Liberia, main decimal file, 1945–1949; Davis to Mrs. C. A. Freeman, 4 Aug. 1948, letters miscellaneous 1948 file, Davis files.

20. Davis to Col. H. J. Shoemaker, 16 Aug. 1948, letters miscellaneous 1948 file, Davis files; special orders no. 99, 1948, memo, Colonel Phillips to Secretary of Army, 7 June 1948, and Kenneth Royall to Harry Truman, 2 July 1948, Davis 201 file.

21. McLendon 1982 interview; Davis to Lee, 2 Aug. 1948, letters miscellaneous 1948 file, Davis files; *Afro-American*, 31 July 1948; *Evening Star*, 21 July 1948; Kenneth Royall to Davis, 13 July 1948, Davis 201 file.

22. Letters can be found in letters miscellaneous 1948 file, Davis files; Omar Bradley to Davis, 16 July 1948, Davis 201 file; *Afro-American*, 31 July 1948.

23. *Afro-American*, 24 July 1948; McLendon 1982 interview.

24. *Afro-American*, 24 July 1948; McLendon 1973 interview; letter, Elnora Davis McLendon to author, 26 Nov. 1982; Davis, "Family Tree;" McLendon 1982 interview.

25. Lee to Davis, 29 July 1950, and Davis to Lee, 28 Sept. and 22 Oct. 1952, Lt. Gen. John Lee correspondence file, Davis files (hereinafter cited as Lee file).

26. Lee to Davis, 24 Feb. 1956, Davis to Lee, 11 Jan. 1957, Lee to Davis,

16 Jan. 1957, and Davis to Lee, 1 Apr. and 7 Nov. 1957—all in Lee file, Davis files.

27. Thomas White to Davis, 22 May 1950, speech file, Davis files; memo to Davis, 12 Dec. 1951, Davis 201 file.

28. Gabriel Dennis to Davis, 29 Oct. 1951, speech file; Davis to Tubman, 16 Mar. 1952, letters miscellaneous 1954 file; Davis to Lee, 28 Sept. 1952, Lee file; and Davis to Tubman, 21 Sept. 1952, letters miscellaneous 1954 file—all in Davis files.

29. Davis to Lee, 19 Nov. 1952, Lee to John F. Dulles, 24 Nov. 1952, and Davis to Lee, 19 Nov. 1952, Lee file; Davis to Howard Snyder, 11 Jan. 1953, speech file; and Davis to Lee, 9 May 1953, Lee file—all in Davis files.

30. Davis to Lee, 1 Mar., 14 Apr., and 23 May 1955, and Lee to Jock Hoghland, 30 May 1955, Lee file, Davis files.

31. President, Board of Commissioners, to Francis G. Addison, Jr., 24 Mar. 1952, Addison Committee records, RG 351, NA (hereinafter cited as Addison records); *Washington Post*, 28 Sept. 1952; Addison to Davis, 5 May 1952, and Davis to B. L. Robinson, 9 Nov. 1952, Addison records; District of Columbia, Citizen's Advisory Committee on Public Works, *Our Nation's Capital: Report of the Citizens' Advisory Committee on Public Works for the District of Columbia, September 26, 1952*, p. 63; memorandum for the minutes, 30 Sept. 1952, Addison records.

32. *Annual report of the Citizens' Advisory Council, for the Period July 1, 1952-June 30, 1953*, Addison records.

33. U.S. Code, title 36, sec. 123; Sherman Adams to Davis, 4 June 1953; and Davis to Adams, 8 June 1953—all in 1953 file, Davis files.

34. Marshall to Davis, 27 July 1953, 1953 file; itinerary, 1953 tour, trip 1954 file; and Davis to Lee, 22 Nov. 1953, Lee file—all in Davis files; memo for the chairman, American Battle Monuments Commission, 1 Nov. 1953, memorandum for American Battle Monuments Commission, 1951–1953, file 300.6, records of the American Battle Monuments Commission, RG 117, WNRC (hereinafter memos from this source are cited as ABMC memo).

35. Minutes, American Battle Monuments Commission meeting, 11 Dec. 1953, American Battle Monuments Commission records, Washington, D.C. (hereinafter cited as ABMC records); Davis to Lee, 1 Apr. 1957, Lee file.

36. Memo 187, 21 Jan. 1954, memo 188, 3 Feb. 1954, and memo 189, 11 Mar. 1954, ABMC memo; minutes, American Battle Monuments Commission meeting, 18 Mar. 1954, ABMC records.

37. BOD, Jr.–ASD 30 May 1981 interview; Davis to Lee, 23 May 1955, Lee file, Davis files; McLendon 1982 interview; Davis to Lee, 11 Dec.

1955 and 7 Nov. 1957, Lee file, Davis files; letter, Elnora Davis McLendon to author, 26 Nov. 1982; *NYT*, 31 Aug. 1958.

38. Memo 225, 10 May 1956, and memorandum for the Chairman, 24 Sept. 1956, file 300.6, ABMC memo; Davis to Lee, 20 Sept. 1956, Lee file, Davis files.

39. Kenneth O'Donnell to Davis, 19 June 1961, personnel file, Davis files.

40. McLendon 1973 and 1981 interviews; Davis to Maj. Burton Lewis, 25 Feb. 1960, and Davis to Jay Wilkins, 27 Nov. 1961, personnel file, Davis files; McLendon 1982 interview.

41. McLendon 1973 and 1982 interviews; BOD, Sr., interview; permanent casualty file, Davis 201 file.

42. *Jet*, 17 Dec. 1970, scrapbook, Davis Papers (hereinafter clippings from this are cited as scrapbook); *Washington Post*, 1 Dec. 1970; *NYT*, 1 Dec. 1970; *Washington Post*, 1 Dec. 1970; *Washington Daily News*, 1 Dec. 1970, scrapbook.

CHAPTER 9. CONCLUSION

1. BOD, Jr., 1972 interview; Moss interview; William Miles, "A Different Drummer: The Officers," telecast on PBS in May 1983.

2. Charles Loeb, *Cleveland Call and Post*, 5 Dec. 1970; *Journal* (Middletown, Ohio), 9 Dec. 1970; *Chicago Daily News*, 30 Nov. 1970; *Philadelphia Tribune*, 1 Dec. 1970; *Atlanta* (Ga.) *Inquirer*, 5 Dec. 1970—all in scrapbook.

3. BOD, Sr., interview.

4. Smith, *When Jim Crow Met John Bull*, p. 154.

5. For an opposite view of Davis's impact see Gilbert Ware, *William Hastie: Grace under Pressure* (New York: Oxford University Press, 1984), p. 101.

Bibliography

UNPUBLISHED MATERIALS

National Archives

RG 15: Records of the Veterans Administration
    Pension files
RG 59: General Records of the Department of State
    Decimal file, 1910–1929
    Main decimal file, 1930–1939
    Main decimal file, 1940–1944
    Main decimal file, 1945–1949
RG 77: Records of the Office of the Chief of Engineers
    Post Plans
RG 94: Records of the Adjutant General's Office, 1780s–1917
    Compiled military service records
    Document file, 1889–1904: Records of the Record and Pension Office
    Document file, 1890–1917
    Letters received, 1863–1894, Appointment, Commission and Personnel Branch
    Muster rolls of volunteer organizations: Spanish-American War
    Orders and Circulars
RG 107: Records of the Office of the Secretary of War
    Assistant secretary of war files
    General correspondence, secretary of war, 1932–1942
    Secret correspondence, 1932–1942
    Subject file, assistant secretary of war, civilian aide to the secretary
RG 111: Records of the Office of the Chief Signal Officer
    Orientation film-production case files
RG 165: Records of the War Department General and Special Staffs
    G-1, secret-classified general correspondence, 1920–1942
    Military Intelligence Division, 1920s–1930s
    Office of Chief of Staff 201 files

Operations Division files
War College Division, general correspondence, 1903–1919
RG 319: Records of the Army Staff
    Office of the Chief of Military History files, typescript, Ulysses Lee,
        "Employment of Negro Troops
RG 331: Records of Allied Operational and Occupation Headquarters,
    World War II
    SHAEF Records
RG 351: Records of the Government of the District of Columbia
    Addison Committee records
    1877 Tax Book, District of Columbia
RG 391: Records of the U.S. Regular Army Mobile Units, 1821–1942
    Ninth Cavalry, military histories of officers, 1898–1919
RG 393: Records of U.S Army Continental Commands, 1821–1920
    General orders, special orders, and circulars
RG 395: Records of U.S Army Overseas Operations and Commands,
    1898–1942
    Department of Visayas, general correspondence, Jan.–Nov. 1901
    Department of Visayas, general correspondence, Dec. 1901–Sept. 1902
    General orders, special orders, and circulars, San Joaquin, Iloilo, Panay
RG 407: Records of the Adjutant General's Office, 1917–
    Central decimal file, 1917–1925
    Central decimal file, 1926–1939
    Central file, 1940–1942
    Central file, 1943–1945

National Archives Microfilm Publications (NAMP)

RG 29: Records of the Bureau of the Census
    Seventh Census of the United States, 1850, NAMP M432
    Eighth Census of the United States, 1860, NAMP M653
    Ninth Census of the United States, 1870, NAMP M593
    Tenth Census of the United States, 1880, NAMP T9
    Twelfth Census of the United States, 1900, NAMP T623
RG 59: General Records of the Department of State
    Numerical and minor files of the Department of State, 1906–1910,
        NAMP M862
    Records of Department of State Relating to Internal Affairs of Liberia,
        1910–1929, NAMP M613
RG 94: Records of the Adjutant General's Office, 1780s–1917
    Returns from Regular Army cavalry regiments, 1833–1916, NAMP
        M744
    Returns from United States military posts, 1800–1916, NAMP M617

RG 165: Records of the War Department General and Special Staffs
   Record cards to the correspondence of the War College Division and
      related General Staff and Adjutant General Offices, 1902–1919,
      NAMP M1023

Regional Federal Archives

Franklin D. Roosevelt Library, Hyde Park, N.Y.
   Official file 2369
Harry S. Truman Library, Independence, Mo.
   Official file 1532
National Personnel Records Center, St. Louis, Mo.
   Davis, Benjamin O., Sr., 201 file
Washington National Records Center, Suitland, Md. (WNRC)
   RG 92: Records of the Office of Quartermaster General
      miscellaneous file, 1922–1936
   RG 117: Records of the American Battle Monuments Commission
      memorandum for the American Battle Monuments Commission
         Pilgrimage Gold Star
   RG 159: Records of the Office of Inspector General
      files
   RG 168: Records of the National Guard Bureau
      Ohio National Guard
   RG 287: Publications of the U.S. Government
      National Guard Regulations under the Constitution and the Laws
         of the United States, 1922
      National Guard Regulation no. 40, 1 Apr. 1927
      National Guard Regulation no. 20, 8 July 1938
   RG 332: Records of U.S Theaters of War, World War II
      European Theater of Operations Records
   RG 338: Records of U.S Army Commands, 1942–
      Adjutant General's Section
      AGO miscellaneous records, ETOUSA
   RG 394: Records of U.S. Army Continental Commands, 1920–1942
      Fourth Corps Area, general correspondence
      Fifth Corps Area, general administrative file, 1921–32

Other Sources

American Battle Monuments Commission. Records. American Battle
   Monuments Commission, Washington, D.C.
Bulletin of Wilberforce University, Annual Catalog, 1937–38. Wilber-
   force University Archives.

Collegiana—The Cub's Bible, 1935. Tuskegee Institute Archives.
Davis, Benjamin O. Papers. In the possession of Mrs. James McLendon, Chicago, Ill.
   Correspondence files
   "The Family Tree and Early Life," n.d.
   Five-year diary
   "History of Special Section, Office of the Inspector General, 29 June 1941 to 16 November 1944
   Return of Live Birth, District of Columbia, no. 23066
   Scrapbook
Logan, John A. Papers. Manuscript Division, Library of Congress.
Lowe, Farrell D. Letter to author, 12 Nov. 1980.
McLendon, Elnora D. Letters to author, 11 Aug. 1981, 11 May, 6 Aug., and 26 Nov. 1982.
Miles, William. "A Different Drummer: The Officers." Documentary, telecast 1983.
Moton, Robert R. Papers. Tuskegee Institute Archives.
National Association for the Advancement of Colored People. Papers. Manuscript Division, Library of Congress.
Ohio Adjutant General. Records. Ohio Historical Society, Columbus, Ohio.
Petre, Gabriel. Letter to author, 12 Nov. 1980.
Scarborough, William. Papers. Wilberforce University Archives.
Stimson, Henry L. Diaries. Microfilm ed. Manuscripts and Archives, Yale University Library, New Haven, Conn.
Taft, William H. Papers. Manuscript Division, Library of Congress.

Interviews

Brown, Charles, with author, 26 Apr. 1981
Davis, Benjamin O., Jr., with author, 8 Aug. 1972 and 24 Nov. 1987
Davis, Benjamin O., Jr., and Agatha S. Davis, with author, 23 and 30 May 1981
Davis, Benjamin O., Sr., with author and Edward M. Coffman, 2 June 1968
Eaker, Ira C., interview, 10–12 Feb. 1975, USAF oral-history interview, Albert F. Simpson Historical Research Center, Maxwell Air Force Base
Fisher, Aaron, with author, 14 July 1981
Hargrove, Hondon, with author, 8 July 1981
Krouse, John, with author, 17 July 1980
McLendon, Elnora Davis, with author, 3 Nov. 1973, 2 May 1981, and 23 Oct. 1982
Moss, Carlton, with Barbara Reed, Aug. 1980
Polk, Prentice H., with author, 18 July 1980

Ph.D. Dissertations

Daugherty, Robert L. "Citizen Soldiers in Peace: The Ohio National Guard, 1919-1940." Ohio State University, 1974.

Ross, Rodney A. "Black Americans and Haiti, Liberia, the Virgin Islands, and Ethiopia, 1929-1936." University of Chicago, 1975.

Satcher, Buford. "Blacks in Mississippi Politics, 1865-1900." Oklahoma State University, 1976.

PUBLISHED MATERIALS

Books

Black, Lowell D. *The Negro Volunteer Militia Units of the Ohio National Guard, 1870-1954: The Struggle for Military Recognition and Equality in the State of Ohio.* Manhattan, Kans.: Military Affairs/Aerospace Historian Publishing, 1976.

Boyd, William H., comp. *Boyd's Directory of the District of Columbia.* Washington, D.C.: W. H. Boyd, 1858.

Cripps, Thomas. *Black Film as Genre.* Bloomington: Indiana University Press, 1979.

Dalfiume, Richard M. *Desegregation of the U.S Armed Forces: Fighting on Two Fronts, 1939-1953.* Columbia: University of Missouri Press, 1968.

Dyer, Frederick H. *A Compendium of the War of the Rebellion,* Vol. 3: *Regimental Histories.* Des Moines, Iowa: Dyer Publishing Co., 1908.

Fletcher, Marvin E. *The Black Soldier and Officer in the United States Army, 1891-1917.* Columbia: University of Missouri Press, 1974.

Frazier, E. Franklin. *Black Bourgeoisie.* Chicago, Ill.: Free Press, 1957.

Green, Constance M. *The Secret City: A History of Race Relations in the Nation's Capital.* Princeton, N.J.: Princeton University Press, 1967.

Gropman, Alan L. *The Air Force Integrates, 1945-1964.* Washington, D.C.: Government Printing Office, 1978.

Hargrove, Hondon B. *Buffalo Soldiers in Italy: Black Americans in World War II.* Jefferson, N.C.: McFarland & Company, Inc., 1985.

Historical Statistics of the United States, Colonial Times to 1970. Washington, D.C.: Government Printing Office, 1975.

Janowitz, Morris. *The Professional Soldier: A Social and Political Portrait.* New York: Free Press, 1960.

Killigrew, John W. *The Impact of the Great Depression on the Army.* New York: Garland Publishing Co, 1979.

Kusmer, Kenneth L. *A Ghetto Takes Shape: Black Cleveland, 1870–1930.* Urbana: University of llinois Press, 1976.

Lee, Ulysses. *The Employment of Negro Troops.* Washington, D.C.: Government Printing Office, 1966.

Logan, Mrs. John A. *Reminiscences of a Soldier's Wife: An Autobiography.* New York: Charles Scribner's Sons, 1913.

MacGregor, Morris J., Jr. *Integration of the Armed Forces, 1940–1965.* Washington, D.C.: Government Printing Office, 1981.

―――, and Nalty, Bernard. *Blacks in the United States Armed Forces, Basic Documents.* Wilmington, Del.: Scholarly Resources, 1977.

Nalty, Bernard C. *Strength for the Fight: A History of Black Americans in the Military.* New York: Free Press, 1986.

Official Register of the United States, 1881. Washington, D.C.: Government Printing Office, 1881.

Official Register of the United States, 1883. Washington, D.C.: Government Printing Office, 1883.

Osur, Alan M. *Blacks in the Army Air Forces during World War II.* Washington, D.C.: Government Printing Office, 1977.

Ruppenthal, Roland G. *Logistical Support of the Armies.* Washington, D.C.: Government Printing Office, 1959.

Smith, Graham. *When Jim Crow Met John Bull: Black American Soldiers in World War II Britain.* New York: St. Martin's Press, 1988.

United States. *Fifth Census: or, Enumeration of the Inhabitants of the United States, 1830.* Washington, D.C.: D. Green, 1832.

Ware, Gilbert. *William Hastie: Grace under Pressure.* New York: Oxford University Press, 1984.

Weigley, Russell F. *Eisenhower's Lieutenants: The Campaign of France and Germany 1944–1945.* Bloomington: Indiana University Press, 1981.

―――. *History of the United States Army.* New York: Macmillan Co., 1967.

Weiss, Nancy J. *Farewell to the Party of Lincoln: Black Politics in the Age of FDR.* Princeton, N.J.: Princeton University Press, 1983.

White, Walter. *A Man Called White: The Autobiography of Walter White.* New York: Viking Press, 1948.

Whyte, James H. *The Uncivil War: Washington during the Reconstruction, 1865–1878.* New York: Twayne Publishers, 1958.

Newspapers

Afro-American, Baltimore, Md.
Cleveland (Ohio) *Gazette*
Defender, Chicago, Ill.

Evening Star, Washington, D.C.
Indianapolis (Ind.) *Freeman*
Journal and Guide, Norfolk, Va.
New York Age
New York Amsterdam News
New York Times
Pittsburgh Courier
Times, London
Tuskegee (Ala.) *Messenger*
Tuskegee Student
Washington (D.C.) *Bee*
Washington (D.C.) *Post*

Magazines

Time

Articles

Coffman, Edward M., and Herrly, Peter F. "The American Regular Army Officer Corps between the World Wars: A Collective Biography." *Armed Forces and Society* 4 (Nov. 1977).

Cripps, Thomas. "Movies, Race, and World War II: *Tennessee Johnson* as an Anticipation of the Strategies of the Civil Rights Movement." *Prologue* 14, 2 (Summer 1982).

———, and Culbert, David. "The Negro Soldier (1944): Film Propaganda in Black and White." *American Quarterly* 31, 5 (Winter 1979).

Dalfiume, Richard M. "Military Segregation and the 1940 Presidential Election." *Phylon* 30, 1 (Spring 1969).

Daniel, Pete. "Black Power in the 1920s: The Case of the Tuskegee Veterans Hospital." *Journal of Southern History* 36 (Aug. 1970).

Dinges, Bruce J. "Court-Martial of Lieutenant Henry O. Flipper." *American West* 9, 1 (Jan. 1972).

Fletcher, Marvin. "The Black Volunteers in the Spanish-American War." *Military Affairs* 38, 2 (Apr. 1974).

Julian, Joseph. "Jim Crow Goes Abroad." *Nation,* 5 Dec. 1942.

McGuire, Phillip. "Desegregation of the Armed Forces: Black Leadership, Protest and World War II." *Journal of Negro History* 68, 2 (Spring 1983).

Villard, Oswald G. *Christian Century,* 18 Dec. 1940.

Government Documents

American Battle Monuments Commission. *Lorraine American Cemetery and Memorial.* 1975.

District of Columbia, Citizen's Advisory Committee on Public Works. *Our Nation's Capital: Report of the Citizen's Advisory Committee on Public Works for the District of Columbia, September 26, 1952.*

U.S., Congress, House of Representatives, House Document no. 2, Vol. 9: *Report of the Lieutenant-General Commanding the Army and Department Commanders, 1902,* 57th Cong., 2d sess., 1902–1903.

———. House Document no. 140: *Pilgrimage for the Mothers and Widows,* 71st Cong., 2d sess., 1929–1930.

———. House Report no. 571: *Pilgrimage of Mothers and Widows of Soldiers and Sailors in European Cemeteries,* 71st Cong., 2d sess., 1929–1930.

———. House Report no. 1337: *Mothers and Widows of Deceased Soldiers, Sailors, Etc., to Visit Cemeteries in Europe,* 71st Cong., 2d sess., 1929–1930.

———. *Congressional Record,* 71st Cong., 2d sess., 1929–1930.

———. *Congressional Record,* 78th Cong., 2d sess., 1944.

U.S., Congress, Senate. *A Bill To enable the Mothers and Unmarried Widows of the Deceased Soldiers, Sailors, and Marines of the American Forces Interred in the Cemeteries of Europe to Make a Pilgrimage to These Cemeteries,* S. 5332, 70th Cong., 2d sess., 1928–1929.

———. *A Bill to Authorize the Secretary of War to Retain Brigadier General Benjamin O. Davis, United States Army, on Active Duty with Combat Troops,* S. 1656, 77th Cong., 1st sess., 1941.

———. *A Bill to Authorize the Advancement on the Retired List of Colonel Benjamin Oliver Davis to the Grade of Brigadier General,* S. 2826, 80th Cong., 2d sess., 1948.

Laws

Public Law 952, 70th Cong.

Index